INTERNATIONAL RELATIONS THEORY AND INTERNATIONAL LAW

International law is playing an increasingly important role in international politics. However, international relations (IR) theorists have thus far failed to conceptualise adequately the role that law plays in politics. Instead, IR theorists have tended to operate with a limited conception of law.

An understanding of jurisprudence and legal methodology is a crucial step towards achieving a better account of international law in IR theory. But many of the flaws in IR's idea of law stem also from the theoretical foundations of constructivism – the school of thought which engages most frequently with law.

Adriana Sinclair rehabilitates IR theory's understanding of law, using case studies from American, English and international law to critically examine contemporary constructivist approaches to IR and show how a gap in their understanding of law has led to inadequate theorisation.

ADRIANA SINCLAIR teaches international relations theory, international political history and globalisation at the School of Political, Social and International Studies at the University of East Anglia.

D1474168

INTERNATIONAL RELATIONS THEORY AND INTERNATIONAL LAW

A Critical Approach

ADRIANA SINCLAIR

CAMBRIDGE
UNIVERSITY PRESS

CAMBRIDGE UNIVERSITY PRESS
Cambridge, New York, Melbourne, Madrid, Cape Town, Singapore,
São Paulo, Delhi, Dubai, Tokyo, Mexico City

Cambridge University Press
The Edinburgh Building, Cambridge CB2 8RU, UK

Published in the United States of America by Cambridge University Press, New York

www.cambridge.org
Information on this title: www.cambridge.org/9780521116725

First published 2010

Printed in the United Kingdom at the University Press, Cambridge

A catalogue record for this publication is available from the British Library

ISBN 978-0-521-11672-5 Hardback
ISBN 978-0-521-13346-3 Paperback

For Lukman and Latimah

CONTENTS

ACKNOWLEDGEMENTS

I always wondered why acknowledgements were quite so fulsome. Then I wrote this book and realised that acknowledgements are, in essence, an apology to all the friends, family and colleagues you have variously ignored, snapped at or forced to read drafts.

In particular I would like to acknowledge the intellectual support of: my doctoral supervisors, Nicholas J. Wheeler and Michael Foley, who may not recognise much of what remains; Michael Byers, for providing generous intellectual support, dinner parties and postdoctoral research fellowships at the Liu Institute for Global Issues, University of British Columbia, and Finola O'Sullivan, for being kind enough to give me a book contract.

Finally, special thanks must go to Alex Brown for reading the entire manuscript, and to my parents, Lukman and Latimah.

Introduction

This is not a book that provides easy answers. It is a book that aims to challenge our unthinking assumptions about law. It has three audiences. Most obviously, this is a book for international relations (IR) theorists who work on international law. It is motivated by a desire to correct what I see as serious errors which produce poor theorisation of international law and its place in international politics. But it is also a book for *all* IR theorists. International law is now pervasive in international politics; it is hard to think of an area of international politics which remains unaffected by it. Witness how the world since 9/11 has been shaped by law. The language and conduct of politics has become increasingly legalised. But more than this, an understanding of law at a general level is crucial for all IR theorists because legalism percolates through every level of our society. It is both what we understand justice to be and how we achieve it. It frames our understanding of human relations and gives a language of rights with which to articulate them. The questions this book raises go the heart of jurisprudence and how we understand law's relation to politics. Focusing on the cross-over between international law and international politics, this book will also provide some useful insights for lawyers concerning both international politics and how IR theorises it.

This book is divided into two halves: a theoretical first half followed by an empirical second. I will start by exploring IR theory's best efforts to understand international law. This, I argue, is constructivism and chapter 1 is an in-depth engagement with constructivism's theoretical foundations in the work of Nicholas Onuf and Friedrich Kratochwil. Their work also merits inclusion because it explicitly addresses the questions of law and international law and therefore offers two of the best accounts of international law in both constructivism and IR theory more broadly.

Having set the scene I introduce the notion of a common-sense idea of law. I argue that we all internalise certain messages about law and, unless we are legally trained, our understanding of law will not develop beyond them. Chapter 2 fleshes out what these ideas might be and unpicks them.

It also serves a second purpose: to introduce the reader to the basics of legal methodology. The reason for this is that, unless IR theorists have at least some basic knowledge of how law actually works, we cannot hold more theoretical ideas about law with any accuracy. We must learn to walk before we can run. A knowledge of international politics unfortunately will not translate into a knowledge of international law, and the assumption that it will has produced some dubious theorisation.[1]

The third and final chapter in the theoretical half continues in a similar vein. Just as some knowledge of legal methodology is needed, so too is some knowledge of 'critical' jurisprudence.[2] The majority of IR theorists who write about law are familiar with natural law theory and legal positivism. There is far less familiarity with legal thinking outside of this mainstream. The purpose of chapter 3 is to correct this but also to be more ambitious than that. Many of the questions raised by critical jurisprudence will reappear throughout the empirical second half. What is the relationship between law and society? And between law and power? How do we view society: as consensual or conflictual? Critical approaches also question how law works in practice. What is the difference between law in books and law in action? Critical thinkers reject the methodology of formalism and charge that law does not operate with the certainty or determinacy formalism says it does. Instead, critical approaches argue that law is indeterminate and, for some, law is *radically* indeterminate. This means that there is no logical or necessary connection between the facts of the case, the law and the decision. The outcome of any legal case is arbitrary. And, because it is not law which determines decisions, it must be something else.

And this question of indeterminacy is crucial. The radical indeterminacy thesis led many legal thinkers to reflect more deeply on how they could reconcile the day-to-day reality of law with the charges laid by the critical approaches. The question in essence is how indeterminate law is and for many 'middle way' thinkers law is not completely determinate. The nature of legal argumentation, the principles the laws enshrine, and the socialisation and professionalism of legal practitioners limits

---

[1] Abbott, Keohane, Moravcsik, Slaughter and Snidal, 'The Concept of Legalization', 401–19; Finnemore and Toope, 'Alternatives to "Legalization"', 743–58.
[2] I use the term 'critical' approaches because, while this covers a broad church of approaches, from American legal realism to feminism or Marxism, they do share one key trait: they define themselves to contradistinction to natural law theory and legal positivism. Their intellectual *raison d'être* is to critique and challenge the assumption of natural law theory and legal positivism, hence my labelling of it as critical jurisprudence.

law's potential indeterminacy. In Thompson's words, social relations are expressed 'not in any way one likes, but *through the forms of law*'.[3] And this implies that the forms of law restrict the possible range of arguments put forward, what will be convincing and, ultimately, the legal decision itself. And it is not simply the case that the decision is not arbitrary but that there is a connection between the limitations that the legal form places on decision-making and justice. But is this true? Does law contain the seeds of its own limitation? And does this limitation translate into justice?

Having set up these questions, I turn to the empirical second half and its three case studies: *Brown* and desegregation in America; rape legislation and reform in the United Kingdom; and torture since 9/11. Each case study raises different questions about our understanding of law. *Brown* represents law as it should be and is one of its finest moments. *Brown* is a legal icon and holds a hallowed place in American culture. On 17 May 1954 the Supreme Court ruled that segregation was unconstitutional and remedied a long-standing social injustice. Or so the story goes. The reality of *Brown* is somewhat different. First of all, the suit was not a class action: it only applied to the five school districts that were party to it. Moreover, only desegregation in *schools* was deemed unconstitutional, not the entire policy of segregation itself. Segregation was not actually overturned until 1957 in *Simkins* v. *City of Greensboro*,[4] and the first clear statement of its overturning by the Supreme Court was not until 1970.[5] And finally, *Brown II*,[6] the Supreme Court's ruling on remedy, intentionally made implementation slow. State authorities were charged with desegregating with 'all deliberate speed' which in practice gave cover for time-wasting and procrastination. This was *not* an unintended consequence of *Brown* but its precise purpose: the Supreme Court had strayed dangerously far into politics in finding desegregation to be unconstitutional. *Brown II* attempted to soften the blow to the South by giving the Southern states ample time to get used to it. As a consequence, no significant desegregation happened until at least a decade after *Brown*.[7]

---

[3] Thompson, *Whigs and Hunters*, p. 262, emphasis added.

[4] 149 F Supp 562, 564 (MD NC 1957), aff'd *Greensboro* v. *Simkins*, 246 F 2d 425 (4th Cir 1957).

[5] *Oregon* v. *Mitchell*, 400 US 112 (1970).

[6] *Brown* v. *Board of Education*, 349 US 294 (1955).

[7] In the ten years from 1954 to 1964 the percentage of African American children in elementary and secondary school with white children only rose by 1.199%, from 0.001% to 1.2%. In the ten years after 1964, this percentage rose by an incredible 89%, from 2.3% to 91.3%.

In 2001 Balkin asked America's top legal experts to play Supreme Court judge and rewrite *Brown*. In Bell's dissenting opinion, he argues that the decision did not go far enough and did little for African Americans. It was white Americans who benefited from *Brown* because the decision enabled them to 'solve' the race problem in America in one fell swoop. Law, in Bell's argument, functioned to soothe white America's conscience while in reality failing to improve the daily lives of African Americans. Law did not produce social justice; it just masked the reality of de facto injustice.

In contrast to the high drama of *Brown*, we will turn to a more mundane case study: rape legislation and reform in the United Kingdom. This is valuable because it provides an insight into how courts rule in actual cases and, crucially, views them together to discover broader trends. There is a danger in trying to understand law that we focus on individual cases and spend our time picking them apart and analysing rulings. When we do this we cannot see the wider, systemic effects a case may have, or how wider systemic factors may impact upon it. Exploring the legal treatment of rape over a thirty-year period, and attempts to solve the 'rape problem', provides us with a vantage point from which to view the operation of law in society.

It also gives us an opportunity to assess how effective reform has been. The legal treatment of rape, from reporting to trial, has been the focus of repeated reform and yet the 'rape problem' seems more acute than ever: a low conviction rate, a high attrition rate, juries plagued with 'rape myths'. Can reform succeed? And if it cannot, does this mean that the law is not capable of providing justice to rape victims? Or are we expecting too much from the law: to transform a complex and deeply embedded set of ideas about men, women and appropriate sexual behaviour?

My third case study concerns the return to torture in the wake of 9/11 and it gives me the opportunity to return again to constructivism. While chapter 1 explores constructivism's theoretical foundations and its treatment of law, chapter 6 will bring in more contemporary constructivist research and explore the norms literature, specifically the idea of norm evolution. In norm evolution, as the name implies, norms evolve from being held by a small number of actors to spreading throughout a community. Once a certain number of actors adopt the norm, a tipping point is reached and the norm cascades throughout the rest of the community: all that remains is legalisation and internalisation. In the legalisation stage, treaties are signed and ratified and the norm becomes enshrined in law. But law also works to internalise the norm, first by giving it the legitimacy of law and, secondly, by punishing transgression. Law is depicted as a terminus; a final stamp of approval after the political battle has been won.

The case of torture post 9/11 questions this picture. The norm against torture was considered as the archetypal internalised norm. As Sussman argues: 'In philosophical and political discussion, torture is commonly offered as one of the few unproblematic examples of a type of act that is morally impermissible without exception or qualification.'[8] It was also a powerfully legalised norm: numerous treaties and conventions prohibited it and it was, and arguably still is, a peremptory norm from which no derogation is permitted. But derogation happened. Chapter 6 will explore how and what this means for our understanding of law. It will also ask whether the norms literature's failure to see the possibility of normative backsliding, either in theory or in practice, is caused by its undertheorised understanding of law.

Constructivism's perception of law owes much to the common-sense idea of law. Law is seen as (a) good. It is 'a force of linear progress, a beacon to lead us out of darkness':[9] the darkness of politics. In this respect more sophisticated constructivist ideas of law stray towards the middle way: that you cannot argue anything you like (and win). But the case of torture powerfully challenges this assumption. The Office of Legal Counsel *did* argue precisely what it wanted. The prohibition on torture was absolute and the legal norm against torture had achieved the highest level of legal normativity: torture was a peremptory legal norm. It is almost impossible to find an international legal norm of comparable strength. And yet it was overturned with shocking ease. And what is most striking is that its overturning happened because of and through the forms of law. The law and its method were sufficiently flexible to justify that which it prohibited. These restrictions may not be as powerful as we would hope, nor do they give law the capacity to solve society-wide injustice. Relying upon the assumption that law contains within it the seeds of its own limitation, and thereby justice, produces questionable theory.

The problem is two-fold. First, a lack of engagement with law leads IR theorists to fall back on common-sense ideas of law that see it in broadly benign ways. Secondly, constructivism's theoretical foundations

---

[8] Quoted in Bellamy, 'No Pain, No Gain'?, 121–48, at 129.
[9] Smart, *Feminism and the Power of Law*, p. 12.

predispose it to seeing law as operating in the same way as social norms: i.e. that social norms evolve through a process of articulation and argumentation between actors who are more-or-less equal. The first problem is ignorance, the second is constructivism. I hope that by removing some of the former, the latter will be improved.

1

The theoretical foundations of constructivism and its treatment of law

Introduction

This chapter will provide the bedrock of the book: it will introduce and explore what I consider to be the best efforts of international relations (IR) theory to understand law in general and international law in particular. As noted in the introduction, IR theory has not engaged with the question of law in any sustained manner. The school of thought which has, I believe, made the greatest attempt to understand law is constructivism, and within constructivism, two authors in particular stand out: Onuf and Kratochwil. There are two reasons for this. First, both authors were instrumental in the creation and development of constructivism as a school of thought. In exploring their work therefore, I will be exploring the theoretical foundations of constructivism. The theoretical focus of their work also predisposes it to addressing questions about the nature of society, norms and ultimately law. Constructivist analysis was definitively shaped by Keohane's injunction to answer empirical questions of international politics.[1] Throughout the 1990s therefore a substantial portion of constructivist work was empirically oriented and this drew attention away from questions of law. I will return to more empirical constructivist work in chapter 6 to see what role law plays in their analysis and specifically address the question of normative backsliding.

But, to return to Onuf and Kratochwil, there is a second reason for selecting them from all other constructivist writers: they explicitly write about law. As noted in the introduction other IR theory accounts of international law suffer from two flaws. Moreover, they approach the question of law in an explicitly theoretical way and this gives us a far better chance of answering the questions

---

[1] Finnemore and Sikkink, 'Taking Stock', 391. Keohane was speaking at the International Studies Association Annual Convention in 1988.

about international law that IR theorists are interested in answering: what should we expect law to be able to do for us? What is law's causal power?

This chapter will start by exploring the work of Onuf then turn to Kratochwil before drawing them together. I will argue that there are a number of significant similarities between Onuf and Kratochwil's work and that they share a number of flaws and ultimately these flaws have percolated through into later, empirical constructivist work and its understanding of law.

ONUF

Introduction

Onuf's landmark book, *World of Our Making*,[2] announced the birth of constructivism and aimed to do no less than reconstruct the discipline of IR. Such a reconstruction is necessary because IR fails in one of its central tasks: understanding that our social reality is constructed. Onuf's task is to investigate what IR has so far taken for granted: that rules themselves are a matter of language.

Language for Onuf is the key to understanding rules, and in turn, understanding the social world. It enables Onuf to connect individual conduct and social rules. Onuf quotes Fish's observation that: 'ruleness, in which any normativity hinges, begins in speech'.[3] By making an assertion, you do something social but you must have an audience; they may accept or reject the assertion but they must be there. Utterances which nobody hears have no social import. Provided that speech acts have an audience, they may themselves change the world. In fact, for constructivists the social world and words are mutually constitutive, and the key to understanding how the world works lies in unpicking this process of mutual constitution. For Onuf the way to do this most effectively is through a systematic analysis of rules with the aim of producing a fully fleshed out 'topology of rules'.[4]

Onuf sets out to create this system using Habermasian speech act theory.[5] According to Habermas, a speech act is the 'act of speaking in

---

[2] Onuf, *World of Our Making*.
[3] Fish quoted in Onuf, *World of Our Making*, p. 85.
[4] Onuf, 'Do Rules Say What They Do?', 386.
[5] Habermas, *The Theory of Communicative Action*.

a form that gets someone else to act'.[6] Language is therefore performative rather than merely descriptive and Onuf uses Habermas's tripartite division of speech acts into locutionary, illocutionary and perlocutionary acts:

> Through *locutionary acts* the speaker expresses states of affairs; he says something. Through *illocutionary acts* the speaker performs an action in saying something . . . a statement, promise, command, avowal, or the like . . . 'I hereby promise you (command you, confess to you) that p [propositional content – state of affairs].' Finally, through *perlocutionary acts* the speaker produces an effect upon the hearer. By carrying out a speech act he brings about something in the world . . . to say *something*, to act *in* saying something, to bring about something *through* acting in saying something.[7]

Rules

Onuf defines rules as 'general, prescriptive statements'.[8] Speech acts acquire normativity and become rules through frequent iteration and acceptance. As time goes by and the statement is repeatedly expressed and accepted, a speech act may be institutionalised as a rule. Whether or not a rule or would-be rule is accepted depends on how well it fits with the context and this is why an analysis of rules, rather than context, is more productive. In fact, attempting to theorise context may be a fool's errand: 'Recourse to the context of a rule's use may help resolve some ambiguities, but introduces others. Context tends to invade a rule's content even as it aids in clarifying the rule's function, and the rule begins to lose its distinctive position in offering guidance.'[9] Those, such as Kratochwil, who look at discourse instead of rules 'flounder because they have not found anything functionally distinctive in what they construe as specifically legal discourse'.[10] The best way to 'get at' context or culture is therefore to study rules and Onuf does this by looking at practices: '[a]ll the ways in which people deal with rules'.[11] We can infer what rules are by looking at practices. However, practices are not just a realisation or an operationalisation of rules. They are 'the content of carrying on'[12] in relation to rules and this includes being aware of them

---

[6] Onuf, 'Constructivism: A User's Manual', p. 66.
[7] Habermas quoted in Onuf, *World of Our Making*, p. 83.
[8] Onuf, 'A Constructivist Manifesto', p. 7.
[9] Onuf, 'Do Rules Say What They Do?', 396.   [10] *Ibid.* 404.
[11] Onuf, 'Constructivism: a User's Manual', p. 59.
[12] Onuf, *World of Our Making*, p. 152.

in a practical or even reflective way. It is through practices that people change rules and alter outcomes[13] and every response to a rule has an effect on that rule and its position.[14] This produces a picture of human society as constantly in flux and as fluid, in which every individual has a degree of power over the rules which make up their world. No one is powerless.

Agency

This brings us to the question of agency and where it is located. Onuf argues that while rules tell us how to 'carry on' they 'cannot provide closure for the purposes of carrying on because rules are not the sufficient agency whereby intentions become equivalent to causes'.[15] Rules provide guidance; they do not determine behaviour. In most situations multiple rules can potentially apply (just like the law) and individuals have to choose which one to follow.

But, Onuf argues, we cannot construct just anything we like; we are limited by 'materiality', that is, material and social limits.[16] We have to recognise these limits and 'evaluate the consequences of ignoring or defying' them.[17] It is unclear precisely what would count as a material or social limit and Onuf is not explicit. He hints at two, opposing meanings. First, he writes that: 'Human beings, using whatever equipment nature and/or society provides, construct society, and society is indispensable to the actualisation of whatever human beings may "naturally" be; society constructs human beings out of the raw materials of nature, whether inner nature or, less problematically, the outer nature of their material circumstances.'[18] He also refers to 'our sensory experience of the world and of our bodily selves in that world'[19] which reinforces the sense that material limits are physical or biological. This is backed up by his choice of examples: we are unable to fly because we do not have wings.[20]

But according to Zehfuss, when Onuf argues that the material is a limit, he legitimises it: 'His view of how we make our world seems to pay insufficient attention to how this asymmetry is already invested into what he calls the raw materials of our constructions. He therefore

---

[13] *Ibid.* p. 101.   [14] Inter alia Zehfuss, *Constructivism*, p. 165.
[15] Onuf, *World of Our Making*, p. 51.   [16] Onuf, 'A Constructivist Manifesto', p. 9.
[17] *Ibid.* p. 9.   [18] Onuf, *World of Our Making*, p. 46.   [19] *Ibid.* p. 292.
[20] Onuf, 'Constructivism: A User's Manual', p. 64.

seems to favour those who are privileged already, who have the means to present the way things are as "reality".[21] But for Zehfuss what constitutes a 'material limit' is a political act. Witness the way in which women's biology was used to justify excluding them from the franchise, for example. Yet, according to Zehfuss, Onuf's approach cannot recognise this and he presents the 'material limits' as uncontestable, unchangeable and apolitical. This idea of materiality has two implications: first, that all people are essentially the same and, secondly, that all people are similarly located within their society.

And yet there is a second sense of materiality for Onuf and it reveals a second side to his theory. In this second sense, Onuf writes that resources are the material component in all human endeavour and moreover that rules constitute a resource themselves. This would seem to imply that it is economic, social or political factors that can hold us back and that the way in which a society is organised, and the rules it has, advantages some over others. In this way rules inevitably produce rule and rule is always exploitative.[22] Rules establish stability in social institutions by privileging certain people over others.[23] Stability is created and maintained because those at the top work hard to maintain the status quo.[24] Onuf argues that this is what we mean when we speak of order: not fairness or equality, but hierarchy. He writes that: 'When we speak of order, we chose a fiction to believe in. "Order" is a metaphor, a figure of speech, a disguise. It is constituted by performative speech and constitutes propositional content for such speech.'[25]

Thus we can see two contradictory sides to Onuf's theory. First, there is his taxonomic quest to produce a topology of rules. Here he focuses solely on language and treats rules technically, seeming to be uninterested in either the political ramifications of rules or the political nature of context. But then Onuf makes his second theoretical move: that rules inevitably produce rule.

His approach to rules treats them technically and abstractly. He writes that '[a]lthough social rules necessarily have authors and histories,

---

[21] Zehfuss, *Constructivism*, p. 195.   [22] Onuf, *World of Our Making*, p. 122.
[23] *Ibid.* p. 122.
[24] According to Zehfuss: 'despite Onuf's concern with the problem of privilege, we do not gain extensive insight about this phenomenon through his approach. Given Onuf's preoccupation also with rule, it is surprising that he categorically refuses to discuss the dimensions of power' (*Constructivism*, pp. 185–6).
[25] Onuf, *World of Our Making*, p. 155.

neither need to be known for rules to work as such'[26] and that rules can and should be the sole focus of analysis.[27] But he then writes: 'because authoring rules tangibly bears on the arrangement of power and privilege in any order, rule authors have a stake in mixing up discourse types. For them the ideal is an order that appears not to be authored at all.'[28] Rules and rule are inextricably interlinked yet he treats them quite differently. Rules are to be studied technically and in isolation from context and questions of hierarchy or power relations have no place here. But his approach to rule, which he sees as an inevitable consequence of rules, is quite different. Rule *is* hierarchy and Onuf argues that society is stabilised by the efforts the privileged make to maintain their position, and they do this *through* rules. This inevitably creates a tension, and this is clear in Onuf's refusal to analyse context because it would simply be too difficult. Moreover, considering context when trying to analyse a rule simply confuses matters. In 'Do Rules Say What They Do?' Onuf states that the 'correspondence between rules and discourse may be difficult to trace'[29] and implies that this is because those in positions of power and privilege are deliberately muddying the waters: 'Directives will be cloaked in metaphors and instructions cast analytically.'[30] Similarly, Onuf's assertion that for the powerful within society (or rule authors as Onuf terms them above) the ideal is an order which appears not to be authored at all. Arguably this is precisely the end his taxonomic approach achieves. By the end of *World of Our Making* Onuf realises that he must choose one approach over the other.

Yet there is no reason for Onuf to do this. The subject matter of rules and rule themselves are not in tension; it is only Onuf's differing approaches to them that put them in opposition. If Onuf extended his political reading of rule to rules then the tension would disappear. In doing this, Onuf could maintain his emphasis on words *and* the political commitments to the notion of rule.

What would conflict however is Onuf's notion of agency. The idea that individuals can remake the(ir) social world has become the hallmark of constructivist analysis producing many upbeat accounts of how groups of individuals have managed to rearticulate social norms and out-manoeuvre significantly more powerful opponents.[31] As Onuf puts it in the title of his landmark book, it is a *World of Our Making*. But clearly,

---

[26] *Ibid.* p. 80.
[27] Onuf, 'Do Rules Say What They Do?', 407.   [28] *Ibid.* 408.   [29] *Ibid.* 408.
[30] *Ibid.* 408.   [31] See chapter 6.

from his argument about rule, it is not a world of *our* making but a world that is *made for us* by the privileged and powerful within society. Onuf appears torn, or at least unclear, about his idea of agency. His use of speech act theory leads him to argue that in speaking we are affecting the world, and that we are all able to speak and express ourselves. As Onuf writes: 'My words (set in train actions that) change the world.'[32] Seen in this way, we are all equally active and powerful within our society. Moreover, we are all involved: 'We can always agree to change a rule; others can join in the agreement; it may become generally accepted.'[33] We as individuals engage with rules rationally and consciously. We also appear to maintain a critical distance from rules and we always have the option of rejecting a particular rule. We may be in a minority of one, but we are still intellectually able to do it. In other words, we are not socialised into rules so deeply that our adherence to them is unthinking.

Or, for that matter, unarticulated: Onuf's theory cannot 'see' a rule or proto-rule if it is not.[34] Yet surely the most powerful norms of all need not be articulated. They are simply accepted as normal or natural or are internalised and are subconscious.[35] Onuf's emphasis on articulation thus restricts analysis to what is surface and fails to see the deeper assumptions which make our world. Take, for example, the clearly articulated law that it is wrong/illegal to force someone to have sex against their will.[36] This rule is so well enshrined that it has become a law: the very highest level of normativity that Onuf sees. If we follow Onuf's argument about speech acts, it must be that the idea has been articulated and accepted so many times that it has become formalised and institutionalised into a law. Yet the force of this normative prescription is frequently undermined by other unspoken ideas about women.

---

[32] Onuf, *World of Our Making*, p. 93.   [33] *Ibid.* p. 84.

[34] Although Onuf states that 'rules need not be stated to be considered as such' (*World of Our Making*, p. 88) he is referring here to rules you make for yourself, in his example, the decision to go to church once a week. He continues that: 'I take it as sufficient that the commitment is capable of public statement and the person making the commitment would not shirk from making it publicly' (ibid), thus the emphasis on articulation remains and it is clear that non-articulated statements are the exception that prove the rule.

[35] See chapter 6. Subsequent constructivist analysis oscillates between these two competing ideas of norms.

[36] See chapter 5's discussion of government attempts to counter dominant perceptions of, or norms about, rape, rapists and rape victims in rape trials. In constructivist terms, the government is seeking to alter the social norms about rape and to do so through the law and the setting of the trial.

Witness court reporting where rape complainants were asked about what colour their past boyfriends were, if she lived with the father of their children, if her children shared the same father. These questions were unrelated to the rape complaint: their purpose was to undermine the complainant's credibility. Indeed, the law clearly states that irrelevant material, including irrelevant sexual history evidence, should not be allowed into the courtroom. But they are because such tactics work.[37] They work because there is the unarticulated premise that a white woman who dates black men, a woman who does not live with the father of her children, a woman who has children by more than one man, is not to be trusted.

Clearly, articulating such ideas is taboo and they either are not explicitly articulated or only rarely so. Because Onuf sees normativity as being created by repeated iteration and acceptance, this would mean that such ideas would have little normative power. But they obviously do. Another explanation could be that the norm in play here is not the right to sexual autonomy but a more powerful and longstanding norm concerning property. The far older and well-established idea is that women are property, owned by either their father or husband and, as Sir Matthew Hale infamously argued in the seventeenth century, a woman gives irrevocable consent to sex in her marriage vows.[38] Historically a married woman was the property of her husband and this invoked the far older, far more powerful norm of property as dominium: uncontrolled use. This idea of property as dominium dates from Roman times and under it: 'Not only could the owner ... exclude others, he could also use and convey his property freely.'[39] The social rule of sexual autonomy is a far more recent invention: marital rape only became a crime in 1991. Two conclusions should be drawn from this: first, a historical long view is needed and secondly, a view which can see unarticulated prejudices is essential. I shall return to these issues in the empirical second half of the book.

This problem here is what I call the unarticulated major premise and the articulated minor premise. So while it is no longer acceptable to argue that women are inferior to men, there is still, for example, an

---

[37] Temkin, 'Prosecuting and Defending Rape', 219–48.

[38] DeLaMothe argues that scholars most often credit Sir Matthew Hale, the English jurist, with creating the concept of marriage as a defence to rape under the implied consent doctrine of subordination. DeLaMothe, 'Liberta Revisited', 861.

[39] Kratochwil, 'Sovereignty as *Dominium*', p. 25.

obsessive focus on female celebrities' bodies and women still earn less than men. The major premise can no longer be articulated but it is supported by a myriad of minor premises which can. Taking the articulation of each minor premise on its own, for example the *New York Times'* ridiculing of Jessica Simpson for gaining weight, seems cruel but it is hardly a dominant normative structure designed to oppress all women.[40] This is another reason why abstraction is dangerous. Something can look quite innocuous on its own but when it is seen as part of a wider pattern of articulation its true significance and causal power is revealed. And this only becomes meaningful when viewed from a historical perspective.

All this sits awkwardly with Onuf's idea of agency. He remains committed to the idea of individual agency and I believe that his attribution of too much agency to the individual undermines the political aspect of Onuf's work, which I consider to be more valuable. This is compounded by his choice of examples (e.g. 'I promise that I will fix the stairs').[41] All his examples centre on the individual in hypothetical situations. There are no examples of how society may instruct us to behave because society is not seen as an actor for Onuf, only as that which is acted upon. Nor does he see the diffuse form of causation, only efficient cause.[42] Onuf is also unable to see these types of instructions because they are unarticulated. As a result Onuf is potentially unable to see the vast majority of social rules that make up his idea of rule. In order to see the ways in which rule truly operates, Onuf would have to renounce the individualism of his theory and cease to focus on the individual as his referent object and secondly, renounce his emphasis on articulation and the speech act theory that goes with it. In fact, Onuf could have his 'rule' and maintain his constructivist insight that words make the world and vice versa if he were to adopt a more subtle approach to the ways in which social norms are expressed and shape our lives. Instead, constructivism has taken off on the back of the headline claim that our words make the world and therefore we can re-make our world. This implies a radical agency which is simply unavailable to the majority. Only the powerful and privileged, I argue, have the power to re-make the world. It is a world of *their* making. But what is most disappointing is that Onuf's contradictions made it possible for subsequent constructivists to

---

[40] Sean Delonas' cartoon, 28 January 2009, *New York Times*, available at www.nypost.com/opinion/cartoons/delonas.htm, accessed June 2009.
[41] Onuf, *World of Our Making*, p. 93.   [42] See Kurki, *Causation in International Relations*.

take the technical insights of his work and leave the political behind: to take the rules but leave the rule. Ultimately this book argues that this is where constructivism and the constructivist idea of law have gone wrong.

International law

What does this mean for law and for international law in particular? Onuf spent a great deal of time writing about law, specifically international law. Unfortunately, the majority of this work has centred on the question of whether international law is law. This is unfortunate for two reasons: first, it is a question that is of limited interest to IR theorists and secondly, it has been asked and answered by jurisprudence for many years.[43] In brief, Onuf claims that: 'The classification scheme produced by applying speech act theory to rules will, in turn, show that the international order is a legal one'[44] and he concludes that: 'Orders are legal in the degree that their rules are effectively supported.'[45] He identifies three criteria to 'lawness'. First, the degree to which rules are formalised; secondly, the degree to which the external dimension of support for rules is institutionalised; and thirdly, the presence of officers.[46]

A far more interesting question to explore would have been the application of Onuf's idea of rule to law. Instead, Onuf chooses to focus on abstract and taxonomic questions of international law and neglects the second element of his theory. Thus his aim is to produce a 'scheme for aligning rules with types of speech acts [which] attempts to stake out fresh ground for a taxonomy of laws by discovering a finite set of mutually exclusive ways in which rules themselves say what they do'.[47] Crucially, Onuf sees legal and non-legal rules as essentially the same: they differ only in that legal rules have reached a certain level of formalisation and institutionalisation. The taxonomic division of social rules can therefore be applied to legal rules. In his work with Peterson, Onuf argues that there are three broad categories of activity which are fundamental to making the human condition a social one: naming and relating, having and using, and enabling and making unable. These activities 'have social meaning if and because they are rule-governed'.[48] This in turn produces three rule types: first, those for designating posi-tion, known as instructions or, when legal, principles. Next there are

[43] Onuf's approach differs only in that he uses Habermasian speech act theory.
[44] Onuf, 'Do Rules Say What They Do?', 386.   [45] Onuf, *World of Our Making*, p. 128.
[46] *Ibid.* pp. 138–40.   [47] Onuf, 'Do Rules Say What They Do?', 404.   [48] *Ibid.* 404.

rules which allocate possession or use, called conferrals, and regulations when legal. Finally, there are rules which exercise control, which are known as directives, whether legal or not.[49]

To Onuf 'all social arrangements constituted by rules of these three types, whatever their mix, are subject to formalisation and that all rule-related practices are subject to institutionalisation'.[50] Once a rule reaches a certain level of 'formalisation and institutionalisation, such as enactment and at least partial enforcement, then they *are* law'.[51] Formalisation and institutionalisation are therefore what separate non-legal rules from legal rules. For Onuf: 'This threshold is neither arbitrary nor indeterminate. Enough formalisation and institutionalisation must take place that such rules can perform a definite function of their own.'[52] Rules are made to be performatively sufficient and refer back to their own authorship for their standing. Hence rules *do* say what they do. In short, rules, at least legal ones, tell us all we need to know and consequently we need look no further.

Conclusion

In their special issue of *International Organization* on legalisation,[53] Abbott, Keohane, Moravcsik, Slaughter and Snidal make a similar argument to Onuf's: that legal rules are characterised by three elements: obligation, precision and delegation. The more obligation, precision and delegation a rule has the more legal it is. While this would appear to be an eminently sensible and logical argument, it is misguided. In a swift and thorough-going critique Finnemore and Toope argue convincingly that there is no correlation between these three elements and legality. The factual reality simply does not tally with the theory put forward by Abbott et al. The same can be said of Onuf's taxonomy. In fact, if the missteps of the legalisation special issue and Onuf's approach tell us anything it is that attempting a taxonomy of law is a fool's errand. It has simply been impossible, at least so far, to produce a taxonomy which is accurate but parsimonious enough to be of any analytical value. And for IR theorists trying to get to grips with international law, the primary

---

[49] Each different category of legal rules has its legal force: Onuf, 'Do Rules Say What They Do?', 410.
[50] *Ibid.* 405.   [51] *Ibid.* 405.   [52] *Ibid.* 405.
[53] Abbott, Keohane, Moravcsik, Slaughter and Snidal, 'The Concept of Legalization', 401–19.

concern is finding analytic tools which work and which make analysis possible and easier. Zehfuss's assessment of Onuf's taxonomic endeavour is devastating: 'Onuf's categories may be pure and comprehensive ... but, other than satisfying his personal preference for neat ordering, what is their purpose?'[54]

But I return again to the worrying flaw in Onuf's work: his failure to apply his notion of rule to law. In brief, what would it look like if he did? (This is what Marxist and critical accounts of international law do.) First, Onuf argues that rule is an inevitable consequence of rules and he implies that whoever makes the rules makes them in their own interest. Rules therefore produce and maintain a hierarchy. We could also go a step further and argue that we need to look at rules themselves with a critical eye. If they function to produce hierarchy, can they really be neutral, apolitical and technical? Should we be looking for evidence of bias within the rules themselves? Should we even look beyond the wording of individual rules themselves to the structure of law itself, in both its sociological make-up and the argumentative logic which it espouses?[55] Having taken us from rules to rule Onuf then steps back from the unavoidable conclusion of his theory: that the law is neither neutral nor apolitical and no amount of technical taxonomy is going to change it.

KRATOCHWIL

Introduction

Kratochwil's work offers one of the most sustained and in-depth engagements with the question of rules, norms and law. His work is also unusual in that he explicitly seeks to address questions of law and, given his legal training, he is eminently well-placed to do so. He is also a constructivist. While his work and that of Onuf share some key elements in that they are both constructivists, they also differ in important respects and these differences produce quite markedly different theories.

Kratochwil's aim is to cast 'a fresh and unobstructed look of how ... norms and rules "work," i.e., what role they play in moulding decisions'.[56] Kratochwil believes that action is, in general, rule-governed and all norms share one characteristic: they are problem-solving. This

---

[54] Zehfuss, *Constructivism*, p. 187.

[55] Chapter 4 on desegregation in America and chapter 5 on rape reform explore some of these broader questions.

[56] Kratochwil, *Rules, Norms and Decisions*, p. 4.

means that they simplify choice situations 'for actors with non-identical preferences facing each other in a world characterised by scarcity'.[57] Rules and norms link individual autonomy to sociality[58] by providing guidance and acting as a problem-solving device. They do this in three ways: they may rule out certain forms of behaviour; they may create schemes or schedules for coordinating the enjoyment of scarce resources; or they provide the basis for a discourse in which the parties discuss grievances, negotiate solutions and ask for third party mediation.[59] Rules therefore 'simplify choice-situations by drawing attention to factors which an actor has to take into account'[60] and they influence the choices we make through the reasoning process and impart 'rationality' to situations.[61] But norms are not merely 'guidance devices', as Kratochwil terms them, in that they are not just rules we come up against telling us to do or not to do things. They are more than that; they constitute our social world. They are 'the means which allow people to pursue goals, share meanings, communicate with each other, criticise assertions, and justify claims'.[62] They are the very fabric of our world. It therefore makes sense to study them but Kratochwil believes that we cannot do this directly. Instead, we must study the processes of deliberation and interpretation[63] and it is through these processes, and the language in which we articulate and express them, that we can understand the impact of rules and norms on decisions.

Intersubjectivity

In order for action to be meaningful it must be located in an intersubjective context. This applies in two senses. First, we as individuals find meaning in it. We can never escape our intersubjective context, and everything we do and everything we understand others to be doing is always refracted through the lens of intersubjectivity. The intersubjective context is our world and it gives everything in it meaning. Secondly, social theorists like Kratochwil find explanation in it. In order to understand why and how people make the choices and decisions they do, you

---

[57] *Ibid.* p. 14.   [58] *Ibid.* p. 70.   [59] *Ibid.* p. 70.   [60] *Ibid.* p. 72.
[61] *Ibid.* p. 10. Interestingly Kratochwil never phrases or frames this as 'people have a natural tendency to obey rules' and he never uses that particular, active construction. This would seem to be a fairly natural conclusion to draw but Kratochwil never does so.
[62] *Ibid.* p. 11.   [63] *Ibid.* p. 11.

must look at the intersubjective context. Crucially, this does not for Kratochwil mean trying to get inside people's heads. Rather intersubjective context can be studied scientifically through language. In Kratochwil's words: 'the social world is intrinsically linked to language and ... language, because it is a rule-governed activity, can provide us with a point of departure for our inquiry into the function of norms in social life'.[64] In common with Onuf, language provides the key to understanding. For Kratochwil intersubjectivity means that individual actions and decisions can be analysed and dealt with en masse. It makes them logical rather than idiosyncratic, plural and impossible to analyse. Human action becomes predictable and comprehensible. Kratochwil refers to this as the 'unprejudiced assessment of the empirical evidence'[65] and it makes a taxonomic understanding of the social world possible.

How does the intersubjective context develop? Kratochwil says that: 'Common understandings can be arrived at through the stabilisation and evocation of generally shared expectations among actors in a specific situation. The medium of understanding is then neither logical cogency nor semantic truth, but rather *claims to the validity of norms* on the basis of which actors can communicate, coordinate their actions, and adjust their preferences.'[66] What is important for Kratochwil in the process of communication and reasoning is not necessarily logical – after all, both moral and legal reasoning become relevant and necessary when no 'logical' solution is available. What matters, according to Kratochwil, is the starting point of an argument.[67] The premises from which an argument starts and how the argument or debate is framed are crucial for arriving at a decision.[68]

The process and nature of argumentation also shape its outcome because the '"logic" of arguing requires that our claims satisfy certain criteria'.[69] Both legal and moral reasoning display a process of principled argumentation which leads to an equally principled application of the respective norms. The process and nature of argumentation creates a path and it is this path dependency that distinguishes reasoned decisions from random choices. However, path dependency does not mean there is no element of choice or fluidity, as in an algorithm. While an algorithm establishes an unequivocal structure, a path allows for 'chance elements at turning points' and 'the influence of past decisions'.[70] This means that paths are traceable but not necessarily predictable.[71]

[64] *Ibid.* p. 6.   [65] Kratochwil, 'Thrasymachos Revisited', 347.
[66] Kratochwil, *Rules, Norms and Decisions*, pp. 31–2.   [67] *Ibid.* p. 38.
[68] *Ibid.* p. 37.   [69] *Ibid.* p. 12.   [70] *Ibid.* p. 238.   [71] *Ibid.* p. 238.

So any eventual outcome will also be shaped by two factors: first, the choice of the narrative which contextualises the argument;[72] and secondly, the process and nature of argumentation itself. While the latter is not a matter of choice, the narrative is. Indeed, the choice of narrative can be crucial.[73] Yet Kratochwil never says who chooses the narrative; only that it is chosen. How do these narratives work?

Kratochwil calls these narratives or starting points 'topoi' or commonplaces and defines them thus: 'a topos is ... a shared *judgement* in a society that enables the respective actors to back their choices by means of accepted belief, rules or preference, or general classification schemes'.[74] Topoi thus not only establish 'starting points' for arguments, but locate the issues of a debate in a substantive set of common understandings that provide for the crucial connections within the structure of argument.[75] Because they reflect our common-sense understandings, these general topoi are 'persuasive'. We fall back upon them when 'technical knowledge about an issue is lacking or has become problematic'.[76]

Topoi can be both general, in that they are akin to common sense, and specific in that they can relate to a particular area of practical reasoning, like the law. Topoi essentially enable us to relate our existing knowledge to new information and thereby make sense of it and situate it within our world view. Thus '[i]t is through such a topical "ordering" that everyday language can mediate between different areas of knowledge'.[77] The essential function of topoi is as a means for appraisal. Clearly there are many topoi, both general and specific, and Kratochwil concedes that no system could accommodate all of them. He argues that topoi are ordered by the pairing of opposing topoi. For example, the topos of 'more is better than less' would be paired with 'quality is better than quantity'.[78] A legal example would be the pairing of *voluntas* (the will of the legislator) with *lex scripta* (the letter of the law).[79] The clarity and understanding that topoi offer us are therefore not without complexity. Confusion and contestation are inherent in the nature of topoi and reasoning with them. In this respect Kratochwil is not trying to provide us with the answer, only with a better understanding of how the reasoning process works.

---

[72] *Ibid.* p. 213.   [73] *Ibid.* p. 213.   [74] *Ibid.* p. 218. Emphasis in original.
[75] *Ibid.* p. 219.   [76] *Ibid.* pp. 219–20.   [77] *Ibid.* p. 220.   [78] *Ibid.* p. 233.
[79] *Ibid.* p. 233.

Change

Because Kratochwil argues that a speech act will only succeed when it fits with the existing rules and norms, change is problematic. Kratochwil argues that change happens when the 'beliefs and identities of . . . actors are altered thereby also altering rules and norms that are constitutive of their political practices'.[80] Change happens when actors, through their practices, change the rules and norms that constitute political interaction and social reality. Although meanings can be contested there remains a significant part which must be uncontested. This uncontested part provides the frame in which debate takes place. Without some level of consistency and agreement between actors, argumentation and resolution cannot happen. For Kratochwil contestation can only happen at the margins, otherwise our social world would become meaningless. This means that change can only ever be incremental. It also means that intersubjective context is inherently conservative and this in turn renders the individual's ability to re-make the/her world minimal.[81]

The causal power of norms

Kratochwil is very clear that norms shape behaviour or influence it, but never cause it. Indeed, for Kratochwil it is the positivistic treatment of norms as causes that has fatally flawed conventional understanding of social action and norms.[82] Their causal power, such that it is, lies in the effect norms have on actors' reasoning and subsequent actions. Norms influence actors by shaping their perceptions and the argumentative logic that defines a particular issue or debate. This would seem to imply that norms influence and shape the world around us in ways we are unaware of, at least some of the time. Yet Kratochwil is unwilling to argue that we are anything less than perfectly free and conscious agents. He holds fast to the notion that we may disregard social norms if we so choose. Yet even if we did, the fact remains that the intersubjective context which we are defying or may be seeking to rearticulate remains set against us. In our heads *we* may be free of a particular social norm, but the overarching intersubjective context continues nonetheless. Our life

---

[80] Koslowski and Kratochwil, 'Understanding Change in International Politics', 216.
[81] This is sharply at odds with what has been constructivism's unique selling point: the argument that we are able to re-make our social world.
[82] Kratochwil, *Rules, Norms and Decisions*, p. 5.

Kratochwil and the law

Just as you need to understand argumentative reasoning in order to understand the intersubjective context, if you want to understand the law then you must understand legal reasoning. Legal reasoning provides the key and in many respects Kratochwil's arguments regarding rules and norms can be applied directly to legal rules. This is certainly Kratochwil's approach. After studying the role of rules and norms in general he then concludes that 'legal norms are not different from other norms by some intrinsic characteristic (such as sanctions, etc.), but become so only through the process of application'.[96] In so doing Kratochwil takes a new approach to understanding law. He is unhappy with existing accounts of law and argues that law should be understood as neither a 'static system of norms nor as a set of rules which all share some common characteristic such as sanctions'.[97] Equally so, it is 'mistaken to depict law simply as a process in which claims and counter-claims are made'.[98] Instead law is a 'choice-process characterised by the principled nature of the *norm-use* in arriving at a decision through reasoning. What the law *is* cannot therefore be decided by a quick look at statutes, treaties or codes ... but can only be ascertained through the *performance* of rule-application to a controversy and the appraisal of the reasons offered in defence of a decision.'[99] In other words, justice is continually being remade and discovered in every legal decision. Instead we should see it as 'a particular branch of practical reasoning'[100] which is governed by the context of legal topoi: in essence the legal version of the legal intersubjective context.[101] So it is legal reasoning or rhetoric which makes the law distinct as a branch of practical reasoning. Law is a particular kind of reasoning[102] and this form of reasoning unites *all* legal systems: common, civilian, domestic

---

[96] Kratochwil, *Rules, Norms and Decisions*, p. 251.   [97] *Ibid.* p. 18.

[98] *Ibid.* p. 18. Compare with the view of law as process articulated by lawyers like Higgins in her book *Problems and Process*.

[99] Kratochwil, *Rules, Norms and Decisions*, p. 18.

[100] *Ibid.* p. 18.   [101] This is my term, not Kratochwil's.

[102] According to Kratochwil: 'The fact that even the common law, whose law of evidence is usually identified with the jury trial, exhibits fundamentally "rhetorical" features suggests a more systematic root for these similarities. It is not the rather weak "diffusion" of Roman legal doctrine ... but rather the requirements of the discursive [sic] treatment of claims which accounts of such a coincidence' (Kratochwil, *Rules, Norms and Decisions*, p. 230). It is inherent in the nature of law. 'The common rhetorical tradition which views legal action as a contest between two *pleadings* leading to an authoritative judgement establishes the

and international. The essence of law is its reasoning process and this is what makes it distinct from non-legal reasoning and unifies seemingly disparate legal systems. It also simplifies the task of understanding how law works and reveals the flaws of the traditional ways of understanding law.

Such accounts have erred in focusing too much on the outcome of a case and ignoring the process of argumentation that produced the decision. This has led traditional accounts of law to rely upon the idea of subsumption when explaining how legal decision-making works. Subsumption is the 'common but naïve view'[103] that a judge applies a norm to a case by subsuming the relevant case under the general norm. But in reality there will always be more than one factual reading of a case[104] and the task at hand for the judge is to interpret the facts and the law. This is what it means when you say that legal reasoning is analogous: analogies are drawn between the case at hand and previous cases. An analogy will be more successful the better it fits the facts and the law. The job of the opposing lawyers and the judge is appraisal of a range of analogies. For Kratochwil the idea of analogies 'lie[s] at the heart of legal reasoning and illuminate[s] a wide variety of jurisprudential problems'.[105] This is important because it means that legal decision-making and the application of law to a case is not yes/no or on/off, but more like a question of percentages and relative fit. Judges therefore are not simply applying norms to a case (subsumption) but 'select among the presented interpretations which are tendered by the parties to a controversy'.[106]

The reliance upon analogies subsequently makes legal reasoning extremely path dependent, just as in ethical and normative reasoning.[107] Indeed, path dependency is more evident in legal reasoning because there is an explicit and recorded series of pleadings and rebuttals, as well as authoritative decision-making. Legal decisions also differ from non-legal ones in that there are certain ethical principles which all legal professionals have to heed and this, along with the path dependency which is inherent in reasoning, serve as 'a backdrop to understanding

---

commonality between continental and common law. Furthermore, it is the notion of proof as an *argumentum*, rather than as a more deductive entailment of inductive generalisation which constitutes the judicial "style" of reasoning common to both legal cultures' (p. 230).

[103] Kratochwil, *Rules, Norms and Decisions*, p. 220.

[104] This is something the common-sense interpretation of law outlined in chapter 2 fails to see. See chapter 2.

[105] Kratochwil, *Rules, Norms and Decisions*, p. 223.   [106] *Ibid.* p. 227.   [107] *Ibid.* p. 214.

and as a "frame" for the practice of legal arguing'.[108] Law is also path dependent in another sense: the historical decisions of courts influence later legal decisions.[109]

Kratochwil's reliance upon analogies and the path dependency of legal reasoning means that the context is of crucial importance. Here Kratochwil returns to the notion of topoi that he develops in his discussion of rules and norms in general choice situations. While Kratochwil does not use the notion of an intersubjective context in a specifically legal sense, nor does he clarify the precise relationship between legal topoi and the intersubjective context, we can infer that legal topoi, just like non-legal topoi, are part of it and help to constitute it.

It is topoi that enable us to link the facts with the law invoked by providing 'starting points' for arguments and locating the debate within a substantive set of common understandings that Kratochwil argues 'provide for the crucial connections within the structure of the argument'.[110] Topoi can be both general in that they are akin to common sense and specific in that they can relate to a particular area of practical reasoning, like the law. Topoi essentially enable us to relate bits of knowledge we have with new information and therefore make sense of it and situate it within our world view. Thus '[i]t is through such a topical "ordering" that everyday language can mediate between different areas of knowledge'.[111]

So how does this work when applied to a court case? There are a number of stages. First, the controversy must be put into legal form, in Kratochwil's words 'hammering it into legal shape through the pleas of the parties and through the decisions during the pre-trial procedures'.[112] Next, different accounts or descriptions of the case will be offered by opposing sides. According to Kratochwil the characterisation of an act 'stands in a close nexus to relevant norms governing a case'[113] and as a result, how an act is characterised can be crucial. We cannot place just any characterisation we like on something: any account we give must satisfy certain requirements of 'the communicative situation of the practical discourse'.[114] Within the legal forum a more specific appraisal is needed and this is only possible through the discursive application of specialised, legal topoi. Moreover the procedural rules and practices which tell us how the case should be run, as well as providing 'assurances that . . . a case is looked at from different angles',[115] are also topoi. Finally, topoi are found in the decision itself which 'depends for its persuasiveness

---

[108] *Ibid.* p. 238.   [109] *Ibid.* p. 243.   [110] *Ibid.* p. 219.   [111] *Ibid.* p. 220.   [112] *Ibid.* p. 227.
[113] *Ibid.* p. 227.   [114] *Ibid.* p. 228.   [115] *Ibid.* p. 228.

largely upon a careful weaving of legal and common-sense arguments into one strand of thought. They "back" the decision and its characterisation of the case.'[116]

Topoi therefore are crucial to a case at every stage: at the general level (as in initial characterisation), in the specifically legal appraisal of the case, in the procedures of the case, and in the decision itself. As Kratochwil says: 'It is through this embeddedness of the specialised "legal" language in the practical discourse that the importance of topoi as backings or groundings for decisions become visible.'[117] Yet as Kratochwil argues the path dependency of reasoning, legal or otherwise, does allow for some fluidity and that the same results can be reached by different routes.[118] Throughout the process of a case practical judgements will be made on factual situations: facts and norms are applied to one another and it is, in Kratochwil's view, this 'artfulness' that is the heart of legal reasoning and the key to understanding what the law is and how legal rules and norms work and mould decisions. Justice therefore is not, according to Kratochwil, an attribute of the formal principles contained in positive law but 'is the result of reasonable and principled use of the norms in making practical judgements about factual situations'.[119] This means that for Kratochwil justice is recreated in each case. This is why the 'law' and 'justice' stand in a certain relationship of tension in Kratochwil's opinion: 'it is only through the authoritative decision of a court that it can be established what is fair and reasonable in a particular case'.[120] Justice does not lie in the invariant principle for formal justice but in *field-dependent criteria* of what counts, for instance, as a good faith effort' etc.[121] Kratochwil has no doubt that 'justice' will be found and served in each court case. Just as rationality is only relative to the intersubjective context, so too is justice only justice if it fits with commonly held ideas of what justice is.

Law creation by judges should not concern us either because this is not norm creation *de novo* but rather is 'path and field dependent in that dogmatic (systematic) considerations and/or precedential "starting-points" provide the context in which the decision has to be made'.[122] In doing this Kratochwil justifies one of the biggest taboos in jurisprudence: judge-made

---

[116] *Ibid.* p. 228.   [117] *Ibid.* p. 228.
[118] *Ibid.* p. 240. Kratochwil does not mention that a different result might be produced, a key theoretical move made by legal realists and critical legal scholars.
[119] *Ibid.* p. 240.   [120] *Ibid.* p. 240.   [121] *Ibid.* p. 241, emphasis in original.
[122] *Ibid.* p. 241.

law. Mainstream jurisprudence holds fast to the notion that judges do not make law but only apply it. They are little more than legal technicians, impartially applying the legal rules, as provided by the common law and the legislative body. Only elected representatives have the right to make law. Yet Kratochwil rejects this as fiction and argues that not only do judges make the law but this is nothing to be concerned about. This places all the theoretical weight on the legal context. Kratochwil trusts that the legal intersubjective context will operate solely to produce justice and fairness but by locating *all* the explanatory weight in this legal normative world, Kratochwil removes any chance we have to critique it. There is nothing outside of the legal normative context which can be brought to bear upon it.

For Zehfuss, Kratochwil's idea of the intersubjective context legitimises any and all action by reference to norms. This stunts our critical faculty and both masks and abrogates the responsibility of the individual. Kratochwil is perfectly able to recognise the reality of how a court case works, for example, but he fails to see that this might involve power relations or hierarchy in any significant way. His vision of the social world is entirely innocent.

To take the legal example further, Kratochwil's picture of how a court case works is devoid of anything critical. We evaluate and appraise facts, we apply different topoi – general and legal – in the process of argumentation and decision. But nowhere do we judge our fellow human beings with anything other than complete respect and fair-mindedness. Kratochwil writes that 'no description of an action is acceptable that hides or evades the effect our actions have on others' interests. These considerations provide the reasons for the privileged status of some accounts over others',[123] i.e. honest or disinterested ones. He does not challenge the idea that good legal arguing or reasoning is enough: provided what happens in court meets these standards then we have nothing to worry about.[124]

Kratochwil fails to see how entering the legal forum alters the actors and the dispute. He quotes Stone:

> People not only walk and punch, they trespass and commit battery. They are not persons simpliciter, but buyers and sellers. The legal language answers the fundamental question of jural ontology . . . The language too determines what attributes of the world are to be noticed: monetary value and certain mental states have gained a place as have pain and suffering and consent.[125]

---

[123] *Ibid.* p. 228. [124] *Ibid.* p. 241.
[125] Christopher Stone quoted in Kratochwil, *Rules, Norms and Decisions*, p. 229.

Kratochwil fails to pick up on the implication of Stone's insight: that certain values are privileged over others and only certain types of 'person' are seen and served by the legal system. The world as seen from the standpoint of the law is partial, not complete. Not only does it transform us as we enter it, but it removes parts of our identity that it does not deem relevant.[126] Intention may be attributed where there was none, consent inferred, inferences drawn from silence. Witnesses and defendants do not have the right to simply say what they want but may only respond to the questioning of legal professionals, unless they choose to defend themselves. Human experiences are altered and channelled into the appropriate legal form, bits sheared off, bits added on.[127] An individual's experience in court can be frustrating, humiliating or silencing.

Nor are the values of the legal system neutral, as Kratochwil himself admits: 'the characterisation of actions ... is not a description at all, but rather an *appraisal*; it is an evaluation of "facts" in terms of some normative considerations ... [pure observation is not possible] an "objective" fact is not the thing described but rather the intersubjective *validity* of a characterisation upon which reasonable persons can agree'.[128] The problem however with this admission is that Kratochwil relies upon the intersubjective context to mitigate against bias and unfairness, but it does not necessarily follow that just because values or norms are shared that they are right or just or fair.

He also writes that 'legal institutions have *their own* values and logic'[129] but what this actually means for Kratochwil is that 'equity, reason, etc., imbue law with ethical traits, [and] it is also true that thereby ethics is *juridified*'.[130] It is simply the case that fairness, equity and reason from ethics are introduced to law and in return are put in a certain, juridical form. There is no questioning of what the values of legal institutions might be: it is simply assumed that they *are* equity and reason, and so on. There is no indication that legal institutions may be prejudiced in any way, or even that the sociological make-up of such

---

[126] This is a long-standing criticism made by feminists; see chapter 5.

[127] According to Rock: 'Trials are ceremonial, disciplined, and staged, and they unfold in set order. Participants come forward at their proper times to perform their stylised parts. Every appearance must be choreographed precisely and unambiguously. Were that not so, there could be allegations of misconduct and appeals for retrials.' (Rock, *The Social World of an English Crown Court*, p. 27.)

[128] Kratochwil, *Rules, Norms and Decisions*, p. 229.   [129] *Ibid.* p. 242.   [130] *Ibid.* p. 242.

institutions might be worryingly narrow.[131] Legal institutions are simply neutral. So when Kratochwil talks of the logic of legal institutions what he means is 'how different rules of, for instance, contract law, torts, etc., fit together, provides important clues about the constraints of judicial law-making'.[132] It is Kratochwil's faith in the intersubjective context that has the potential to undermine his entire theoretical edifice; or so I shall try to argue in this book.

International law

Given Kratochwil's tendency to miss the critical, does his analysis of international law fare any better? Unfortunately, not markedly so. Because Kratochwil believes that it is the nature of reasoning that unites all legal systems, the same basic assumptions about domestic law are extended to international law. However, Kratochwil does explicitly reject the domestic analogy, which he finds misleading. While the reasoning process that underpins international law may be the same as that which underpins domestic systems, the international legal system is still unique with unique challenges.

In many respects Kratochwil treats international law as *sui generis*. He writes that it exists 'simply by virtue of its role in defining the game of international relations. It informs the respective decision-makers about the nature of the interaction and determines who is an actor; it sets the steps necessary to insure the validity of their official acts and assigns weight and priority to different claims.'[133] Moreover it cannot be seen as domestic law writ large: there are simply too many significant differences between the two. Most significantly the legal process cannot be separated from the political process and this means that the impartiality of legal reasoning that Kratochwil sees as characterising the domestic system is impaired by the lack of authoritative decisions about how the law should operate. The absence of an authority which can establish once and for all what the law is and to rule on legal disputes, means that the international legal system risks being completely paralysed by disputes to which no definitive

---

[131] In England and Wales, of the twelve Lords of Appeal in Ordinary only one is a woman, the five Heads of Division are all men and three of the thirty-six Lords Justice of Appeal are women. Even at the most junior end of scale – Deputy Masters, Deputy Registrars, Deputy Costs Judges and Deputy District Judges – women make up only 34%. Data correct as of 1 April 2008. Source: www.judiciary.gov.uk/keyfacts/statistics/women.htm. Accessed June 2009.

[132] Kratochwil, *Rules, Norms and Decisions*, p. 243.   [133] *Ibid.* p. 251.

resolution is possible. Because the international legal system lacks the apparatus and structure of a domestic legal system, it must find substitutes, such as Advisory Opinions and the writings of legal scholars.[134]

International legal fora face a particular difficulty 'because judges and courts are primarily institutions entrusted with the protection of interest funnelled through the domestic legal order'.[135] This difficulty leads to some peculiar tensions in transnational legal disputes when domestic courts have to wear two hats at the same time, i.e., that of a domestic institution and that of an international agency. Moreover, principles are invoked *ad hoc* because the interaction of norm and more specific rules is only weakly articulated in the transnational arena. In the absence of a clearer identification of the international legal order's needs, interest adjustments rarely go beyond the short-term *particular* weighing of the concrete interests in a *particular* case. This inhibits the growth of normative 'solutions' or 'structures'.[136] It is therefore reasonably fair to characterise the international arena as a primitive system.[137]

Moreover, we should not view non-compliance in international law in the same way as we would view it in the domestic arena. Precisely because the means of peaceful change in the international arena are new and, by and large, ineffective, the violation of a legal norm is often not a pure act of lawlessness but rather part of a larger bargaining game for change. Given the far closer links between politics and law in the international arena Kratochwil notes that 'differentials of development and power still matter' and he recognises that there is an 'imbalance of power resulting from the unequal distribution of resources and know-how'.[138] This insight however only applies to the international legal system and Kratochwil recognises no such equivalent hierarchy in domestic society.

In sum then the 'bloodlessness' of Kratochwil's account of politics and society is also present in Kratochwil's picture of international law. While he recognises power and hierarchy in the international system, he sees this as a consequence of the lack of an overarching sovereign. Moreover, he sees the international legal arena itself as relatively benign: transgression and non-compliance are not lawlessness but part of a process of bargaining. In the legal arena, compliance is therefore very similar to

---

[134] Article 38(1)(d) of the Statute of the International Court of Justice lists 'judicial decisions and the teachings of the most highly qualified publicists of the various nations as subsidiary means for the determination of rules of law'. See: www.icj-cij.org/documents/index.php?p1=4&p2=2&p3=0#CHAPTER_II.
[135] Kratochwil, *Rules, Norms and Decisions*, p. 246.
[136] *Ibid.* p. 246.   [137] *Ibid.* p. 247.   [138] *Ibid.* p. 255.

speech act theory in the domestic arena. At base, the actors are just collectively working out the rules of the game. It seems more brutal at the international level because international society is far less evolved and is younger than domestic society. As in his theory of society generally, Kratochwil recognises that power and hierarchy exist but he sees them as relatively insignificant. Where Onuf is forced to choose between the critical and the technical, Kratochwil keeps both but denudes the critical aspect of any real significance.

Conclusion

There are several similarities between Onuf and Kratochwil's work and both share common flaws. First, both rely heavily on context or society. The success or failure of proposed norms depends upon their 'fit' with the existing context. Change therefore can only happen incrementally. For both Onuf and Kratochwil this reliance on society, or context as they refer to it, is unproblematic because both assume that what society thinks, holds to be true or will accept is right. Neither consider the possibility that the dominant ideas within a society may be wrong or unjust. Rather, because society holds them they are, by definition, right. This acceptance serves to legitimise the status quo. In part this may be because neither author wants to engage with complex analysis of context: both explicitly decline to do so on the grounds that it is complex and apt to confuse analysis, rather than enlighten it. While this is an understandable and possibly necessary decision to make, I think this ultimately handicaps their theories. Granted, both can produce logical and relatively parsimonious theories. Yet when they are applied to society and to account for the emergence, operation and evolution of norms, they are of limited use.

I argue that the 'unreality' of both approaches stems in large part from the desire to produce a taxonomy of rules and norms. Their purpose is technical and in viewing norms and society technically they have sheared off anything potentially political. What I mean by 'political' is essentially 'personal' in the sense that one person sees the world in a different way to the next. Prejudices, ignorance and preferences all shape our behaviour. Because both Onuf and Kratochwil use Habermasian speech act theory, they see human understanding and reasoning as working in rational ways. Individuals are aware of their normative context and consciously reason about and choose between competing norms. Individuals always have the option of disregarding a norm. Neither author considers that this may come at a cost. Nor do they believe that certain norms can become so embedded that we do not see them and could not ever rationally challenge them or refuse them. Instead, we operate in the perfect, technical unreality of the Habermasian speech act theory. And it is this understanding of how individuals relate to their normative context that leads both authors to attribute a high degree of agency to individuals.

But this is a picture of the world as viewed by its elites. It is a world of individuals who are empowered through wealth, education, class, race, nationality and gender. While Onuf sees the critical path before him in his notion of 'rule', he wants to hold both parts of his theory simultaneously. This means seeing the world as composed of technical and rational operating rules but also believing that rules produce rule, that is, hierarchy and oppression. If rules do this, then they will inevitably become embroiled in and reinforce rule. They will no longer be neutral and our understanding of them cannot be in purely technical terms. If we are to truly understand the normative world, our understanding of rule must colour our understanding of rules. There cannot be a hermetically sealed divide between the two.

Such a divide and the subsequent intellectual gymnastics is not necessary for Kratochwil: he simply does not see the critical potential which his theory, at times, points him towards. Instead, Kratochwil can focus, undisturbed by reality, on the elaboration of a technical roadmap of how the world works. And it is this emphasis on technicality to the exclusion of anything political or critical that causes constructivism's, and consequently IR theory's, inability to see both law and society as they truly are, rather than how we would logically want them to be.

2

Challenging the common sense idea of law

The language of judicial decision is mainly the language of logic. And the logical method and form flatter that longing for certainty and for repose which is in every human mind. But certainty is generally an illusion, and repose is not the destiny of man.

Oliver Wendell Holmes[1]

Introduction: setting the scene

This chapter starts by identifying the dominant popular perception of law and picking apart and exploring its individual elements. For want of a better term, I have called this the common sense idea of law as this is most frequently how this picture of law is referred to. I do not mean to suggest that this picture of law is held only by those without the benefit of a legal education. Most academics, regardless of disciplinary allegiance, would exempt themselves from this category. Instead this is a popular narrative about law and is held by many members of the legal profession. It is also extremely powerful. In part, this is the power of the designation of 'common sense': who would disagree with common sense? But its power also stems from being so powerfully intertwined with the evolution of jurisprudence: the common sense idea of law is essentially a popular understanding of formalism. Formalism reigned supreme during the nineteenth century but it has been around in some form since the twelfth century. All this changed in the twentieth century when it was overwhelmingly rejected by academia. This rejection has yet to cross over into the popular imagination for two reasons: (i) the formalist idea of law fits perfectly into our understanding of the modern state, the separation of powers and the rule of law; and (ii) a convincing and suitably fitting alternative has yet to be found.

---

[1] Holmes, 'The Path of the Law', 465–6.

An important feature of the formalistic common sense idea of law is an idea of how legal reasoning and decision-making work. The emphasis is almost exclusively on deductive reasoning, to the exclusion of the other types of reasoning employed by legal professionals, namely inductive reasoning and analogical reasoning. Indeed, the insufficiency of the sole focus on deductive reasoning by formalism was the path to its eventual debunking. Legal realists challenged the notion that law was simply the application of general legal rules or principles to particular fact situations. According to Menand, Holmes, perhaps *the* pre-eminent legal realist, 'liked to tell his colleagues on the Supreme Court, when they were conferring about a case, that he would admit any general principle of law they proposed, and then use it to decide the case under discussion either way'.[2] However, Holmes believed that specific legal rules would determine results in most cases and that the possibility of judicial legislation only occurred in a penumbra of cases where the application of the rule was unclear. In *Southern Pacific* v. *Jenson*, Holmes conceded that: 'I recognize without hesitation that judges do and must legislate, but they can do so only interstitially.'[3] However, other realists, like Frank, believed that legal principles and rules could not determine a legal decision and that to claim that they did was to fool oneself and fool the public.[4]

The legal realists were on to something. In reality legal reasoning extends beyond just deductive reasoning and beyond just legal rules and principles. In so-called 'hard cases', where the law 'runs out' (that is to say, there is no directly applicable law) lawyers and judges will use non-legal factors to make their case and reach their decision. It is the *recognition* of the entry of non-legal factors into legal decision-making that caused such a problem, arguably because the reigning jurisprudential orthodoxy of formalism had no way of accounting for them or theorising them.

Throughout the twentieth century the debunking of formalism via the question of the role of non-legal factors in legal decision-making became widespread throughout non-mainstream scholarship. The significance of these non-legal factors lay in what they could be. Initially, when

---

[2] Menand quoted in Bix, *Jurisprudence*, footnote 20, p. 181. Holmes famously argued that: 'General propositions do not decide concrete cases' (*Lochner* v. *New York*, 198 US 45 at 76 (1905) (Holmes J., dissenting)).

[3] *Southern Pacific* v. *Jensen*, 244 US 205 at 221 (1917).

[4] See Frank, 'Are Judges Human?', 80.

recognition was new, theorists envisaged these non-legal factors as public policy. Traditionally, the notion that politics entered into the law was strictly taboo and this idea persists today.[5] Legal realism was radical and new in suggesting that law should be a tool for achieving certain social goals and that, even if the law could and did determine the result of a case, it could still be that the law should be changed. Within the context of 1920s and 1930s America, where American legal realism originated, the possibility of achieving social engineering through law was viewed in a generally positive light. This initial optimism did not last. Scandinavian legal realism, the other variant of legal realism, emphasised instead the reality of legal decision-making as one man deciding the fate of another.[6] Reducing the operation of law to its starkest terms made the law appear arbitrary as never before. The non-legal factors began to include the personal prejudices of the individual judge and judges themselves came under scrutiny. No longer the guardians of justice and impartial adjudicators, they were old, white, middle- to upper-class men. The institution of law itself was challenged: how did law relate to society and the political elite? Judges were undoubtedly part of the elite. Was law just a way of the elite maintaining its privileged position in society, under the guise of doing justice? With the emergence of critical legal studies[7] and feminist accounts[8] of law, systematic and structural factors like capitalism, racism and patriarchy became part of law's ontology. In the face of such powerful forces, law and legal reasoning are unable to provide significant resistance and legal reasoning is seen as arbitrary by critical jurisprudence and unable to produce justice. All it could do is produce the consistency that is a side-effect of maintaining an unjust social order.

While the critical approach to law spread rapidly through the left-wing intellectual ghettos, the mainstream continued much as before. Because critical legal studies emerged only in the 1980s, mainstream responses to it are relatively recent. Essentially this counter-argument revolves around the argument that law and legal reasoning are not as susceptible to the

---

[5] For the belief that judges do not make law see *Willis* v. *Baddeley* [1892] 2 QB 324.

[6] The Scandinavian legal realists include Hägerström, Olivecrona, and Ross. See Hägerström, *Inquiries into the Nature of Law and Morals*, Olivecrona, *Law as Fact* and Ross, *On Law and Justice*.

[7] Hutchinson and Monahan, 'Law, Politics, and the Critical Legal Scholars'; Kairys, *The Politics of Law*; Fitzpatrick and Hunt (eds.), *Critical Legal Studies*; Gordon, 'Law and Ideology', 14–18 and 83–6; Goodrich, *Reading the Law*.

[8] MacKinnon, *Feminism Unmodified*; MacKinnon, *Toward a Feminist Theory of the State*; Naffine, *Law and the Sexes;* Naffine and Owens (eds.), *Sexing the Subject of Law*; Smart, *Feminism and the Power of Law*; Smart, *Law, Crime and Sexuality*.

charge of arbitrariness as critical legal studies believes. Doubtless there are some bad judges, some bad decisions and some level of prejudice (though such responses never conceive of this prejudice as being institutional) but surely not in every case? This would imply a level of consistency and ordering that even mainstream legal scholars now recognise as fictional. Scholars like MacCormick argue that the fact that judges must justify their decisions acts as a constraint. Moreover, both logic and the nature of language restrict them from producing decisions which are patently biased. Because critical legal studies condemns all law and legal decision-making as arbitrary and potentially dismisses all of law, it does not see the constraints which are implicit in the law. In short, critical legal studies goes too far and does so at the cost of intellectual accuracy. Mainstream responses therefore depict themselves as an eminently more sensible and accurate representation of law, and based in the substantive reality of actual cases and real decisions, rather than taking a theoretical and abstracted high point which makes a broad-brush rejection of all law possible. The challenge of this chapter and broadly of this book is to decide which elements to take from each side.

The remainder of this chapter demonstrates to IR theorists that many of our implicit ideas about law, which flow through into analysis of international law, reflect the formalistic common sense idea of law. Relatedly the chapter aims to introduce IR theorists to the basics of legal reasoning before adding in layers of complexity and in the hope of providing them with a more complex yet more accurate understanding of law. It is hoped that by providing a grounding in both legal reasoning and jurisprudence that IR theorists will question their own assumptions about law and ultimately move towards a richer and more accurate understanding. To this end, chapter 3, on critical jurisprudence, functions as a second half to this chapter, extending the focus on jurisprudence to critical variants.

The common sense view of law

The common sense idea of law becomes hardwired into our psyches as part of our socialisation. As Mansell, Meteyard and Thomson argue: 'The newspapers confirm it, the police confirm it, the government confirms it, *Lord of the Flies* confirms it. Law, we are taught, is what protects and preserves civilisation from chaos.'[9] According to Davies, 'many people

---

[9] Mansell, Meteyard and Thomson, *A Critical Introduction to Law*, p. 3.

will ... have internalised the official message about law and culture, simply because of the power of prevailing ideologies'.[10] It is difficult to get away from this common sense view simply because by the time we encounter other ideas of law it has already taken such a strong hold in our minds that it is difficult to conceive of alternative ideas of the law.[11] The power of the common sense idea of law lies in the belief that it is simply depicting reality, rather than constituting it, but as Mansell, Meteyard and Thomson point out, 'law in our society is maintained in the form in which it is *because* of our perception of law, *because* of our common sense'.[12]

Shklar's idea of legalism holds that moral conduct is a matter of rule-following and that all human relations can be put into the form of claims and counter-claims over rights and duties flowing from those rules. This ethos has percolated throughout our society from the highest courts in the land to the village green. It shapes our conceptions of domestic law and the way we understand human relations. We understand the world through the idea of rights, so much so that envisaging justice as anything other than the 'equal application of rules'[13] is almost impossible. This is both what justice is and how we achieve it. The common sense idea of law depicts legal rules as both necessary and neutral and as applied by impartial legal technicians. It is the Western world's assumptions about law which in turn have become the globally dominant idea of law. It is not only a way of resolving disputes but of being in and seeing the world.

Although the common sense idea of law is defined in slightly different ways by different authors, Goodrich argues that it will always have two core elements:

> the legal institution itself has maintained a virtually uninterrupted doc-trinal belief in the distinctiveness of law, a belief in its unity and its separation from other phenomena of social control. The two claims, those of unity and of separation, have traditionally been closely linked in legal doctrine; law is kept separate and distinct from other institutions and forms of control precisely by virtue of being a unity, by virtue of having an 'essential' characteristic which distinguishes law from all else.[14]

Law is seen as separate from everyday life and the social situations it is called upon to resolve. This is what Shklar means when she refers to law

[10] Davies, *Asking the Law Question*, p. 168.
[11] Mansell, Meteyard and Thomson, *A Critical Introduction to Law*, p. 3.
[12] *Ibid.* p. 6.   [13] Shklar, *Legalism*, p. 109.   [14] Goodrich, *Reading the Law*, p. 4.

as being 'there'. To clarify: 'To be "there" it [the law] must be self-regulating, immune from the unpredictable pressures of politicians and moralists, manned by an impartial judiciary that at least tries to maintain justice's celebrated blindness. That is why it is seen as a series of impersonal rules which fit together neatly.'[15] This separation from politics and non-legal factors is part and parcel of the representation of law as operating in a formal way, like mathematics or geometry. Moreover, like the natural sciences, legal rules are clear, predictable and politically neutral. Law operates impartially and is nothing more than the routine application of rules to the facts by legal technicians.[16] As Kairys points out in his version of the common sense idea of law, 'the law on a particular issue is pre-existing, clear, predictable'.[17] The job of lawyers therefore is to discover the relevant rules and apply them in order to determine legality and to ensure that actions conform to the rules. Indeed, the operation of law is rather routine and 'any reasonably competent and fair judge will reach the "correct" decision'.[18] The separation of law from non-legal factors is a key part of our idea of law, namely that it is a superior mode of social action to politics: what Shklar calls the policy of justice.

According to Cotterrell all legal theories are united in their desire to demonstrate the unity of law:

> It may involve trying to identify a consistent moral or cultural foundation of legal regulation which validates and gives moral meaning . . . [or] it may entail trying to show how the entirety of legal rules and regulations can be seen as part of a single rational structure, or how legal reasoning entails consistent methods or epistemological assumptions . . . It may involve a search for purposive unity of law, so that all its elements are to be interpreted and evaluated in terms of some fundamental objectives (for example, social, moral . . .) which they are thought to serve.[19]

According to Cotterrell, closely connected to the need to demonstrate the unity or consistency of law is the need to separate law from its context and to distinguish the legal from the non-legal. He argues that this is because it is assumed that the task of clarifying what law is and how it operates is rendered simpler by closing off non-legal factors from

---

[15] Shklar, *Legalism*, p. 35.
[16] There is considerable overlap between the popular conception of law and the rule of law. I discuss the rule of law below.
[17] Kairys (ed.), *The Politics of Law*, pp. 1–2.
[18] *Ibid.* pp. 1–2.   [19] Cotterrell, *The Politics of Jurisprudence*, p. 9.

analysis and is therefore an implicit goal of many legal theories.[20] This Shklarian tendency to think of law as 'there' as a discrete entity, which is discernibly different from morals and politics, is rooted in the legal profession's views of its own functions, and according to Shklar forms the basis of most of our judicial institutions and procedures.[21] This idea in turn is reinforced by the structure of legal education and the nature of legal methodology. It also means that the law can therefore be understood without reference to the societies in which it evolved and which it continues to regulate. Law has an integral history of its own and one that can be understood without reference to social context. Law evolves according to a logic of its own. For Shklar, legalism cannot see law as a product of its social context and influenced by the different historical epochs through which it evolves, because to do so would reveal that the laws we have are a consequence not only of those different historical eras, but also of the interests of the powerful throughout history. To both Cotterrell and Shklar this deliberate isolation of the legal system is the expression of a preference, rather than a logical necessity of legal reasoning or judging human actions; it is the result of legalism.

Formalism

As suggested above the primary influence on the common sense idea of law is formalism, which claims that legal decision-makers both are and should be constrained to follow the law as it is, not as it should be. Existing law should be their only guide and consideration. Bix identifies two elements to formalism: first, legal concepts and principles are neutral and secondly, general legal concepts or rules can determine results in particular cases.[22] A judge will therefore decide a case by discovering the appropriate legal rule and applying it, a process which requires and uses only deductive reasoning.[23] It is the job of the legislature is make law, not the judge, and for a judge to have the discretion to interpret laws would

---

[20] *Ibid.* pp. 12–14.   [21] Shklar, *Legalism*, p. 9.   [22] Bix, *Jurisprudence*, pp. 180–1.
[23] Formalism poses unique challenges for common law systems which rely heavily on precedent. What distinguishes common law systems, like the England and the United States, from civil law systems is the binding nature of precedent and the reliance upon case law as a source of law. When deciding a case, a judge will look at previous cases and will be bound by previous decisions by courts of higher standing. This means that much of the law is essentially made by judges, either as new law or simply as the repetition and reinforcement of existing legal interpretation. Civil law systems also rely on precedent but it is not binding, merely persuasive.

violate the separation of powers upon which the rule of law modern state rests. It is assumed that the processes that produced the laws have exhausted all possible normative and policy considerations and that once a proposed law comes into force it is no longer up for contestation. Its form, content and meaning are fixed. The law is therefore a closed system both normatively and logically.[24]

Formalism has been soundly rejected in jurisprudence for most of the twentieth century, so much so that it has become a term of abuse and short-hand for an inaccurate and myopic theory of law. As Bix puts it: 'If it was once subversive to think that extralegal factors influence judicial decisions, it now seems naïve to doubt it.'[25] According to Posner the rejection of formalism stemmed from three of its characteristics.[26] First, its conceptualism and scientism. Formalism sees law as a set of principles and legal reasoning as a branch of exact inquiry. Secondly, the static quality of formalism, 'its penchant for treating the cases from which the principles of law are inferred as a set of data having no chronological dimension and the principles themselves as timeless, like the propositions of Euclidean geometry'.[27] And finally, the separation of law from life: the formalists' data is judicial opinions, not the problems and practice of social life.

Despite this, however, formalism is still a powerful force in contemporary understandings of law. For a start it has clearly had a significant influence on the layperson's idea of law. Moreover, many of the core assumptions held and defended by legal professionals are formalistic, like the idea that judges do not legislate. Whilst most legal professionals will concede that, in certain limited circumstances, judges do make law, the vast majority ardently defend the general principle. Indeed, for legal professionals the prospect of indeterminacy is so worrying that it is deliberately minimised. Many do so simply because if the belief that judges had the latitude to make law as and when they pleased became widely accepted within society, then the power and legitimacy of the law would be called into serious doubt. The primary concern of most legal professionals is the desire to maintain their autonomy because this insulates them from political interference.

---

[24] Clearly there are links to legal positivism. Positivism focuses on what law is whereas formalism focuses on how law operates.
[25] Bix, *Jurisprudence*, p. 184.   [26] Posner, *The Problems of Jurisprudence*, pp. 15–16.
[27] *Ibid.* p. 16.

Part of the reason that formalism has played such an important role in contemporary jurisprudence, including those who support and those who deny it, is that for several hundred years it was simply an essential set of assumptions to hold about law. Prior to the emergence of secularism the legitimacy and power of law came directly from God and the Church. As the power of the Church began to be rolled back, law had to find a new source of power and legitimacy which was separate from the Church. Simply put, law had to rely upon itself and the way it did this was to emphasise two things about itself: the logical consistency of the legal system and its separation of non-legal influences, like religion or politics. In other words, unity and separation. Law was fair, logical and impartial. Its decision-makers were not influenced by any considerations other than the law, and society could trust the law and legal practitioners to do justice. Without formalism, the continued legitimacy of the law would have been severely compromised in the move towards secularism. Given that formalism was an important idea of law from the twelfth to the nineteenth century, it is unsurprising that the twentieth century's debunking of it has not succeeded in eradicating it completely.

The other main reason for the continued relevance of formalism lies in the rule of law. Historically formalism has been essential to the rule of law and the dominant conception of the modern state. Hutchinson and Monahan call the rule of law 'a rare and protean principle of our political tradition ... it has withstood the ravages of constitutional time and remains a contemporary clarion-call to political justice. Apparently transcending partisan concerns, it is embraced and venerated by virtually all shades of political opinion'.[28] It manages to be the central jewel in liberalism's crown but is also seen by the left as an 'unqualified human good'.[29] It comprises two aspects: restraint and regularity. Raz similarly identified two aspects: (i) that people should be ruled by law and obey it; and (ii) that the law should be such that people will be able to be guided by it.[30]

Dicey defines the rule of law as 'the universal subjection of all classes, to one law'.[31] For Harris it: 'requires that every governmental action must be justified by legal authority, and that the operation of government itself is carried out within a framework of legal rules and

---

[28] Hutchinson and Monahan, *The Rule of Law*, p. 1.
[29] Thompson, *Whigs and Hunters*, p. 266.   [30] Raz, 'The Rule of Law and Its Virtue', 198.
[31] Dicey quoted in Naffine, *Law and the Sexes*, p. 51.

principles.'[32] But Hayek interprets it slightly differently: '[G]overn-
ment in all its actions is bound by rules fixed and announced
beforehand – rules which make it possible to foresee with fair certainty
how the authority will use its coercive powers in given circumstances,
and to plan one's individual affairs on the basis of this knowledge.'[33]

Raz in turn compiled what is taken to be the definitive list of
criteria for the rule of law. Laws should be prospective, rather than
retroactive; they should be stable and not change too frequently: this
helps everyone to know what the law is; there should be clear rules
and procedures for making new laws; the independence of the judiciary must be guaranteed; principles of natural justice should be
observed, especially those concerning the right to a fair trial; courts
should have the power of judicial review; the courts should be acces-
sible to all; the discretion of law enforcement and crime prevention
agencies should not be allowed to pervert the law.[34] Not every criter-
ion has to be met but the majority should be for a system to count as
having the rule of law.

It is easy to see why Shklar wrote that the term has gone the way of
similarly commonplace terms like democracy and justice and 'has become
meaningless thanks to ideological abuse and general over-use'.[35] The term

---

[32] Harris, *An Introduction to Law*, p. 69. The modern articulation of the rule of law
originated with Dicey. In *The Law of the Constitution*. Dicey divided the rule of law
into three subheadings: the absence of arbitrary power in any individual or department
of government; equality before the law, or the equal subjection of the officials of
government to the courts; and the ordinary common law applicable to all British
subjects; the fact of the constitution being part of the ordinary law of the land (Adams
and Brownsword, *Understanding Law* (2006)).

[33] Hayek quoted in Raz, 'The Rule of Law and Its Virtue', 195. Although Dicey first
articulated it in 1885 and Shklar traces it back to Aristotle, Berman claims that, in
some respects at least, the idea that law transcends politics has been consistently
articulated in Western Europe since the twelfth century (Berman, *Law and Revolution*,
p. 9). According to Berman the idea of the rule of law is central to the idea of the secular
state that emerged from the Papal Revolution. According to Berman the rule of law had
three main sources of support: first, prevailing religious ideology in which popes
and kings made law but only as God's deputies; secondly, the prevailing economic and
political weakness of rulers and the pluralism of authorities and jurisdictions; and
thirdly, the high level of legal consciousness and sophistication that came to prevail
during the twelfth and thirteenth centuries (*ibid.* p. 293). As Berman writes: 'It was well
understood that the preservation of legality required not merely abstract precepts of
justice, equity, conscience, and reason but also specific principles and rules' (*ibid.* p. 293).

[34] Raz, 'The Rule of Law and Its Virtue', 198–202.

[35] Shklar, 'Political Theory and the Rule of Law', p. 1. Raz agrees, writing that 'promiscuous
use' has meant that 'no purist can claim that truth is on his side and blame the others of
distorting the notion' ('The Rule of Law and Its Virtue', 196).

for Shklar exists in a 'political vacuum'.[36] Three different ideas of the rule of law can be discerned. First, there is the formal approach, which is the most widespread. Formalists hold that the law must be prospective, well-known, certain and apply generally and equally to all. Provided these criteria are satisfied, the formalist view asks no questions about the content of the law. The substantive interpretation, on the other hand, does and argues that, for the rule of law to exist, the law must protect some or all individual rights. Finally, the functional approach to the rule of law focuses on the functions performed by government officers: if they have a lot of discretion to decide cases then the rule of law is low, if they are restricted in their actions then the rule of law is high.

The rule of law is necessary because law itself creates the possibility of arbitrary power; as Raz argues, 'the rule of law is designed to minimise the danger created by the law itself'.[37] The idea of the rule of law is negative in two senses. First, conformity to it does not cause good except through avoiding evil and, secondly, the evil which is avoided could only be caused by law itself. It is crucial for Raz that the rule of law does not become confused with the rule of the good law:[38] a non-democratic legal system based on denial of human rights, racial segregation, sexual inequalities and religious persecution may very well conform to the rule of law. The rule of law does not a good legal system make. It is conformity that is assessed, not content or consequence.

The rule of law is principally concerned with the form of law, rather than its content: laws must not impose impossible demands, they should be prospective, not retroactive; laws should be consistent with each other; they should be public, clear and constant over time.[39] Provided a law meets the checklist of requirements its content is unimportant. The belief in the rectitude of a governance of laws, not men, has long been considered the mark of a civilised society.[40] The idea of the rule of law retains

---

[36] Shklar, 'Political Theory and the Rule of Law', p. 1.

[37] Raz, 'The Rule of Law and Its Virtue', 206.

[38] Raz, 'The Rule of Law and Its Virtue', 209.

[39] This list is Fuller's. See Fuller, *The Morality of Law*. See also Raz, *The Morality of Freedom*. This idea of law has been attacked from both the right and the left. In Hayek's version of the rule of law it is only the minimum of rules needed to allow individuals to go about their business without colliding with each other, see Hayek, *Constitution of Liberty*. There has been a sustained attack on the concept of the rule of law from the left, which sees it as a mask for oppression and exploitation, and has developed into a separate debate. See Unger, *Law in Modern Society*, and 'The Critical Legal Studies Movement', 561–675; and Kairys, *The Politics of Law*.

[40] MacCormick, 'Rhetoric and the Rule of Law', p. 163.

a powerful resonance in today's society and the common sense of law bears its imprint.

Legal reasoning in the common sense idea of law

Syllogism and deductive reasoning

The classic pattern of legal reasoning follows what is known technically as a syllogism. Syllogistic reasoning takes the following form.

If	$A = B$	major premise
And	$B = C$	minor premise
Then	$A = C$	conclusion

To put it in legal form:

It is an offence to exceed the speed limit
Exceeding the speed limit is what the defendant has done
It is an offence to do what the defendant has done

Syllogistic reasoning is deductive in nature, that is, it starts with a general principle and applies it. In both formalism and the formalistic common sense idea of law, it is only deductive reasoning that is employed by legal decision-makers and professionals, not the alternative form of inductive reasoning. However, while the application of a general legal rule or principle to a particular fact situation would appear on the face of it to be solely deductive, in reality an inductive element is unavoidable. Inductive reasoning operates in the opposite direction to deductive reasoning. Deductive reasoning starts with the general and reasons towards the specific. Inductive reasoning starts with the specific and reasons towards the general. It involves making a number of observations and using them to formulate a principle of general application.

While formalism sees no place for inductive reasoning in the law, in reality it is commonplace. As MacCormick points out, deductive reasoning can only be the sole method of reasoning in 'easy' cases: those in which either: '(a) no doubt as to interpretation of the rule or classification of facts could conceivably have arisen; or (b) no one thought of raising and arguing a point which was in truth arguable; or (c) where such an argument has been tried but dismissed as artificial or far-fetched by the Court.'[41] In 'hard' cases,

---

[41] MacCormick, *Legal Reasoning and Legal Theory*, p. 199.

where evaluation must turn to non-legal sources or where competing legal explanations must be assessed, there must be, in Farrar and Dugdale's words, 'an evaluation which goes beyond the law itself and which must be made in accordance with the "law behind the law", i.e. the basic underlying values of the legal and ultimately social system'.[42]

Indeed in case law, as opposed to statute law, 'the lawyer will have to examine several cases to find a major premise which underlies them all. He will have to reason from particular case decisions to a general proposition'.[43] When a lawyer advises on the application of case law to a particular situation she will employ inductive reasoning first in order to find a general proposition of law, and then use deductive reasoning to determine how it applies to the facts. Likewise, when deciding cases judges will use both types of logic. So if inductive logic is so widely used, why is it absent from the formalist picture of law? Quite simply because it does not fit with the formalist idea of law as the application of general rules and principles to fact situations. Equally excluded from formalism is reasoning by analogy.

Reasoning by analogy

According McLeod, analogical reasoning 'involves saying that, if a number of different things are similar to each other in a number of different, specific ways, they are, or should be, similar to each other in other ways as well'.[44] Analogical reasoning characterises the doctrine of precedent, which requires that cases with similar facts should be treated as being similar in law. The challenge of reasoning by analogy is to identify which points need to be similar, and how similar they need to be. In other words, assessing the correct level of generality. To illustrate, take the case of *Donoghue* v. *Stevenson*.[45] May Donoghue claimed that she contracted gastroenteritis after she drank some ginger beer that, unbeknownst to her, contained a dead snail. The case established the precedent that manufacturers owe a duty of care to their customers. However, the task when assessing the application of *Donoghue* v. *Stevenson* to subsequent cases is determining the correct level of generality. Does the precedent only relate to dead snails, noxious foreign bodies or any foreign body? Does it pertain only to ginger beer, all drinks, all consumable products, or simply all products? Must illness or harm be

---

[42] Farrar and Dugdale, *Introduction to Legal Method*, p. 86.   [43] *Ibid.* p. 79.
[44] McLeod, *Legal Method*, p. 16.   [45] [1932] AC 562.

caused, or maybe just revulsion? Is the mere presence of a foreign body enough?

Clearly, there is no exact test or delineating point at which the level of generality is too great or too little. For MacCormick, however, while sufficiency of analogy can never be exactly or definitively determined, this does not prevent it from being 'a real and important'[46] test. Reasoning by analogy therefore 'is not strictly logical. It is a looser form of reasoning which raises broader issues'.[47] Moreover, as Farrar and Dugdale point out, the debate about the similarities and dissimilarities between cases is 'only the tip of the iceberg. Underneath is the complex question of the desirability and expediency in extending the rule to the new fact situation. This is a question of policy and the values accepted by the legal system both in relation to the instant case and in relation to society at large'.[48] Two processes are therefore at play in analogical reasoning: analysis and justification, and it is in the latter that subjectivity is unavoidable.

Precedent

Analogical reasoning also involves an unavoidably subjective assessment of the similarity or difference between the case at hand and previous cases which may be relevant. These previous cases may be more than just relevant however; they may be binding or precedential.[49] Precedent, the logic by which all legal systems – common or civilian – operate,[50] means that the reasoning and decisions of preceding cases are not simply a guide but can actually be binding. This is known as *stare decisis*, or to give it its full name *stare rationibus decidendis*, meaning 'let the decision stand'. This latter term is actually the more accurate description because it is the

---

[46] MacCormick, *Legal Reasoning and Legal Theory*, p. 192.
[47] Farrar and Dugdale, *Introduction to Legal Method*, p. 80.   [48] *Ibid.* p. 87–8.
[49] When precedent and statute conflict, statute takes priority.
[50] One of the key differences between a civilian and common law system is the role of precedent. In common law systems precedent is binding. That means that prior decisions of higher ranking courts must be adhered to. In civilian systems, precedent is not binding but merely persuasive. In civilian systems the primary source of law is the Code, not case law. What this means in reality is that civilian judges use previous decisions to guide them in applying the Code. Judges may therefore interpret the Code in a completely different way but because all legal systems value consistency more highly than almost any other value bar justice (though this is debatable), this is relatively unusual. As we shall see the differences between how precedent operates in practice in the two systems are less marked than theory depicts.

reasoning (*rationibus*) that is binding, not the decision. However, not all legal decisions are binding. Instead, there is a hierarchy of 'bindingness'. A court must follow the decisions of higher courts, but not courts which are equal or lower.

The value of precedent lies in the consistency that it produces. Continually referring back to past decisions makes the law and the decisions it creates remarkably consistent. Holland and Webb argue that precedent is 'really the lawyer's term for legal experience. We all tend to repeat things we have done before: law is essentially no differ-ent.'[51] As a consequence law is strongly path dependent, but the reality is less rigid than the doctrine of precedent depicts. First of all, several precedents will, at least initially, be relevant. This is what the opposing sides do: find a precedent which fits the verdict they want the court to reach and which can be argued to be relevant. Opposing sides may even agree on the precedent that is relevant and simply disagree over the material facts (i.e. the facts that are central to the decision). And even where there is one, clearly relevant precedent the judge may still decline to apply it. Judges may deem a precedent to be 'awkward' and therefore do not have to apply it. This provides a judge who is sufficiently deter-mined not to apply precedent strictly with a means of so doing.[52] Judicial discretion also extends into relying upon policy in reaching their deci-sion: an anathema for formalists. This, according to Holland and Webb, 'can range from the pragmatic, such as the so-called "floodgates principle" ... to the political'.[53] The judiciary has been extremely wary of admitting this because it would mean that judges were making law rather than just applying it because of the violation this would imply of the separation of powers. Yet in reality judges do sometimes use policy as their guide. Judges may also cite general principles of justice or equity in their decision-making and use them to justify reaching a certain decision.

Flexibility and legal Reasoning: how legal reasoning actually works

Clearly then the formalist and common sense depiction of law only portrays a part of what legal reasoning is and fails to acknowledge the flexibility inherent within it and available to legal decision-makers.

---

[51] Holland and Webb, *Learning Legal Rules*, p. 111.   [52] *Ibid.* p. 242.
[53] The 'floodgates principle' is that doing something once will 'open the floodgates' for others to do the same. *Ibid.* p. 242.

Flexibility is introduced in a number of ways. Most straightforwardly rules do not interpret themselves and potentially all rules are open to interpretation. If this were not the case, no dispute would ever turn to law. It is inherent in the legal process that both parties to a dispute will be sufficiently certain of the truth of their claim and the legal merits of their case to go to court, even though only one can ever win.[54] Of course, which rule is selected as relevant also implies choice, albeit one that may be constrained by logic or the appearance of justice. Precisely how that rule is formulated and interpreted also imports flexibility. Finally, there is the vexed question of the distinction between matters of fact and matters of law. As Green argues: 'No two terms of legal science have rendered better service than "law" and "fact" ... They are the creations of centuries. What judge has not found refuge in them? The man who could succeed in defining them would be a public enemy.'[55] This is because the doctrine of binding precedent only applies to matters of law, not matters of fact. According to MacCormick, if a judge wants to avoid making a certain legal finding he has 'an obvious escape hatch. He can simply say that he does not find certain facts proven.'[56] In practice it is almost impossible to draw a clear dividing line between matters of law and matters of fact, even if legal professionals wanted to. In fact, McLeod argues that this 'giving up' extends to academia: 'It is not altogether surprising, therefore, that academic commentators tend to unite in scepticism as to whether the law-fact distinction has any practical utility as a basis for predicting judicial outcomes.'[57]

Ultimately the depiction of legal reasoning and legal decision-making in the common sense idea of law is inaccurate. As Wisdom has put it, legal reasoning is 'not a chain of demonstrative reasoning. It is a presenting and re-presenting of those features of the cases which severally co-operate in favour of the conclusion ... The reasons are like the legs of a chair not the links of a chain.'[58] For Farrar and Dugdale legal reasoning is not an '"ineluctable logic", but a composite of the logical relations seen between legal propositions, of observations of facts and consequences, and of value judgements about the acceptability of these consequences'.[59] Predicting how courts will rule, particularly in hard cases, is almost impossible and this

---

[54] This point belongs to Holland and Webb, *ibid.* p. 88.
[55] Leon Green quoted in McLeod, *Legal Method*, p. 41.
[56] MacCormick, *Legal Reasoning and Legal Theory*, p. 36.
[57] McLeod, *Legal Method*, p. 40.
[58] Wisdom quoted in Farrar and Dugdale, *Introduction to Legal Method*, p. 82.
[59] Farrar and Dugdale, *Introduction to Legal Method*, p. 112, original emphasis removed.

undermines one of the central elements of the rule of law: that law is constant over time. However, while the rule of law can only see this flexibility and lack of predictability as a problem to be solved, the simple truth is that some degree of flexibility is both desirable and necessary in law. A perfectly consistent and precedent-following system would be unbearably static and would quickly lose touch with the society it regulates. Just as society changes, the law must change too and it can only do this if it is flexible. Indeed, the central tension, even if it is unacknowledged by formalism or the common sense idea of law, is that between consistency and justice. We can also see the importance of certainty in this idea of law. Indeed, legalism's most basic aim is certainty and it is through certainty that individual freedom is best guaranteed.[60] This idea is common to most conceptions of the rule of law.[61] As both the common sense idea of law and the rule of law say: law should be predictable. This predictability is essential if the law is to shape human behaviour, otherwise people could not use it as a guide or to plan their future.[62] We must know with confidence what the law is so that we can modify our behaviour accordingly and constantly changing laws are seen as both the hallmark and tool of tyrannical regimes.

Anti-formalism and the middle way

Despite the success of the anti-formalist critique there are many scholars who think that this rejection of formalism has gone too far. The flexibility that is inherent in legal decision-making and reasoning is simply not significant enough to sustain the radical anti-formalist critique. According to MacCormick: 'There is a certain sort of not altogether uncommon silliness which, observing the veracity of such observations as these [about appearance], leaps to the conclusion that appearances are all that is to it. That could be true, but would require proof of a kind which has yet to be offered.'[63] Moreover, Berman argues that the critical approaches pose a significant

---

[60] Shklar, *Legalism*, p. 95. [61] Simmonds, *Law as a Moral Idea*.

[62] Raz considers the right to be able to plan one's future as a fundamental aspect of human dignity, 'The Rule of Law and Its Virtue', p. 204.

[63] MacCormick, *Legal Reasoning and Legal Theory*, p. 17. He writes that: 'It would be a very radical version of "rule scepticism" which suggested that statutes and case law are in all circumstances so indeterminate as to impose no limits whatever on possible ranges of "interpretation" or "explanation". No one has ever advanced such a theory' (*ibid.* p. 197). Of course this was written in 1978 and before the emergence of critical legal studies. MacCormick sees his work as setting 'a course between these two extreme positions' (*ibid.* p. 265): Dworkin's ultra-rationalism which leads him to assert that there is one right answer to every legal case, and Ross's Scandinavian legal realism which declared law to be indeterminate.

danger to both law and justice because they delegitimise and undermine law. By declaring law to be arbitrary the critical approaches have made justice and fairness harder to achieve, not easier, by encouraging contempt for it. According to Berman, the result is that '"fairness" has lost its historical and philosophical roots and is blown about by every wind of fashionable doctrine'.[64] By denying the autonomy, integrity and ongoingness of the legal tradition, anti-formalism poses a real danger to justice.

Worse still, this dismissal of law is based on a misunderstanding of what law is. To anti-formalism the 'language of law is viewed not only as necessarily complex, ambiguous, and rhetorical (which it is) but also wholly contingent, contemporary, and arbitrary (which it is not)'.[65] Legal realism and critical legal studies fail to see the restrictions placed upon both judges and lawyers by the system itself. Lawyers are constrained in their interpretation of the law by the need to prove that the law is 'capable of bearing a meaning consistent with the desired decision'.[66] Judges are constrained by the need to justify their decisions and the knowledge that their decisions, at least the controversial ones, will be subject to scrutiny. According to Farrar and Dugdale three factors influence how a judge reaches a decision: first, the legal arguments offered by the parties' counsel; secondly, his own personal views; and thirdly, '[p]erhaps the most important influence on his choice is the knowledge that he will have to justify his decision in a reasoned judgement'.[67] There is considerable pressure on judges to live up to the public perception of them as impartial determiners of disputes. Not only are 'the watch-dogs of the public interest ... continually alert to yap at their heels if they appear to do any other thing'[68] but judges have internalised this role for themselves. According to MacCormick, 'there are therefore strong pressures – apparently very effective pressures – on judges to appear to be what they are supposed to be'.[69]

Judges are also constrained by legal logic. As MacCormick points out: 'Courts neither do nor ought to apply statutes in less rather than more obvious senses unless they have good reason to do so.'[70] Of course, the element of choice remains but the idea that judges *en masse* decide cases solely on their personal whims is ridiculous: 'That judges *could* so behave

[64] Berman, *Law and Revolution*, p. 41.   [65] *Ibid.* p. 41.
[66] MacCormick, *Legal Reasoning and Legal Theory*, p. 206.
[67] Farrar and Dugdale, *Introduction to Legal Method*, p. 81.
[68] MacCormick, *Legal Reasoning and Legal Theory*, p. 17.
[69] *Ibid.* p. 17.   [70] *Ibid.* p. 206.

Conclusion: how to understand law

This chapter set out to introduce, unpick and challenge the common sense idea of law. In concluding, I want to highlight a number of threads that this chapter has started and which will play out in the remainder of the book. Most straightforwardly this chapter has argued that legal reasoning and legal method do not work in the way that the common sense of law thinks they do. It is far more complicated and subtle than the simple application of rules and while most IR theorists would instinctively question that simplicity, their natural scepticism does not inform their analysis of international politics or international law within it. I do not mean to argue here that IR theorists have simply accepted the common sense idea of law. Rather, the common sense idea of law has coloured their unthinking assumptions because IR theorists do not in general spend much time thinking about the theory of law, and are prone to fall back on popular perceptions to what the law is and how it operates.

Most IR theorists see law in a manner broadly similar to MacCormick's middle way: there is some fluidity but also a number of restrictions. A lawyer cannot argue anything she wants but is constrained in her interpretation of the law by the need to prove that the law is capable of bearing a meaning consistent with the desired decision. The fluidity, or indeterminacy, of law, is also limited by the need for law to appear just. If the law were not seen to be just the majority of the time, it would lose credibility and people would start to disobey. On some level judges, lawyers and the powerful instinctively feel the need to maintain law's credibility by not turning it into a sham.

I am sceptical of such an argument. First, I do not believe that this is a calculation actors make. People rarely accept short-term defeat for long-term gain. Secondly, given the foregoing section on the nature of legal reasoning and legal method, while I do think that law has some consistency, I think it is overstated by the common sense idea of law. The empirical second half of this book raises the question of the determinacy of law, social justice and legal change. In chapter 4, I explore the end of segregation in the United States and the landmark *Brown* v. *Board of Education* decision.[91] The dominant narrative of *Brown* is that it was the decision that ended segregation. However, reconciling *Brown* with *Plessy*,[92] the Supreme Court ruling that had deemed segregation as

---

[91] *Brown* v. *Board of Education*, 349 US 294 (1955).
[92] *Plessy* v. *Ferguson*, 163 US 537 (1896).

constitutional less than sixty years earlier, raises a serious question about the determinacy and consistency of law. Where chapter 4 raises the possibility of a different understanding of law, chapter 5 explores it through the issue of rape legislation and reform in the United Kingdom. Over thirty years of reform have yet to solve the 'rape problem' and chapter 5 raises the question of the limitations of law to address or change complex social phenomena. In the dominant narrative of *Brown*, law was the path to racial equality and social justice. The experience of rape reform, however, despite long attempts at reform, shows that some problems at least are very resistant to resolution. So much so that law may not be *able* to provide justice where such complex and well-established social norms are concerned.

And in chapter 6 we return to the belief that you cannot simply argue anything you like. I will argue that the Bush administration attempted to create a new legal paradigm, altering established legal practice regarding the treatment of prisoners of war (and even their classification) and justify a policy of torture. The Bush administration's lawyers radically undermined the assumption that legal reasoning and method will be a brake on the perversion of law. They were able to argue the direct opposite of the very well-established law against torture and *used the law to do so*. However strongly lawyers now discount the Office of Legal Counsel's legal logic as 'bizarre', the torture memos have irreversibly altered the legal standing of torture.[93] By simply arguing that 'enhanced interrogation techniques' were legal, they provide a basis in law, however contested, to defend and justify the use of torture.

But these ideas are yet to come. First I want to provide some additional knowledge to strengthen, or maybe complicate, our idea of law: critical jurisprudence.

---

[93] Luban, 'Liberalism', *VLR*.

3

Introducing critical jurisprudence

The 'centre of legal gravity lies ... in society itself'[1]

Introduction

Before I go any further I must explain what I mean by 'critical juris-prudence'. Historically, jurisprudence has been dominated by two main schools of thought: natural law theory and legal positivism. For many the debate between them continues to define modern jurisprudence.[2] According to Scott J. Shapiro: 'For the past four decades Anglo-American legal philosophy has been preoccupied – some might say obsessed – with something called the "Hart-Dworkin" debate.'[3] Most introductory texts to jurisprudence divide jurisprudence into three categories: natural law theory, legal positivism and sociologically influenced theories of law.[4] While this latter unwieldy label covers a broad church of approaches, from American legal realism to feminism or Marxism, they do share one key trait: they define themselves to contradistinction to natural law theory and legal positivism.[5] Their intellectual *raison d'être* is to critique and challenge the assumption of natural law theory and legal positivism, hence my labelling of it as critical jurisprudence. Because it is such a broad church certain groups would not call themselves, and should not be called, 'critical'. I hope that, as I engage with the varying schools of 'critical' jurisprudence the differences between them will become clear. But toward the end of more clarity, I will start with Lon L. Fuller's influential story of the Speluncean Explorers.

---

[1] Eugen Ehrlich quoted in Freeman, *Lloyd's Introduction*, pp. 522–3.
[2] See Hart, *The Concept of Law* and Dworkin, *Taking Rights Seriously*.
[3] Shapiro, 'The "Hart-Dworkin" Debate'.
[4] See for example Bix, *Jurisprudence: Theory and Context*.
[5] Such approaches frequently refer to natural law theory and legal positivism as the 'mainstream'. Much of critical approaches' ire is targeted at liberalism, which they see as inherent to mainstream approaches.

Fuller creates five fictional judges of a hypothetical case in order to illustrate competing schools of legal thinking. His imagined case concerns a group of men, who were exploring underground caves when a landslide blocked their only way out. When the men were rescued twenty-three days later, it was found that the leader of the expedition, Roger Whetmore, had been killed and eaten by his fellow explorers. It emerged that Whetmore himself had been the first to suggest that if they were to survive one of them would have to be sacrificed. It was also Whetmore who suggested drawing lots with dice he happened to have with him. The others agreed but before the dice were cast Whetmore decided he wanted to wait another week before resorting to murder and cannibalism. At this point the others accused him of a breach of faith and killed him. They were indicted for murder, the sentence was death.

Of Fuller's five judges Chief Justice Truepenny, Judge Keen and Judge Tatting are positivists of varying hues, Judge Foster is a natural law theorist, and Judge Handy represents broadly sociological jurisprudence. Chief Justice Truepenny opens the deliberations by arguing that the court was right to convict the men because it was the only course of action open to them. He states that 'the language of our statute is well known: "Whoever shall wilfully take the life of another shall be punished by death"... This statute permits no exception.'[6] To Truepenny the facts of the case are beyond doubt – the men wilfully killed Whetmore and all knew their action to be illegal. Given that the statute permits no exception, the extraordinary circumstances in which the men found themselves should not alter the verdict. The law is clear and has been correctly applied. Yet Truepenny is unhappy at the fate of these men and urges the other judges to ask for clemency from the Chief Executive. Thus to Truepenny the law has operated as it should within its limited realm. The question of justice is not for him to decide, it is a matter for the Chief Executive. Truepenny sees himself as a mere enforcer of law, whatever that law may be. Questions of justice and morality are simply not his job.

Judge Keen shares many of the same assumptions. He says that the difficulties of this case 'all trace back to a single source, and that is a failure to distinguish the legal from the moral aspects of this case'.[7] Keen further argues that: 'I respect the obligations of an office that requires me to put my personal predilections out of my mind when I come to interpret and apply the law';[8] and that, as a judge, he has 'sworn to apply,

[6] Fuller, 'The Speluncean Explorers', pp. 61–71.   [7] Ibid. pp. 67–8.   [8] Ibid. p. 68.

not my conceptions of morality, but the law of the land'.[9] Keen's decision differs from Truepenny's in that he does not ask for clemency. Rather he believes, as Truepenny does, that the law is sufficiently clear and fits the case well enough for the conviction to stand. Yet whereas Truepenny applies the law but feels uneasy about condemning the defendants to death, Keen does not. He argues that '[h]ard cases [like this one] may even have a certain moral value by bringing home to the people their own responsibility toward the law that is ultimately their creation, and by reminding them that there is no principle of personal grace that can relieve the mistake of their representatives'.[10] Here Keen puts the responsibility for the law back onto the people and warns them that the clemency of the Chief Executive (the personal grace of the quote) does not abrogate them of their responsibility. The case of the explorers is therefore unfortunate but just. The men knew murder was illegal and punishable by death. If they were unhappy with the law they should have resisted it before they became murderers themselves. They cannot expect a principle that they tacitly agreed to and would probably still believe to be a vital moral principle to be overturned in their case. In short, they have no one to blame but themselves.

Whereas both Truepenny and Keen are sure that a relevant piece of law exists and was applied to the case, Judge Tatting is not. Tatting is unconvinced that the crime under appeal was really murder and argues that the indictment should never have been for murder. Instead, in the light of the mitigating circumstances, a lesser charge should have been appended. Tatting remarks that if it were a crime to eat human flesh, then this would have provided a more appropriate indictment. To Tatting murder simply does not reflect the crime and no other charge exists. In other words, law has 'run out' and fails to cover the admittedly extraordinary circumstances of the case in hand. Tatting concludes that both he and the law are incapable of resolving the moral dilemma posed by the case and he withdraws from the decision.

In stark opposition to Judge Tatting, Judge Foster, the natural law judge, denies that either men or judges can abrogate their responsibility for hard moral choices. In further contrast to both Keen and Tatting, Foster views law as part of society and as embedded within its social context. Consequently the law itself should not be applied to a case in such a way as to 'compel us to a conclusion we are ashamed of'.[11] Such a result, even mitigated by Chief Justice Truepenny's request for clemency,

---

[9] *Ibid.* p. 67.   [10] *Ibid.* p. 69.   [11] *Ibid.* p. 61.

seems to Foster to be 'an admission that the law of this Commonwealth no longer pretends to incorporate justice'.[12] Compare this to Truepenny's belief that it should be left to the Chief Executive to ensure 'justice' is done. Whereas Truepenny and Keen believe that law should be free of non-legal influences, including even justice it would seem, Foster argues that the very *purpose* of law is justice.

The final judge to deliver his opinion is Judge Handy. He argues that the other judges are making the case appear more difficult than it really is. The issue at hand is not one of abstract legal theory but 'what we, as officers of the government, ought to do with these defendants'.[13] It is simply a question of what one group of men should decide to do with another group of men who have broken society's legal rules. Arcane discussions of legal principle, purpose, and theory merely mask the reality that 'government is a human affair and that men are ruled, not by words on paper or by abstract theories, but by other men'.[14] Further '[t]hey are ruled well when their rulers understand the feelings and conceptions of the masses. They are ruled badly when that under-standing is lacking.'[15] Because law is a social institution and a means of social organisation, it should reflect what society wants. To do otherwise is to reject the context from which law emerges, a fatal arrogance that creates human misery and wrecks governments. Law is not certain or clear-cut and where we face moral dilemmas it is only right that we look to the wider moral context. He rejects the criticism that public opinion is 'emotional and capricious ... based on half-truths',[16] countering: 'can anyone pretend that these decisions [of the judiciary, rather than the public] are held within a rigid and formal framework of rules that prevents factual errors, excludes emotional and personal factors, and guarantees that all the forms of law will be observed?'[17] Law, Handy asserts, is not a science and should not be de-personalised as if it were, for to do so is to mask the simple fact of what it is: men controlling other men. Consequently, Handy believes the court should follow public opinion that he believes is overwhel-mingly in favour of acquitting the men or of giving them a token punishment, and declares the men innocent. Handy's decision splits the court evenly, with two allowing the conviction to stand, two clear-ing the men, and one failing to rule. The conviction and the death sentences were therefore confirmed.

[12] *Ibid.* p. 61.   [13] *Ibid.* p. 69.   [14] *Ibid.* p. 70.   [15] *Ibid.* p. 70.   [16] *Ibid.* p. 71.
[17] *Ibid.* p. 71.

The sociological movement

What is significant about Handy's ruling, and distinguishes him from the other judges, is his insistence upon law as a social phenomenon. He rejects both the natural lawyers' mysticism and abstraction, and the positivists' myopic focus on 'words on paper', arguing that both obscure the reality of men being ruled by other men. There are two core assumptions: the rejection of formalism and the move to context from the foundation and start point of the sociological movement in law. This section will briefly trace the emergence of sociological jurisprudence and the development of legal realism, in both its American[18] and Scandinavian[19] variants. It will assess what the move to context can tell us about the relationship between law and its political and moral context. This section will seek to demonstrate a growing rejection of the idea of an autonomous, self-contained, apolitical, ahistorical and amoral legal system. By viewing law as porous we challenge the implicit assumption of a consensus model of society and move to a conflict model where law and the legal system serve as an arena for conflict, and raise the possibility of law as a tool of the weak.

Sociological jurisprudence as a school of thought is most often associated with the American jurist Roscoe Pound.[20] In some respects we can see sociological jurisprudence as an off-shoot of natural law. Pound himself termed it 'practical natural law . . . a natural law with a changing or a growing content'.[21] He rejected legal traditionalism which viewed law as a self-contained system through which the logical elaboration of rules might be more systematically formulated. Law was not a self-contained system, separate from its social context. Moreover, 'legal institutions and doctrines are instruments of social control, capable of being improved with reference to their ends by conscious, intelligent

---

[18] The American legal realists include Karl Llewellyn, Jerome Frank and Justice Oliver Wendell Holmes. See Llewellyn, *The Bramble Bush*; Llewellyn, *Jurisprudence*; Frank, *Courts on Trial*; *and* Holmes, The Common Law.

[19] The Scandinavian legal realists include Axel Hägerström, Karl Olivecrona and Alf Ross. See Hägerström, *Inquiries into the Nature of Law and Morals*; Olivecrona, *Law as Fact*; and Ross, *On Law and Justice*.

[20] Doherty writes that Pound 'laid the foundation for post-traditionalism' (Doherty, *Jurisprudence*, p. 187) and that he 'is to be regarded as synonymous with the term sociological jurisprudence' (*ibid. Jurisprudence*, p. 181). See also Pound, *An Introduction to the Philosophy of Law*.

[21] Pound quoted in Hunt, *The Sociological Movement in Law*, p. 17.

effort'.[22] Thus Pound's aim was 'a continually more efficacious social engineering'.[23] Thus we can identify three main strands of Poundian sociological jurisprudence. First, Pound was concerned with the gap between purposively defined goals and the social consequences manifested in the law in action. This developed into a rejection of 'law in books' in favour of 'law in action', that is, what actually happens in the courts. Secondly, Pound held the logical positivist belief that there are objective and discoverable principles or patterns in society. Once these have been discovered law can be made more efficient. This placed a premium on empirical research. Finally, Pound espoused reform, not revolution. Pound did not challenge the necessity or desirability of law but merely sought to make it more 'in tune' with the society it regulated. Pound focused on the effects of law on society, not the social determination of law. In Harris's words: 'Pound's pragmatic jurisprudence equates justice with quietening those who are banging on the gates.'[24]

Whatever the criticisms and flaws of Pound's work his belief that law does not exist, and cannot be studied, in a vacuum represents both a culmination of earlier sociological thought and the guiding light for future jurisprudence. Pound was the first to articulate the belief that law is subject to external forces. Many of the key tenets of Pound's thought are shared by legal realism. There are two schools of legal realism: American and Scandinavian. Both share a rejection of the metaphysical, relying upon empirical realism and a desire to ground philosophical discussions in an observable reality. Consequently empirical research is necessary. Both propound the idea that law must reflect society and be pegged to it in some respects yet they both strongly believe in the Humean injunction to separate the 'is' from the 'ought'. First we shall consider American legal realism.

One of the biggest contributions of American legal realism is rule and fact scepticism. Rule scepticism, developed by Karl Llewellyn, is based upon a rejection of formalism's reliance upon logic and *a priori* reasoning. In 1881 Oliver Wendell Holmes wrote that:

> the logical method and form flatter that longing for certainty and for repose which is in every human mind. But certainty is generally an illusion, and repose is not the destiny of man. Behind the logical form lies a judgement as to the relative worth and importance of competing

---

[22] Pound quoted in *ibid.* p. 15.
[23] Pound quoted in Freeman, *Lloyd's Introduction*, p. 572.
[24] Harris, *Legal Philosophies*, p. 235.

legislative grounds, often an inarticulate and unconscious judgement it is true, and yet the very root and nerve of the whole proceeding. You can give any conclusion a logical form.[25]

Llewellyn elaborated upon this belief further in an article some fifty years later.[26] In providing a manifesto of the American legal realist movement, Llewellyn argues that law is a means to a social end, not an end in itself, and should therefore be evaluated in terms of its effects. Both law and society are in a continual state of flux, though society changes more rapidly. Law must therefore be kept under constant review. This is a key difference from both natural law and positivism, which deny this linkage. Natural law sees law as unchanging and absolute, whereas positivism sees it as divorced from its social reality.

To Llewellyn legal rules and concepts should be distrusted where they purport to describe what actually happens in the legal system and any legal theory which relies upon the assumption that rules govern the decisions of courts should be questioned. Llewellyn also articulated the same emphasis on 'law in action' as Pound. He distinguished between 'paper rules', that is 'law in books', and 'real rules' by which he meant the actual practices of the court. This same distinction is found in Holmes' example of 'our friend the bad man'[27] who does not care 'two straws for the axioms or deductions, but ... does want to know what the Massachusetts or English courts are likely to do in fact'.[28] Jerome Frank built upon this rule scepticism, creating a yet more sceptical and ultra-realist theory of fact scepticism. To *Frank*, rule scepticism did not go far enough:

> [T]he rules, statutory or judge-made, are not self-operative. They are frustrated, inoperative, whenever, due to faulty fact-finding in trial courts, they are applied to non-existent facts.[29]

In other words, because trial courts receive conflicting evidence, the decision-makers, be they jurors, judges or magistrates, must decide whom to believe. This is when personal prejudice, conscious or other-wise, comes into play. How a witness conducts herself on the stand will determine her credibility to a great extent. By muddying the waters to

---

[25] Quoted in McLeod, *Legal Theory*, p. 117.
[26] Llewellyn, 'Some Realism about Realism' extracted in Freeman, *Lloyd's Introduction*, pp. 686–91.
[27] Holmes quoted in McLeod, *Legal Theory*, p. 115.   [28] McLeod, *Legal Theory*, p. 116.
[29] Frank quoted in McLeod, *Legal Theory*, p. 119.

such an extent, the decision-maker is given greater leeway in making their decision.

So what is the significance of these two types of scepticism, and of the sociological move thus far? In short, scepticism denies the autonomous or self-contained nature of law. It demonstrates that factors outside of law impinge heavily upon it. Pound argued that the sociological jurist should avoid engaging in 'logical reconstruction of the meaning expressed by legal texts, but . . . to survey and classify social institutions to which those texts do, or should, give effect'.[30] We should move away from a focus upon the words of the law, and turn our attention instead to the social impact those words actually have. This means that law can be evaluated by a set of criteria which are external to law.[31] This central insight tells us a different story about the relationship between law and morality than that told by traditional natural law or positivism. In this respect Scandinavian legal realism is more explicit than its American cousin. To Hägerström, the 'spiritual father of the Scandinavian realist movement',[32] goodness and badness are subjective. Moreover, even those feelings which are unmediated by law, politics, or social standards of morality, such as love or compassion, are not strong enough to order society. The regulation of society therefore is not about goodness or badness. Similarly Olivecrona argues that law's normativity and the psychological feeling of compulsion are not the result of law or its constitution. Such feelings come from the human psyche and are conditioned in part through the administration of justice via regular infliction of punishment and extraction of damages, as well as through the propaganda that is associated with it. Obedience comes from the 'psychological connexion' of legal rules which are absorbed by our mind and then become moral commands.[33] In other words, we obey because we are socialised to obey and the idea that law is based on abstract justice is 'too openly superstitious'.[34]

There is a clear agenda here. According to Freeman, Hägerström 'dedicated his life to exposing speculative ideas and myths by which man is exploited by man'.[35] Scandinavian realism sought to overturn the traditional belief that moral standards are embodied by law, turning

---

[30] Pound quoted in Harris, *Legal Philosophies*, p. 235.
[31] Natural law theory evaluates law by its adherence to precepts of natural law. Whilst these are external to substantive law, they are still considered as 'law'.
[32] Doherty, *Jurisprudence*, p. 214.
[33] Olivecrona quoted in Freeman, *Lloyd's Introduction*, p. 763.
[34] Olivecrona quoted in *ibid.* p. 762.   [35] Freeman, *Lloyd's Introduction*, p. 732.

this proposition on its head and arguing that it is *law* that dictates morality. In reality there are only a few core rules that become objectified enough to attain the status of being regarded as binding without reference to authority. To Scandinavian realists morality is neither totally objective, depending on an external world of moral reality, nor totally subjective, because its coherence must be testable in the public domain.

So what does the sociological turn in law tell us about the relationship between law and morality, and law and politics? Primarily it views law in its social context, removing its autonomy to a certain extent. It does this by demonstrating the fallacy of the belief that law is not influenced by political or moral factors that are external to it. Once the 'lie' has been revealed, legal realism produces a critical awareness of law's operation and a rejection of existing assumptions about that operation. However, the sociological movement never questions the desirability or necessity of law. Despite its critical perspective neither sociological jurisprudence nor legal realism looks beyond reform. The assumption that underpins both schools is that, essentially, the system works, it just needs a little tinkering. The existence of law and its centrality are never questioned, nor is the relationship between the law and the state, both of which are seen as neutral.

From sociological to 'critical' approaches

The sociological movement can therefore be seen as an inchoate move towards more critical approaches. It marked a rejection of traditional, mainstream approaches underpinned by liberal political philosophy and started to question and challenge the apparent neutrality and necessity of legal orthodoxy. Ian McLeod argues that critical approaches, such as Marxism, critical legal studies (CLS) and feminism, 'proceed from bases other than those which underpin the traditional analysis in ... the positivist and natural law traditions'.[36] That is, so-called critical approaches base their work upon the rejection of the liberal orthodoxy and the liberal model of society. The impact of liberalism has been what Collins terms the fetishism of law which can be seen as a composite of the liberal model of law and against which broadly critical approaches react. Legal fetishism comprises three elements. First, the thesis that a legal order is necessary for social order and that there can be no social order without law. In all but the idyllic small society, the absence of law

---

[36] McLeod, *Legal Theory*, p. 125, emphasis removed.

will inevitably lead to anarchy in the pejorative sense. Secondly, '[l]aw is a unique phenomenon which constitutes a discrete focus of study'[37] with a distinct method and form of reasoning, and a normativity that sets legal rules apart from the simple exercise of force. Thirdly, the doctrine of the rule of law, which Dicey defines as 'the universal subjection of all classes, to one law'[38] but also comprises the need for certainty and predictability in law.[39] Crucially, the rule of law doctrine allows rules to have any kind of content; the emphasis is on exercising power according to rules announced in advance. Critical approaches reject all these elements. While such approaches do accept that while law *might* be necessary, they argue that the assumption that it is has served to naturalise its existence and protect a particular division of power within society.

Cotterrell argues that the guiding motivation of the critique of law is the refusal to 'accept legal doctrine on its own terms; that is, to refuse to accept it in the terms in which it justifies itself (as the unfolding of legal logic; as the self-evident embodiment of rationality; as the purely technical instrument of policies originating from "non-legal" (political) sources)'.[40] Hutchison and Monahan however argue that CLS is not about challenging the idealised model of legal thought that is formalism. They argue that '[t]he CLS critique should not be understood as simply an assault upon formalism – the notion that disputes can be resolved by the neutral application of objective rules'[41] because formalism has been soundly rejected by jurisprudential scholars, as noted in chapter 2. However, CLS does accept that while formalism has been discredited among the academic community, the public generally accept the idealised form of law. As Kairys points out: '[t]he public perception – the crucial perception from the standpoint of legitimacy – is generally limited to the idealised model'.[42] Nobody believes this anymore. Except for the public, whose perception of the law is, according to CLS, that of the idealised form of law, or what I have termed the common sense idea of law. While the occasional miscarriage of justice and ill-judged remark by judges is to be expected, systematic bias and prejudice is not, nor can it be, or the edifice of law would lose all legitimacy.

Thus it is clear that the purpose of critical approaches to law all start from the debunking of what Naffine calls the 'official version of law – what the

---

[37] Collins, *Marxism and Law*, p. 11.   [38] Dicey quoted in Naffine, *Law and the Sexes*, p. 51.
[39] See chapter 2.   [40] Cotterrell, 'Power, Property and the Law of Trusts', p. 78.
[41] Hutchinson and Monahan, 'Law, Politics, and the Critical Legal Scholars', 206.
[42] Kairys, *The Politics of Law*, p. 2.

legal world would have us believe about itself – is that it is an impartial, neutral and objective system for resolving conflicts'.[43] This official version of law also has a preferred person of law, the paradigmatic citizen who is believed to inhabit the idealised social order. This is the 'man of law', the individual taken as central by liberal theory. He is 'assertive, articulate, independent, calculating, competitive and competent ... precisely the qualities valued in the sort of society which law has in mind: a society which is fiercely competitive and composed of similarly self-interested and able individuals';[44] in other words, a liberal society.[45] Clearly, there are two models of society at play here. First, a liberal model, which sees society as characterised by consensus and harmony and where law is seen as representing the shared values of society, adjusting conflicts and reconciling interests to the ultimate benefit of society. The second, critical model sees society as characterised by conflict, rather than consensus, and that law is used to impose the interests of one group over another.[46]

Marxism and the conflict model of society

The most significant conflict model of society is to be found in the work of Marx and Engels. Non-communist society is characterised by the exploitation of the workers by those who own the means of production. The workers are ignorant of their exploitation because they lack the class consciousness which would reveal their widespread and systemic exploitation. This fundamental conflict cannot last forever because it is inherent in the nature of capitalism that the exploitation of the ruled becomes more and more egregious until class consciousness emerges and the revolution is unleashed. To Marxism, this is inevitable.

---

[43] Naffine, *Law and the Sexes*, p. 24.

[44] *Ibid.* p. 22. She does not argue that men constitute a single, undifferentiated category. Rather, the model of the man of law is a combination of attributes and the more of these attributes one possesses the better one will fare in the legal system. Therefore a middle class, educated and articulate woman will fare well but a working class, uneducated black man will not. Naffine's analysis operates on two axes: gender and class. As she writes, '[c]ritics of law's bias against women have been surprisingly silent on the question of legal bias against certain types of men, bias which is informed by issues of gender, as well as class' (*ibid.* p. xii).

[45] This will be returned to below in the discussion of feminism.

[46] Doherty uses a similar division of consensus and conflict models of society. See Doherty, *Jurisprudence*, pp. 182–3.

The Marxist divides society into base and superstructure. The base consists of the conditions of production and the economic relations involved in production. The base is therefore purely economic. The super-structure contains what is left – culture, religion, tradition and law. The base gives rise to and determines the superstructure but the superstructure does not, and cannot, affect the base; influence flows in one direction only. Within this schema the purpose of law is to maintain class domination and preserve economic inequalities. But as Collins argues law is merely 'one aspect of a variety of political and social arrangements concerned with the manipulation of power and the consolidation of modes of production and wealth'.[47] Law is by its nature bourgeois; it cannot be anything else. In communist society law will be redundant, as would talk of justice and rights. This is because in the communist utopia there would be no inequal-ity, so the idea of justice and rights, which would only have meaning against a backdrop of inequality and injustice, would be 'obsolete verbal rubbish'. The concept of a person as essentially a being with a sense of justice and who is a bearer of rights is to Marx a defective concept which is only needed in a defective society.[48] The idea of justice is paradoxical as the demands of justice cannot be satisfied in the circumstances which make conceptions of justice necessary. The idea of justice in capitalist society exists therefore, not because justice is possible or desirable but as a sop to the exploited, a trick to appease them and subvert their revolutionary potential. Law, to Marx and Engels, serves to obscure power relations and mystify the oppressed. Law does not reflect reality but serves as political sleight of hand, both a distraction from reality and a distortion of it. 'Thus, the legal form will refer to the right to enter freely into contracts but in the absence of equality of bargaining power, this freedom is illusory.'[49]

Law then appears to be nothing more than an empty vessel for economic interests. Lawyers have challenged this assumption that the economic base determines all other forms of social intercourse, arguing that law in part constitutes the relations of production and is not just constituted by them. How economic relations and practices are regulated can heavily affect what those practices are and how they operate. Thompson challenges the base-superstructure divide, arguing that '"law" was deeply imbricated within the very basis of productive

---

[47] Collins, *Marxism and Law*, p. 13.
[48] See Shklar's notion of the 'policy of justice' in chapter 2.
[49] Freeman, *Lloyd's Introduction*, pp. 856–7.

relations, which would have been inoperable without law'.[50] Moreover, as McCoubrey points out: 'To concentrate solely upon economics as the base factor is severely to limit the analysis and to interpret all other factors in its light actually involves a distortion.'[51]

But is this a fair reflection of Marx and Engels' thought? Are they really guilty of such crude reductionism? To Freeman, Marx and Engels accept that the reality is more complex than their mechanistic theory allows for and that the superstructure can influence the base, quoting Engels in support: 'One must not think that the economic situation is *cause, and solely active*, whereas everything else is only passive effect. On the contrary, inter-action takes place on the basis of economic necessity, which ultimately always asserts itself.'[52] Thus the superstructure *can* influence the base and legislative decisions *may* be motivated by something other than the economic interests of the ruling class. But as Harris asserts: 'Perhaps the point is ... that the economic basis of class interests will filter out and render ineffective all laws which are not [in the interests of the ruling class].'[53] So while Marx may have been aware of early legislation that *was* contrary to the interests of the ruling class[54] such legislation never really posed much of a threat to the dominant class. As such the oppressed working class should not try to use law as a tool to improve their everyday conditions because this would subvert and dissipate the workers' revolutionary potential. Even if law does offer the potential to lessen the exploitation of the ruled, it ultimately serves the interests of the rulers by quietening them.

Schmitt shares a similar view of law as politics and little else, and provides two important arguments for this chapter: first, a critique of liberalism and liberal legal theory, and secondly, an alternative conceptualisation which denudes law of any autonomy or substance. First, I look at Schmitt's critique of liberalism. According to Schmitt in the liberal *Rechtstaat* statesmen and judges do not rule but merely enforce impersonally valid norms. In Koskenniemi's words 'things happen as if impersonal laws were governing'.[55] Schmitt argues that it is 'pretended' that the constitution is nothing but a system of legal norms and prescriptions; secondly, that this system is a closed one; and thirdly, that it is

---

[50] Thompson, *Whigs and Hunters*, p. 261.
[51] McCoubrey quoted in McLeod, *Legal Theory*, p. 127.
[52] Engels quoted in Freeman, *Lloyd's Introduction*, p. 844, original emphasis.
[53] Harris, *Legal Philosophies*, p. 253.
[54] Harris notes that Marx was aware of early legislation against enclosure. *Ibid.* p. 253.
[55] Koskenniemi, *From Apology to Utopia*, p. 194, n. 4.

sovereign. By depicting law in this way the liberal paradigm clears the way for the juridification of the entire life of the state: a massive extension of power. As this juridification occurs the liberal *Rechtstaat* must put increasing effort into repressing the political and 'compressing all expressions of the life of the state into a series of prescriptions'.[56] The channelling of acceptable expressions and the suppression of others means that the bourgeois *Rechtstaat* can only ever be a partial state, never fully accepting and expressing its political nature.

Schmitt rejects this liberal paradigm for two reasons. First, it is simply not true. In reality, law and decision-making are not governed by 'intangible institutions and systems of norms'[57] but ruled by individuals and organisations with their own institutions and morals. Moreover, liberalism's attempt to depoliticise law and to present itself as neutral and apolitical masks a hidden agenda. This act of attempted depoliticisation is, however, a supremely political act, arguably perhaps *the* most political act, because it subverts resistance. Furthermore, attempting to make the state neutral, as liberalism does, only makes it easier for political groups to inject surreptitiously their own politics. As Schmitt writes, '"liberty" no longer means the in-principle unlimited scope of activity of the individual, but the unlimited exploitation of social power by social organisations'.[58] The second reason for Schmitt's rejection of the liberal paradigm is that it is a legacy of the nineteenth century and simply cannot cope with the changed nature of the state in the twentieth century.[59] Schmitt argues that the underlying premise of liberalism – the dualism of state and society – is anachronistic. State and society have merged to form the political creature of the total state. In the total state, where the political is so prevalent, liberalism is simply not strong enough to temper the political and impose order.

To Schmitt then law is secondary to factual decision, not abstract norms. In the liberal paradigm the location of factual power usually remains hidden and it is only in times of crisis, when the legal order is threatened, that power will manifest itself. Schmitt finds the normativity of liberalism unacceptable because it is ineffective in resolving the life-threatening political crises that he believes are inevitable. Politics is

---

[56] Schmitt quoted in Slagstead, 'Liberal Constitutionalism', p. 108.
[57] Schmitt quoted in *ibid.* p. 112.
[58] Schmitt quoted in Dyzenhaus, *Legality and Legitimacy*, p. 61.
[59] Morrison sums up Schmitt's argument thus: 'the nineteenth-century struggle against royal absolutism and the goal of creating a national identity had kept the contradiction between liberalism and democracy from revealing itself openly' (Morrision, *Jurisprudence*, p. 309).

outside of norms, and legitimacy can only ever refer to the efficacy of a set of power-holders. Schmitt argues therefore that the linkage of a norm and a judge should be jettisoned in favour of the linkage of judge with judge. Legal propositions should be found true if another judge would reach the same conclusion as the first, rather than adhering to unreachable law. As such, homogeneity within the judiciary is vital because Schmitt links the ability to innately understand a legal system (if this is possible) with nationality. Such a re-working of legal reasoning is questionable and Scheuerman argues that Schmitt never precisely outlines his interpretation of normativity precisely because 'his dramatic juxtaposition of the norm to the decision itself is untenable'.[60] The significance of Schmitt's work lies then in both his unmasking of the liberal paradigm, which demonstrates his belief that law is nothing but an empty vessel for politics, and his own alternative, which puts it into action. Indeed, Schmitt's belief that law denuded of any substance or autonomy gives it even less agency than a Marxist interpretation of law. Law is nothing but its context. Yet it is open to question whether we need go this far.

Re-imagining a Marxist theory of law

There is also a second interpretation of Marxism possible if we believe that Marx and Engels did see law as possessing enough substance to challenge the interests of the ruling class. Cain and Hunt argue that: 'The argument that law is by its nature bourgeois is potentially a negative one. It leads to the position that any legally backed achievement of the working class is in fact no more than a consolidation of bourgeois ideology in a bourgeois form – the law.'[61] If this is the case then there is no point in taking the law as an object of struggle. Cain and Hunt reject the exclusively economic focus of Marxist ideology and highlight a much more complex reality where 'changes in relations of re-production, changes in the institutionalised forms of ideology and of politics which serve to reproduce the relations of production, are as appropriate as objects of class struggle as the relations of production themselves'.[62] They deny that this would divert revolutionary fervour, arguing that success in improving the living conditions of the working class would not make them politically inactive and apathetic but would 'unify and strengthen

---

[60] Scheuerman, *Carl Schmitt*, pp. 76–7.   [61] Cain and Hunt, *Marx and Engels*, p. 205.
[62] *Ibid.* p. 205.

[them] ... and so help create the conditions necessary for the transfor-
mation of the relations of production'.[63] To Cain and Hunt reformist and
non-revolutionary political action is *part* of the class struggle, not a
distraction from it. They do not see their position as differing greatly
from the original work of Marx and Engels, only in their estimation of
the chances of success. When both sets of authors are faced with the task
of explaining law which threatens the interests of the ruling class, Marx
and Engels characterise them as insignificant hiccoughs, soon to be
flattened by the sheer weight of economic power, and that winning
against the oppressors is simply not possible. Cain and Hunt on the
other hand, view such victories as part of the class struggle, advancing the
workers along the path to freedom and equality. The reason for these
differing conclusions lies in differing views of law's autonomy. Marx and
Engels deny that law has any autonomy and that it lacks the power and
independence to contradict the influences of the dominant. Cain and
Hunt on the contrary, accept that law has at least limited autonomy and
that while it may serve the interests of the rulers most of the time, that it
obscures the exploitation of the workers, and that bourgeois talk of
justice and rights will rarely be available to those who are politically
and financially excluded, it is nevertheless a tool available to the
oppressed. And such tools are too rare to be rejected.

In sum, Marx and Engels see law as nothing more than a consequence
of society's economic base. Law serves to preserve economic inequalities
and maintain the subordination of the workers. Law's primary function
is to obscure power relations, in other words, to mask law's context and
its true relation to it. In this way law reflects only a certain reality or a
particular part of it. If we contrast Marxism with traditional theories of
jurisprudence it is clear that they represent two extremes of the same
spectrum. At one end, we find natural law and positivism which view law
as separate and separable from its political and moral context. At the
other, we find Schmitt and classical Marxism, both of which deny law's
autonomy, seeing it as nothing but context.

However, Marxist jurisprudence has come in for heavy criticism for its
conceptualisation of law. Rock's criticism merits quoting at length. He
argues that such perspectives:

> offer no understanding of law as a complex and variegated rule-system
> whose origins are frequently as mysterious to elites as to governed. It

---

[63] *Ibid.* pp. 205–6.

offers no vision of a legal system as a series of constraints upon law-giver and ruled alike. It does not refer to legitimacy and authority other than in the context of manipulation and mystification. It does not provide for the elaborate patterns of accommodation that characterise many situations of social control.[64]

Instead it relies upon the anthropomorphic fallacy, or what Rock calls the 'anthropomorphic conspiracy theory', attributing omniscient power to the oppressors and blind ignorance to the oppressed. Law itself is nothing more than a cartoonish tool of manipulation, bearing little relation to the reality of legal complexity. Thompson too shares a dislike of the simplistic nature of the classical Marxist conception of law. He argues that when we examine law and its operation 'we reach then, not a simple conclusion (law = power) but a complex and contradictory one'.[65] As a Marxist, Thompson accepts the central Marxist insight that law is, and has proved to be, a superb instrument by which the rulers are able to impose their will and secure their position. Yet, like all Marxists, Thompson is presented with the question of legislation that inhibits, however slightly, the interests of the rulers. How do Marxists reconcile their belief in law as a tool of the powerful with this empirical reality? Most deny that such victories have the effect their proponents say they do and that they are nothing more than bribes to keep the people quiet. Even if the rulers are discomfited by such instances, ultimately economic forces will out and the legislative victory becomes a drop of fresh water in a sea of salt water.

But Thompson rejects this on three grounds. First, empirical evidence shows that in Thompson's area of focus (the Black Act) the law did serve to 'impose, again and again, inhibitions upon the actions of the rulers'.[66] Secondly, even when the ruled were unable to continue the fight at law 'men still felt a sense of *legal* wrong: the propertied had obtained their power by illegal means'.[67] Law, even when it is either not being used or is not functioning, still remains a means to judge the ruler's action. Crucially 'if we say that existent class relations were mediated by the law, this is not the same thing as saying that the law was no more than those relations translated into other terms, which masked or mystified the reality . . . For class relations were expressed, not in any way one likes, but *through the forms of law*.'[68] Finally, and building upon his first two

---

[64] Rock, 'The Sociology of Deviancy', 144.   [65] Thompson, *Whigs and Hunters*, p. 264.
[66] *Ibid.* p. 264.   [67] *Ibid.* p. 261, emphasis added.   [68] *Ibid.* p. 262, emphasis added.

grounds of dissent, Thompson points out that 'people are not as stupid as some structuralist philosophers suppose them to be'.[69]

Thompson then still believes that law offers the possibility of furthering the interests of the exploited and does not accept the traditionally Marxist view that law can only ever be bourgeois and that what it buys by its talk of justice and rights is obedience and silence. While Thompson believes the small gains are enough, many Marxists would not be satisfied with anything less than revolution. In conclusion it is clear that there are two competing conceptualisations of law and its emancipatory potential, proponents of both can offer evidence that theirs reflects what Marx and Engels actually meant. Is law salvageable? Does it offer the oppressed a weapon or is it merely a palliative? And what does this tell us about law's relation to its political and moral context?

Critical legal studies

Sharing many of the main Marxist beliefs yet offering a more sophisticated examination of the relationship between law and politics is critical legal studies (CLS). CLS emerged in the United States in the late 1970s and its intellectual roots stretch back to both Marxism and American legal realism. Many jurists were unimpressed with Marx's exclusive focus on economics and the lack of any coherent Marxist jurisprudence. Consequently critical jurists tend to be influenced by Marxism in a more general manner. For in-depth legal analysis, many critical lawyers look to legal realism. From legal realism, CLS inherits a scepticism of both rules and facts, yet while legal realists introduced sceptical doubt, they did not follow this insight through to its logical conclusion. To legal realists the law is seen in a positive light and the legal edifice is left unquestioned by realism. CLS, on the other hand, seeks to demonstrate law's lack of value freedom.

Legal indeterminacy

Unger identifies two main tendencies of CLS. The first sees liberalism as a 'system of thought that is simultaneously beset by internal *contradiction* ... and by systematic *repression* of the presence of these

---

[69] *Ibid.* p. 262.

contradictions'.[70] Here, the rule of law is a mask for the basic contradiction in liberal society because law is not, and can never be, determinate. Law therefore:

> is not so much a rational enterprise as a vast exercise in rationalisation. Legal doctrine can be manipulated to justify an almost infinite spectrum of possible outcomes ... Legal doctrine is nothing more than a sophisticated vocabulary and repertoire of manipulative techniques for categorising, describing, organising, and comparing; it is *not* methodology for reaching substantive outcomes.[71]

In this respect, this first tendency has much in common with the second, which argues that law and legal discourse 'reflect, confirm, and reshape the social divisions and hierarchies inherent in a type or stage of social organisation such as "capitalism"'.[72] However, as already noted CLS 'should not be understood as simply an assault upon formalism', because few jurists accept or believe in it anymore. Rather, CLS is all about the contradiction between individual autonomy and communal force that liberalism has failed to resolve, but which liberalism believes can be rationally solved. However, few critical scholars focus solely on legal method; the vast majority base their assessment of the indeterminacy of legal method upon a Marxist or Marxist-influenced notion of society. Gordon, for example, sees that legal discourses 'routinely help to create and maintain the ordinary inequities of everyday social life'[73] and that they 'have the legitimating power they do because they sketch pictures of widely shared, wistful, inchoate visions of an ideal'.[74] Clearly, there are substantial overlaps between these two elements and they can be quite helpfully collapsed. As Fitzpatrick and Hunt argue '[t]he element of cohesion is provided, in the first instance, by a shared rejection of the dominant tradition of Anglo-American legal scholarship, the expository orthodoxy or, more crudely, the "black-letter law" tradition'.[75] The purpose of rejecting the method is because they believe that a different model of society lies beneath it.[76]

---

[70] Kelman quoted in Freeman, *Lloyd's Introduction*, p. 936, emphasis in original. See also Kelman, *A Guide to Critical Legal Studies.*

[71] Hutchinson and Monahan, 'Law, Politics, and the Critical Legal Scholars', 206, original emphasis.

[72] Unger, 'The Critical Legal Studies Movement', 563, n. 1.

[73] Gordon, 'Law and Ideology', 16.   [74] *Ibid.* 16.

[75] Fitzpatrick and Hunt (eds.), *Critical Legal Studies*, p. 1.

[76] See Stone, 'Formalism', pp. 166–205. Stone notes that '[l]ike the treatment of neurosis or the death of God, the critique of formalism seems somehow interminable' (p. 166).

Central to the part that focuses on legal method is the notion of indeterminacy. As Hutchinson and Monahan argue: 'Legal doctrine not only does not, but also cannot, generate determinant results ... Legal doctrine can be manipulated to justify an almost infinite spectrum of possible outcomes.'[77] Kairys offers the following example, using the core legal tenet of *stare decisis*, or the injunction to follow past decisions. In *Amalgamated Food Employees Union* v. *Logan Valley Plaza* (1968) the Supreme Court upheld the right of employees to picket a store involved in a labour dispute even though the owner of the shopping centre did not want the picket to occur. Four years later, in 1972, in *Lloyd* v. *Tanner* the Supreme Court held that an anti-war activist had no right to distribute leaflets in a shopping centre 'even though this centre regularly attracted political candidates by avowing that it provided the largest audience in the state'.[78] In denying the protestor's right to distribute leaflets the Supreme Court reconciled its decision with *Logan Valley* by highlighting that 'speech concerning a labour dispute relates more closely to the activities of a shopping centre than does anti-war speech'.[79] However in *Hudgens* v. *NLRB* the Supreme Court re-wrote the *Lloyd* verdict, arguing that to treat labour speech differently from anti-war speech would violate the norm that the First Amendment freedoms do not depend on the content of the speech. Therefore no one should be allowed to picket a shopping centre. 'The *Hudgens* Court went on to say that it was bound by *Lloyd* (as re-written) and to hold that union members involved in a labour dispute with a store located in a shopping centre do not have a constitutional right to picket in that shopping centre.'[80]

Thus Kairys demonstrates that the idealised model of the legal process is based on the false assumption that there is 'a distinctly legal mode of reasoning and analysis that leads to and determines "correct" rules, facts, and results in particular cases'.[81] Such legalism[82] takes law for granted 'as something to be simply defined and analysed'.[83] Jurisprudence therefore has focused on constructing ever more refined and rigid systems of formal definition yet such a procedure has 'served to isolate law completely from the social context within which it exists'.[84] The main purpose of legalism has been to reify the law and its reasoning, and to

---

[77] Hutchinson, and Monahan, 'Law, Politics, and the Critical Legal Scholars', 206.
[78] Kairys, *The Politics of Law*, p. 12.   [79] *Ibid.* p. 12.   [80] *Ibid.* p. 12.   [81] *Ibid.* p. 11.
[82] The term is Judith Shklar's, see 'Law and Ideology' extracted in Freeman, *Lloyd's Introduction*, pp. 26–9.
[83] *Ibid.* p. 26.   [84] *Ibid.* p. 27.

legitimate the status quo, imbuing the legal edifice with the type of mysticism which, as Marxism points out, serves to mask the true nature of law. But, as much analysis of law has shown, it is not value-free or neutral but as both Marxists and critical lawyers argue it is 'a sophisticated vocabulary and repertoire of manipulative techniques for categorising, describing, organising and comparing'.[85] It is indeterminacy that means law can be used as just such a tool of rationalisation. Such an analysis denies that legal reasoning has 'any distinct existence'[86] and that, simply put 'law is politics. It does not have an existence outside of ideological battles within society.'[87] Despite all these negative characterisations of law, critical lawyers do not write law off. Rather, they argue that once law is reconnected with its political and moral context then peoples' inevitable thirst for equality and fairness will emerge. Whereas some Marxists argue that domination will always occur until we attain the communist utopia, CLS argues, along with Marxists like Hunt and Thompson, that law can be used as a tool of the disenfranchised and dominated.

Feminism: critical jurisprudence in action

One of, if not the, best attempt at a practical agenda of reform is feminism and feminist jurisprudence. This section will focus on radical feminism and not liberal, cultural or post-modern feminism because it is only radical feminism that shares such a critical perspective on law. Feminism shares the same core assumptions as critical legal systems: a critique of the inherent logic of law, a belief in law's indeterminacy and the manipulability of doctrine, and viewing law as playing a role in legitimising particular social relations and combines all this (i.e. the foregoing factors) with empirical analysis. McLeod[88] argues that all feminist jurisprudence possesses two unifying characteristics. First, the belief that society, and necessarily the legal order, is patriarchal. Secondly, 'it seeks to analyse the contribution of law in constructing, maintaining, reinforcing, and perpetuating patriarchy and it looks at ways in which this patriarchy can be undermined and ultimately eliminated'.[89]

One of the central feminist insights is law's historical development. Historically, those who have written, shaped and applied the law have

---

[85] Hutchinson and Monahan quoted in McLeod, *Legal Theory*, p. 128.
[86] *Ibid.* p. 128.   [87] Freeman, *Lloyd's Introduction*, p. 936.
[88] McLeod, *Legal Theory*, p. 129.   [89] Freeman, *Lloyd's Introduction*, p. 1027.

been men. As Finley argues legal language itself is gendered because the primary linguists of law have been 'white, educated, economically privileged men'.[90] Not only have men shaped and defined law but they have 'given it meaning consistent with their understandings of the world and of people "other" than them'.[91] By demonstrating the history of law's development feminists challenge our unthinking acceptance of law as natural, inevitable and neutral. Such an approach forcefully demonstrates the role that context plays in the eventual development of law. By demonstrating that law is historically contingent feminism removes the veil of law's neutrality.

The same treatment has been extended to the definition and separation of the public and private spheres, a central tenet of liberalism. To liberals the public/private dichotomy is an inevitable and universal phenomenon. They accept that some regulation of society is necessary but that freedom is enhanced by limiting law's intrusion into the private sphere. Essentially, we all benefit from the liberal restraint of law. Charlesworth[92] however questions the inevitability of such a split. She characterises the legal regulation of the public sphere as reflecting the interests of elite males. Thus civil and political rights were the first to be protected because they were the abuses that elite males most feared. After all, such men had little to fear in their own households. One of the central legal rights and principles, the right to life, is concerned with the arbitrary deprivation of life *by the state*. Such dangers required regulation, violence within the home or marriage, perpetuated primarily by men against women, did not. Yet this is not simply an unfortunate coincidence – that the private sphere is unregulated and that is where women happen to be – but that the private sphere is unregulated precisely *because* that is where women tend to be. Copelon argues that within the private sphere there operates 'an informal customary system of social control with the explicit or implicit permission of the formal state, constantly bolstering the formal impunity given to gender aggression'.[93] To Copelon such domestic violence is both the result of the structure of patriarchy and the mechanism that keeps it in place.

Law's role in shaping and maintaining women's subordination manifests itself not only in the absence of regulation in the domestic sphere but also in the exclusion of women from the public sphere. Taub

---

[90] Finley, 'Breaking Women's Silence', 892.   [91] *Ibid.* 892.
[92] Charlesworth quoted in Cook (ed.), *Human Rights of Women*, p. 71.
[93] Copelon, 'Intimate Terror', p. 132.

and Schneider argue that the equality norm that provided so many gains in the early years of feminism, now operates to maintain women's limited inclusion. In their words the law is 'legitimising discrimination through the language of equality'.[94] This is because law only offers equality to the extent that women may conform to the male norm. Equality thus validates and enshrines in law the male experience. By focusing attention on equality and encouraging the channelling of energy towards attaining greater equality, attention is distracted from the need for real change in social roles. 'The law can thus purport to guarantee equality while simultaneously denying it.'[95] In many respects the law simply fails to see the dangers that women face and the needs they have. In order for law to serve women therefore a rearticulation of it is needed. Take the two trials of Inez Garcia for example. Inez Garcia was raped by two men. In response Garcia said 'I took my gun, I loaded it, and I went after them,'[96] killing one of the two assailants. She was put on trial for murder. At her first trial she was convicted of second degree murder, avoiding the first degree murder charge because of psychiatric evidence that she did not know what she was doing. The trial was however dismissed because of improper jury direction. At her second trial her male attorney was replaced by Susan Jordan, a radical feminist. Jordan saw her task as to 'translate the male-oriented rule of self-defence into a form that would capture the real experience of a woman facing possible attack by a man'.[97] Jordan successfully rearticulated popular conceptions of what rape is and separated it from gender and sexual implications, recasting it as a violent assault.[98]

It can be argued then that feminism views law and its relation to context in a far more immediate and pressing manner than other theorists at the same end of the spectrum.[99] To feminists the role of power and politics is not natural or inevitable, but nefarious and wrong. A key difference here between the two approaches is whether they view law as a potential tool of emancipation. To those approaches that denude it totally of any distinct existence or social justice separate from politics,

---

[94] Taub and Schneider, 'Perspectives', p. 134.   [95] *Ibid.* p. 123.
[96] Garcia quoted in Freeman, *Lloyd's Introduction*, p. 944. Her attackers had threatened to return and attack her again.
[97] Jordan quoted in *ibid.* pp. 944–5.
[98] See chapter 5. Certain jurisdictions attempted to recast rape as violence but the attempt was widely considered a failure, not least because it confused jurors as to why the defendant was not charged with rape.
[99] The empirical dimension of feminism is explored with reference to rape legislation in the United Kingdom in chapter 2.

such a possibility is denied. While others, such as feminists, certain Marxists and critical lawyers, may share a belief in the manipulation of law by its political context, such approaches do not believe that this manipulation rules out the possibility that law can act in ways contrary to the dominant forces in society, however defined. Part of the explanation for these differences may lie in whether they believe there is an alternate way of achieving a more just society. To Marxists, revolution is the method of transition, with a difference of interpretation over whether revolution is impeded or brought closer by using law to improve the conditions of the workers. Even to Schmitt, a writer of near unparalleled pessimism, a better, or at least more harmonious society can be realised once the camouflage of liberalism is stripped away, though not through law.

Those approaches that do attribute some emancipatory potential to law see it as the sole or primary method of transition. Yet such a belief does not render the task easy or straightforward, as such theories rest upon the notion that legalism seeks to render politics' control of law invisible.

> Law is not, of course, uniquely the tool of the powerful . . . But to be able to wield legal discourses with facility or authority or to pay others . . . to wield them on your behalf is a large part of what it means to possess power in society. Legal discourses therefore tend to reflect the interests and the perspectives of the powerful people who make most use of them.[100]

And regardless of who uses them, legal discourses, that is, ways of speaking about law, are 'saturated with categories and images that for the most part rationalise and justify in myriad subtle ways the existing social order as natural, necessary, and just'.[101] The task at hand is to reveal the contingency that such discourses translate into necessity can be challenged.

Conclusion

Natural law theory posits that there are objective moral standards which should be brought to bear upon the law and legal system. Any form of legal regulation should reflect and incorporate these standards and where regulation and morality diverge, it is morality that is superior and the law must fit to it. While this may seem commonsensical, such a reliance upon

---

[100] Gordon, 'Law and Ideology', 15–16.   [101] *Ibid.* 15.

something so vague as 'morality' or a higher law has historically been used to justify all manner of laws and beliefs. The effect of cloaking law in a 'halo of moral sanctity'[102] is to preclude criticism and the ability to change the law. Legal positivism, on the other hand, seeks to remove natural law's reliance upon factors external to law, insisting instead that law can be made into a closed logical system. The main purpose of the law is simply technical resolution of legal problems. The primary task of legal thinkers is the elaboration of law's rules so that every circumstance can be covered, as and when new circumstances arise. The business of law to positivists is simply the application of impartial rules.

Positivism's attempt to de-contextualise law is reversed by the socio-logical turn in law, which seeks instead to view law in its context. Rather than simply being the 'rules of the game' law is a tool of social engineer-ing which can serve to improve society by reference to policy goals. While the sociological turn does make a major contribution in its belief that law does not exist, and cannot be studied in a vacuum, its overall approach is one of problem solving and moderate reform. It ultimately has faith in law's ability to deliver justice and views law as a good system which just needs perfecting. This is simply a question of a technical adjustment of the means to the ends.

It is clear then that these jurisprudential approaches are based upon a certain model of society and a particular conceptualisation of law: the liberal model of society. This society is characterised by consensus and harmony, and law's purpose is the technical resolution of conflicts to the ultimate benefit of society. Law is natural and necessary for the proper functioning of orderly society and provides an impartial method of resolving the conflicts that will inevitably arise. The law is unbiased and favours no particular person or group, being applied equally to all and being blind to the prejudices and perceptions of the rest of society.

This model of law and society has been challenged by what has been termed for the purpose of this chapter 'critical' approaches. Their under-lying model of society is one based upon conflict, rather than consensus. To critical approaches law does not supply the impartial rules of the game but is itself part of the machinery of domination and hierarchy, and operates to impose the interests of one group over another. The liberal model's assertion that law is impartial and apolitical is a supremely political move designed to obscure the reality of domination and

---

[102] Harris, *Legal Philosophies*, p. 9.

oppression. Law serves to fool the people into believing that they live in a just and fair system where all are treated alike.

For classical Marxists law cannot provide social justice because of its complete indeterminacy. Other approaches however do not go as far and are therefore able to recover the possibility of law as a tool of justice. Law possesses at least some autonomy from politics and it is this autonomy that makes justice possible, at least some of the time. As Bell writes: 'Like the gambler who enters the card game knowing that it is fixed, we are drawn to the courts because they are the only game in town.'[103] Those seeking social change, as in the case of the National Association for the Advancement of Colored People's (NAACP) fight against segregation, know that they may lose most of the time but for the chance of that one vital decision, they keep taking the legal path to achieve social change.[104]

The case of desegregation in America and the NAACP's legal strategy is premised therefore on an understanding of law as a tool for achieving social *change*. By constructing the law and the story of *Brown* in this way, it is hard *not* to see law as effective: there was a concerted legal strategy, a series of cases, and finally, a Supreme Court ruling. Law therefore produced desegregation. However, as Bell argues, we must adopt a more complicated understanding of law. First, we must see social change as broader than a simple legal pronouncement; we must ask harder questions about the nature, history and complicity of law in racism. When we accept the dominant narrative of law as solving the problem of racism in America with a single decision, we fall prey to the delusion of Shklarian legalism: that human relations are put in the language of law and thereby solved. But doing so hides the reality and effects of complex social phenomena like racism.

This is why it is important to counterbalance the hyperbole of *Brown* and reforming zeal created by legal activism with the daily reality of rape cases in the United Kingdom. If *Brown* is the extraordinary, rape law is the mundane. Where the counter-narrative to *Brown* asks the question about law's ability to solve complex social problems, analysis of rape reform explores it. The point of this chapter therefore is not to convince readers that indeterminacy permeates all law, all of the time. It is simply to introduce readers to the radical indeterminacy thesis itself and provide them with a set of questions to take into the empirical part of the book.

[103] Bell, *Silent Covenants*, p. 137.   [104] See Sinclair, 'The Role of Law.'

it: 'Groups must command significant social, political, and economic power before they become attractive candidates for judicial solicitude.'[28] He also notes that between 1900 and 1950 not a single court decision involving race clearly contravened national public opinion.[29] The only decision that came closest to it was *Brown*, which evenly split the American people.

Nor was *Plessy* an anomaly. Indeed, Klarman argues that *Brown* was not a straightforward or obvious decision. 'On the conventional legal materials' Klarman writes '*Plessy* was at least plausible, and it was arguably right'.[30] This is because the Equal Protection Clause does not bar segregation, and the original understanding of the Fourteenth Amendment probably permitted it.[31] Given that the conventional constitutional sources on segregation had not changed since *Plessy* in 1896 *Brown* was not an obvious conclusion. 'As the justices in 1896 almost certainly thought that segregation was good policy, the case was easy. Fifty-eight years later, the Court came out the other way – unanimously.'[32] In short, as Klarman argues, it was not the *legal* context that had changed; it was the *social* one.

The Supreme Court's ruling in *Brown* therefore was not simply about the law or the constitutionality of segregation, because the Constitution was indeterminate on the question of segregation, but about something else. To Bell this 'something else' was the need for America to launder its ideals. He argues that the positive depiction of *Brown* necessarily paints segregation and racism as an 'eminently fixable aberration',[33] rather than a widely practised and supported social institution. Instead of challenging the bases of the *Plessy* framework which legalised segregation, the Supreme Court chose to sidestep it and, as a consequence, the issue of American racism. As Bell argues:

> The *Brown* majority's racism as an unhappy accident of history immunises 'the law' ... from anti-racist critique. That is to say, the majority positions the law as that which *fixes* racism rather than as that which participates in its construction.[34]

---

[28] Klarman, *From Jim Crow to Civil Rights*, p. 450. [29] *Ibid.* p. 450.
[30] *Ibid.* p. 449.
[31] *Ibid.* p. 449. The Equal Protection Clause of the Fourteenth Amendment states that 'no state shall ... deny to any person within its jurisdiction the equal protection of the laws'. In *Plessy* Justice Henry B. Brown argued that the framers intended the clause to apply to civil rights, not social arrangements.
[32] Klarman, *From Jim Crow to Civil Rights*, p. 449. [33] Bell, 'Dissenting Opinion', p. 198.
[34] *Ibid.* p. 198–9, emphasis added.

Such an interpretation enables *Brown* to function as a resurrection of American ideals, and the Supreme Court's place in them, without accepting that it was the Supreme Court and the Constitution that legally sanctioned segregation in the first place. But the simple fact of the matter is that *Brown* did not, and could not, fix American racism, which was a deeply entrenched system in both the North and South. Racism simply served too powerful a purpose. As Bell argues in his dissenting opinion to the rewritten version of *Brown* '[r]acial segregation furthers societal stability by subordinating Negro Americans, which makes it easier for rich white Americans to dominate poor white Americans'.[35] Bell cites Woodward's argument that Southern leaders in the post-Reconstruction era enacted segregation laws mainly at the insistence of poor white people who, given their low social and economic status, demanded these barriers in order to retain a sense of superiority and status. As Bell argues 'in a country that views property ownership as a measure of worth, there are a great many whites with relatively little property of a traditional kind – money, securities, land – who come to view their whiteness as a property right'.[36] Thus the central question for Bell is: 'How could a decision that promised so much and, by its terms, accomplished so little, have gained so hallowed a place?'[37] He concludes that:

> it has gained in reputation as a measure of what law and society might be. That noble image, dulled by resistance to any but minimal steps toward compliance, has transformed *Brown* into a magnificent mirage, the legal equivalent of that city on a hill to which all aspire without any serious thought that it will ever be achieved.[38]

Thus contemporary depictions of *Brown* paint the decision as achieving far more than it was ever truly capable of achieving. *Brown* is expected to carry a great burden: reconciling American ideals with the unpalatable truth of racism. These grand depictions of *Brown* mask the significance it arguably did have, that of giving the NAACP and African Americans the ability to place the difficult question of segregation before the Supreme Court. The Court may have been presented with a *fait accompli*, but there was nothing certain about the NAACP's ability to create the legal conditions in which *Brown* might be possible and to actually move the battle for civil rights into the legal domain. Moreover, by focusing on the constitutionality of segregation the NAACP were able to cut to the

---

[35] *Ibid.* p. 187.   [36] *Ibid.* p. 188.   [37] Bell, *Silent Covenants*, p. 2.   [38] *Ibid.* p. 4.

heart of American ideals in a way that mass mobilisation at that time could not. The remainder of this chapter will address four aspects of *Brown* and the NAACP's litigation strategy: first, the origins and evolution of that strategy; secondly, the legal journey to Brown; thirdly, the opinion itself; and fourthly, differing explanations of why the Supreme Court ruled to declare segregation unconstitutional.

The NAACP's litigation strategy

Brown represented the culmination of over a quarter of a century's legal planning and work by the NAACP. The NAACP itself started life in 1909, formed by a biracial group alarmed at the increase in white violence against African Americans. Its original purpose was to seek 'equal rights and opportunities for all'[39] and it was essentially a political action group. Its initial strategy was to broaden and strengthen the political coalition which had started to emerge around civil rights. In 1930 Nathan Margold headed a small committee set up to decide what strategy the NAACP should adopt in the courts. In 1931 the Margold Report was produced, outlining a proposed litigation strategy. In it Margold argued that the NAACP should not accept the *Plessy* framework. Until that time *Plessy* and 'separate but equal' had been the dominant conceptual framework for segregation and it could be used to demand the strict duplication of facilities, but to Margold, using *Plessy* would mean that 'we should be leaving wholly untouched the very essence of the existing evils'.[40] He believed that the strategy of demanding equalisation and raising the costs of segregation to a prohibitive level would provide limited victories and that newly equalised schools would soon slip back into inequality. The report states: 'it would be a great mistake to fritter away our limited funds on sporadic attempts to force making of equal divisions of school funds in the few instances where such attempts might be expected to succeed'.[41]

Instead of using *Plessy*, which was after all a civil rights loss, Margold advocated the use of *Yick Wo* (1886),[42] one of the few civil rights successes of the nineteenth century. *Yick Wo* held as unconstitutional a San Francisco ordinance that banned laundries in wooden buildings. The ordinance, while appearing to be non-discriminatory, in practice discriminated against Chinese who typically located their businesses in

---

[39] Quoted in Greenberg, *Crusaders in the Courts*, p. 14.   [40] *Ibid.* p. 59.   [41] *Ibid.* p. 59.
[42] *Yick Wo* v. *Hopkins*, 118 US 356 (1886).

wooden buildings. The Court found that the law had been administered 'with an evil eye and an unequal hand'.[43] As Jack Greenberg, Chief Counsel to the NAACP, points out: 'The idea was that if wherever there was segregation there was also inequality, which was invariably the case, segregation, therefore, was unconstitutional.'[44] Margold thus understood the difference between ostensibly colour-blind laws and the reality of bias and discrimination. In other words, the difference between *de jure* and *de facto* discrimination, a crucial element of the NAACP's strategy. The message of Margold's report was that segregation is always accompanied by inequality, making 'separate but equal' a myth. Despite Margold's dismissal of an equalisation strategy using *Plessy*, he understood that, at least initially, a direct attack on segregation would be likely to fail. His report therefore proposes a bifurcated strategy: the use of the doctrine of 'separate but equal' to achieve better facilities for African American school children and attacking segregation itself both indirectly by raising the cost of segregation, and directly by attacking and challenging its constitutionality. The NAACP chose to shelve the latter part of Margold's strategy until the late 1940s when political factors were more favourable and the legal groundwork had been laid.

What did emerge clearly from Margold's report was the importance of education and its role as the focus of NAACP strategy. The easiest stage of education to attack was the highest: graduate and professional schools. Plaintiffs in such cases were educated, ambitious, confident individuals, often without the attachment of families, who were vulnerable to pressure. Moreover, equalisation of university facilities was extremely expensive for the segregated state, and even in the worst case scenario, plaintiffs would be given scholarships to out-of-state universities. In several university equalisation cases, states had to establish entirely new universities or law schools, often just for a single student. In Thurgood Marshall's words, the aim was 'to compel the states to pay for their "luxury"'[45] of segregation. The NAACP's litigation strategy later moved to include salary equalisation cases for African American school teachers in the Upper South. Here too, the NAACP won some crucial victories, proving that the system could be used by African Americans to further their interests. However, the NAACP soon found that the removal of an openly discriminatory law was swiftly followed by laws that were discriminatory in administration – the evil eye and unequal hand of *Yick*

---

[43] Quoted in Greenberg, *Crusaders in the Courts*, p. 57.   [44] *Ibid.* p. 59.
[45] Quoted in Tushnet, *The NAACP's Legal Strategy*, p. 10.

Wo. The simple fact of the matter was that courts were unwilling to enforce the *Yick Wo* precedent and preferred to accept at face value covertly racist laws and administrations. Thus school boards abandoned salary schedules that overtly discriminated on grounds of race, only to adopt schedules that used non-racial criteria, often merit systems, which produced similar results. In such circumstances: 'Clarity became obscurity, as state officials began to construct definitions of equality that preserved the status quo and that judges were willing to accept. Compliance with the law as it was applied by the courts was then accomplished, but little changed.'[46] In the school year 1931–32 African American teachers received 50 per cent less than their white counterparts. In 1945–46, after some key successes African American, teachers' salary was still only 65 per cent of white teachers.

A direct attack on *Plessy*: beyond 'separate but equal'

By the late 1940s it was clear that both university and salary equalisation cases were producing diminishing returns. In 1947, Marshall, who was by this time the Legal Defense and Educational Fund's (LDF)[47] legal counsel, wrote to the NAACP president Roy Wilkins that 'nothing can be gained under the doctrine of "separate but equal"'.[48] He continued that the aim is now 'either equal facilities or the breaking down of segregation'.[49] Three years later the NAACP Board of Directors adopted a resolution stating that all future education cases would seek 'education on a non-segregated basis and that no relief other than that will be acceptable'.[50] And so in 1950 the more radical strand of Margold's initial strategy finally became LDF policy.

Although the NAACP did not officially abandon the aim of compensation until 1950, in the late 1940s the LDF pursued its aim of a Supreme Court ruling that segregation was unconstitutional in several cases. In both *Gaines*[51] and *Sipuel*,[52] the LDF challenged states' assertions that

[46] *Ibid.* p. 103.
[47] On 20 March 1940 the NAACP set up the NAACP Legal Defense and Educational Fund, Inc., also known as the LDF or Inc Fund. It did this to retain tax exempt status for the legal side of its work. It will be referred to here as the LDF.
[48] Quoted in Tushnet, *The NAACP's Legal Strategy*, p. 114. [49] *Ibid.* p. 114.
[50] *Ibid.* p. 136. Greenberg also picks 1950 as the date of the change of strategy.
[51] *Missouri ex rel. Gaines* v. *Canada*, 305 US 337 (1938).
[52] *Sipuel* v. *Board of Regents of University of Oklahoma*, 332 US 631 (1948).

newly created law schools could be equal to their white counterparts.[53] The most significant advance thus far emerged in *Sweatt* v. *Painter*.[54] Heman Marion Sweatt was rejected by the University of Texas Law School on the grounds of race. Suit was filed in May 1946, and the LDF decided to challenge for the first time the school's equality. The Texas court ruled that because the state offered to set up an African American law school, it had discharged its responsibility to provide equal education. The LDF took the case to the Supreme Court, arguing that the African American school that had been set up in the intervening four years was clearly inferior to the white law school in both tangible and intangible aspects.[55] When Texas state authorities offered to set up the law school, Sweatt would have been its only pupil. Consequently, there could be no classroom discussion, no law review and no moot court programme. Even if other students were admitted as the university grew over time the African American school could not supply the same reputation as the white school, nor opportunities for developing contacts. As a consequence, segregation inevitably resulted in educational inequality, breaching the Fourteenth Amendment, and rendering it unconstitutional. The decision was significant because it referred back to the precedent set in *Yick Wo* and accepted its argument that while segregated facilities may appear cursorily equal, in operation they produce inequality.

Sweatt was accompanied by two other cases: *McLaurin*,[56] where an African American student was admitted to white classes but had to sit in an antechamber, and *Henderson*,[57] which challenged segregated dining car services. *McLaurin* was the more significant of the two, reducing segregation to its starkest, and most absurd, terms. The brief argued the sole purpose of admitting McLaurin, then singling him out could only be 'to place a badge of inferiority upon him'.[58] In both *Sweatt* and *McLaurin* the LDF used a two pronged legal and argumentative strategy: a direct

---

[53] *Gaines* failed after the plaintiff disappeared, and *Sipuel* fell through because the plaintiff had indicated that she was willing to attend a segregated school, thus allowing the Court to avoid the issue.

[54] *Sweatt* v. *Painter*, 339 US 629 (1950).

[55] The white university assets were valued at $72 million, the African American at $4 million, per capita investment for African American students was a quarter of that for white students, and the white library had 750,000 volumes, the African American only 82,000.

[56] *McLaurin* v. *Oklahoma State Regents*, 339 US 637 (1950).

[57] *Henderson* v. *United States* 339 US 816 (1950).

[58] Quoted in Greenberg, *Crusaders in the Courts*, p. 71.

attack on 'separate but equal' combined with straightforward inequality arguments. In all three cases the federal government became involved through amicus briefs in support of desegregation with the Attorney General arguing for the overturning of *Plessy*, and that 'separate but equal' was 'wrong as a matter of law, history, and policy'.[59]

The LDF won all three cases. Upon winning the cases Greenberg concluded that: 'The Court's reasoning suggested how next to attack segregated education at elementary, high school, and undergraduate levels – go after the intangibles.'[60] In order to prove such intangibles existed, the LDF had to use social science – psychology, anthropology and sociology. Although this was controversial the LDF was left with little choice. The only way round 'separate but equal', which was, after all, the law, and had a powerful precedent in *Plessy*, was to sidestep it.

The case and the opinion

After nearly twenty-five years of legal groundwork the stage was finally set and in 1954 the LDF filed *Brown*. The case placed Chief Justice Earl Warren in an extremely difficult position. First of all, he believed that a decision of this magnitude needed to be unequivocal, and therefore decided to author the opinion himself. It also needed to be unanimous. This was difficult. Five judges wanted to overturn *Plessy*, four did not, and all were wary of appearing to intrude into politics. In order to achieve his aims Warren had to produce an opinion that appeased all of them. The opinion also had to be non-rhetorical, unemotional, and above all, non-accusatory. Warren believed that he had found a solution in social science, which would allow him to sidestep the question of *Plessy's* constitutionality and simply justify a decision for (limited) desegregation on the grounds of harm caused to African American children. In the infamous footnote eleven, Warren based his opinion on the 'modern authority' of a number of sociological studies. The studies cited were widely derided, in particular Kenneth C. Clark's doll study. Here, African American and white children were given an African American doll and a white doll and asked to chose which one was the 'good doll', which had a 'nice colour', and so forth. Both sets of children favoured the white doll, leading Clark to conclude that African American children felt ashamed of their colour and inferior to white children. However, Chief Justice Warren's opinion failed to mention that African American children

[59] *Ibid.* p. 73.   [60] *Ibid.* p. 78.

living in the segregated South had higher approval rates for the African American doll than African American children living in the unsegregated North. The basic premise of the study, that segregation makes African American children feel inferior, could not therefore be borne out by the study. Despite this, the 'doll study' and the other studies served their purpose: giving Warren grounds for his decision, however tenuous.

These limitations created an opinion in *Brown* that was both narrow and slow. Warren ruled that *Brown* was only applicable to segregation in public schools, leaving *Plessy* untouched.[61] This suggested that *Brown* only viewed segregation as harmful to *children*, making desegregation in this case an exception, rather than an outright condemnation of segregation as a whole. The remedy provided in *Brown II* also served to slow the pace of desegregation considerably. It did this in three ways. First, the expression 'with all deliberate speed' allowed the South to delay desegregation indefinitely.[62] This was intentionally designed to give the South time to get used to the idea. Secondly, the Court limited relief to the parties to the cases. By not making *Brown* a class action, civil rights lawyers would have to undertake court cases to desegregate each individual school district. This would be time-consuming and costly, again slowing the pace of desegregation.[63] Finally, the Court decided that because local school problems varied, federal courts were the best way of enforcing desegregation, allowing states to delay the process almost indefinitely. In other words, as Balkin argued, 'Warren and the Court decided to edge the country toward ending Jim Crow without offering a general theory of why Jim Crow violated the Constitution'.[64] To have done so would have been too confrontational and increased the chances of failure. Warren hoped that by grounding his opinion in social science, he could avoid appearing as if he were condemning the South. There was a very real possibility that the South would openly and vigorously resist the decision, creating a constitutional crisis. Similarly, the Court relied upon the social scientific evidence, rather than a legal basis, because this

[61] *Brown* did not actually overturn segregation. *Plessy* was not actually overturned until 1957 in *Simkins* v. *City of Greensboro*, 149 F Supp 562, 564 (MD NC 1957), aff'd *Greensboro* v. *Simkins*, 246 F 2d 425 (4th Cir 1957) and the first clear statement of it by the Supreme Court was not until 1970 in *Oregon* v. *Mitchell*, 400 US 112 (1970): Balkin, *What* Brown v. Board of Education *Should Have Said*, p. 48.

[62] One estimate believed that segregation would take 100 years to dismantle.

[63] Despite this the Court issued a series of *per curiam* orders affirming lower court decisions involving municipal golf courses, public buses, beaches, etc., extending the ruling to adults.

[64] Balkin, *What* Brown v. Board of Education *Should Have Said*, p. 49.

gave cover to the Court to rule in this way. The idea of psychological harm to children was simply the most palatable way of overturning segregation.

Explaining *Brown*

According to the popular interpretation of *Brown* the Supreme Court's decision was a courageous and radical decision that created significant social change. However, many accounts have emerged that challenge this depiction of the Supreme Court as defenders of the weak. But if desegregation was such a bitter pill for the South to swallow and ran the risk of a constitutional crisis, why did the Supreme Court bother? Dudziak[65] argues that the Truman Administration wanted desegregation because of the Cold War imperative. In the immediate post-war period Truman was keen to shape the post-war world in America's image. This would require large amounts of foreign aid and, in order to sell foreign aid to Congress and the American people, Truman had to paint the ideological divide between the US and USSR in the starkest terms. He did this by emphasising the American way of life – democracy, free elections and institutions, and individual liberty. Yet segregation conflicted with the new stories America needed to tell about itself. Ideologically, a policy of oppressing people because of their non-whiteness proved a major obstacle in selling the American way of life to the Third World. The Soviet Union made as much propaganda capital out of America's hypocrisy as possible. In 1949 the US Embassy in Moscow reported that: '[T]he Soviet press hammers away unceasingly on such things as "lynch law," segregation, racial discrimination, deprivation of political rights, etc. seeking to build up a picture of an America in which the Negroes are brutally downtrodden.'[66] Nor was it just the Soviets who wanted to highlight America's hypocrisy and racism. Both the NAACP and the Civil Rights Congress filed petitions at the United Nations protesting the treatment of African Americans, and charging the US government with genocide, respectively.[67] In short, segregation was a

---

[65] Dudziak, 'Desegregation as a Cold War Imperative', 61–120.   [66] *Ibid.* 89–90.
[67] The NAACP petition died in the Sub-Commission on Prevention of Discrimination and Protection of Minorities due to a combination of US pressure, the influence of Eleanor Roosevelt and misgivings among certain NAACP officials about Soviet support for the petition. The Civil Rights Congress's petition, 'We Charge Genocide: The Crime of Government Against the Negro People', was delivered by Paul Robeson and William L. Patterson in 1951.

public relations disaster and an embarrassment to the North, and in removing it '*Brown* served US foreign policy interests'.[68] Truman therefore placed pressure on the Supreme Court through the filing of amicus briefs, stressing 'the international implications of US race discrimination, and at times focused on the negative impact on American foreign policy that a pro-segregation decision might have'.[69]

Truman's most significant contribution was the Civil Rights Committee which reported in 1947.[70] It recommended desegregation for three reasons: moral, economic and international. Morally, the Committee argued that by not living up to her democratic ideals, America was 'creating a kind of moral dry rot which eats away at the emotional and rational basis of democratic beliefs'.[71] Moreover, in terms of economics the simple fact was that segregation cost.[72] It was hugely inefficient to have duplicate facilities and it demanded an inefficient use of labour. It created a vicious circle where African Americans would be restricted to low income jobs, which in turn reduced their purchasing power, lowering consumer demand, depressing production and creating a lower standard of living for everyone. As the President of the Chamber of Commerce put it: 'You can't sell an electric refrigerator to a family that can't afford electricity.'[73] The issue then was not the denial of civil and political rights on the basis of race, but the loss of all those consumers. Moreover, African Americans had little reason to work hard when they could not progress, and rebellious workers and troubled race relations scared investors away from the South. Finally, internationally, the report stressed the propaganda weapon of segregation and argued that: 'Throughout the Pacific, Latin America, the Near, Middle, and Far East, the treatment which our Negroes receive is taken as a reflection of our attitudes toward all dark-skinned people.'[74]

More significantly for Truman, however, was the growing strength of the African American vote. Migration of African Americans from the South to the North created concentrated areas of African American

---

[68] Dudziak, 'Desegregation as a Cold War Imperative', 65.   [69] *Ibid.* 103.
[70] The Committee's report 'To Secure These Rights: The Report of the President's Committee on Civil Rights' (1947) can be accessed online at www.trumanlibrary.org/civilrights/srights1.htm.
[71] The President's Committee on Civil Rights, 'To Secure These Rights', p. 46.
[72] According to the Department of Health, Education and Welfare in 1953 racial bias cost the US between $15 and 30 billion a year: Rosenberg, *The Hollow Hope*, p. 158.
[73] Quoted in President's Committee on Civil Rights, 'To Secure These Rights', p. 48.
[74] *Ibid.* p. 52.

votes. Approximately 87 per cent of all African Americans who migrated North from 1910 to 1960 settled in the key electoral states of California, Illinois, Michigan, New Jersey, New York, Ohio and Pennsylvania. These seven states accounted for over 70 per cent of the electoral votes needed to elect a president.[75] According to Rosenberg, Truman realised this and points out that: 'it was black votes in California, Illinois and Ohio that provided Truman's margin of victory'.[76] After the decision the government made much use of *Brown*, and within an hour of the decision being handed down, the Voice of America had translated and broadcast the news in Eastern Europe[77] and Eisenhower used it prominently in propaganda.[78]

Brown and civil rights reform: a different reading of *Brown*

When the significant gains offered by a desegregation decision in the Supreme Court are set against the actual rate of desegregation in public schools, and the civil rights movement more generally, we view *Brown* in a different light.[79] It is now widely accepted that in the decade following *Brown* civil rights reform barely advanced at all, primarily because of the inactivity of Congress. It was not until 1964 and the Civil Rights Act, followed by the Voting Rights Act of 1965, that the true legacy of *Brown* emerged. This was coupled with a resurgence of protest activity, most notably in Birmingham, Alabama in April and May 1963. Between 1954 and 1964, then, arguably *Brown* did little to improve the day-to-day reality for most African Americans. What it did do was provide an ideological blow, both to Communist critics and to pro-segregationists in the South. This leads us to a very different reading of *Brown*, undermining its long-accepted position as an instigator of significant social change and the death knell of segregation. In this reading *Brown* gave the appearance of being a moral decision but in truth it simply served foreign policy interests as outlined in the previous section. Other scholars also

---

[75] Rosenberg, *The Hollow Hope*, p. 160.   [76] *Ibid.* p. 161.

[77] Dudziak, 'Desegregation as a Cold War Imperative', 113. This contrasts sharply with the extremely limited news coverage the decision received domestically.

[78] Although Truman started the process of desegregation, Eisenhower reaped the rewards when his presidency started in 1953.

[79] In the ten years from 1954 to 1964 the percentage of African American children in elementary and secondary school with that of white children only rose by 1.199 per cent, from 0.001 per cent to 1.2 per cent. In the ten years after 1964, this percentage rose by an incredible 89 percentage points from 2.3 per cent to 91.3 per cent.

argue that *Brown* did not help civil rights. Tushnet argues that it was protest activities that were 'in the end, more important than judicial decisions',[80] and that focusing money and resources on political lobbying and activism would have produced desegregation much sooner. Essentially, the NAACP's litigation strategy was a waste of time and money. Klarman even goes so far as to argue that *Brown* actually delayed the progress of civil rights. He maintains that the main effect of the decision was a white backlash.[81] '*Brown* produced a southern political climate in which racial extremism flourished'[82] and 'the lesson for ... southern politicians was clear: The more extreme a politician's resistance to the civil rights movement, the greater the rewards he might expect at the polls.'[83] 'Massive resistance' also took a legal form, with the South enacting laws that were a blatant contradiction of the Supreme Court ruling. Mississippi made it illegal to attend a desegregated school, Louisiana passed a law denying promotion or graduation to any student of a desegregated school, and Georgia deprived policemen of their retirement and disability pay if they failed to enforce the state's segregation laws. By 1957, at least 136 new laws and state constitutional amendments designed to preserve segregation had been enacted.[84]

Balkin too shares Tushnet and Klarman's scepticism that the Supreme Court's decision ended segregation and advanced civil rights. He argues that '*Brown* was not so much an outlier as one might imagine',[85] pointing out that the Truman Administration had specifically asked the Court to overrule *Plessy* in *Sweatt*, four years before *Brown*. Nor is the idea that the Court was more radical than the Executive true. Truman had run on a civil rights platform in the 1948 election, and had ordered the desegregation of the military. Finally, Balkin points out that desegregation was hardly unheard of – Major League Baseball had been desegregated in

---

[80] Tushnet, 'Commentary', p. 124.

[81] To Klarman, a non-confrontational and gradualist approach would have been far more successful, seemingly ignoring the reality that Deep South white Americans would never willingly desegregate. In such a climate it is hard to see precisely *how* the civil rights situation would ever have improved for African Americans when it was so deeply entrenched, and progressing at the pace of Southern white Americans. Even when African Americans were significantly oppressed, without rights and little threat to white Americans, there were still extensive civil and human rights abuses. The reality of massive resistance was not a threatened and cowed South but a hate-fuelled, violent response to African Americans demanding no more than their civil and political rights.

[82] Klarman, 'How *Brown* Changed Race Relations', 103.   [83] *Ibid.* 104.

[84] Rosenberg, *The Hollow Hope*, p. 79.

[85] Balkin, *What* Brown v. Board of Education *Should Have Said*, p. 19.

1946[86] and in 1948 Truman ordered the integration of the armed forces.[87] It should be noted too that twenty-seven states did not segregate. Tushnet argues that *Brown* might best be understood as 'enforcing a national political view against a regionally dominant one that happened to have excessive power in Congress'.[88]

Bell too challenges the supposed radicalism of *Brown*,[89] arguing that where *Brown* was concerned, no conflict of interests between white Americans and African Americans actually existed. For a brief period, their interests combined, for white Americans, primarily for international and foreign policy reasons, and for African Americans, offering the attainment of their civil rights. Once the appearance of racial justice had been attained the interests of the two groups diverged once more. But, argues Bell, it is wrong to assume that African Americans and white Americans benefited equally. The professed aim of *Brown*, to remove the psychological harm being done to African American schoolchildren, was not, and could not, be met by the opinion and its remedy. Nor could the anti-defiance strategy which attempted to create desegregated schools and involved the highly unpopular bussing, provide educational equality. Far more preferable would be 'to focus on obtaining real educational effectiveness which may entail the improvement of presently desegregated schools as well as the creation or preservation of model black schools'.[90] As du Bois argued: 'Negro children need neither segregated schools nor mixed schools. What they need is education.'[91] If educational opportunity could be provided by segregated schools then so be it. The people should be put before the principle. In du Bois' opinion:

> A separate Negro school, where children are treated like human beings, trained by teachers of their own race, who knew what it means to be black . . . is infinitely better than making our boys and girls doormats to be spit and trampled upon and lied to by ignorant social climbers, whose

---

[86] The baseball colour line, also known as the 'Gentleman's Agreement' excluded African Americans and Latin players of African descent from organised baseball. The colour line was not breached until 1946 when Jackie Robinson signed for the Brooklyn Dodgers.

[87] Executive Order 9981. Integration was accelerated.

[88] Tushnet, *Taking the Constitution Away from the Courts*, p. 145. The Congress was unable to initiate desegregation because it is organised on the basis of seniority, giving long-serving members of the one-party South considerable power. They could block legislation and punish liberal Democrats and Republicans for pursuing civil rights issues.

[89] Bell, '*Brown v. Board of Education*' 518–33. [90] *Ibid.* 532.

[91] Quoted in Bell, 'Dissenting Opinion', p. 187.

sole claim to superiority is the ability to kick 'niggers' when they are down.[92]

The logic behind this resistance to civil reform lies in the recognition that racism is not the easily uprooted 'bad weed' that some white liberals and African American activists believe it to be. Both du Bois and Bell see racism as intrinsic to America and American life. Racism and prejudice are more than legally enforced or constitutionally enshrined, thus cannot be wiped away by a simple court decision. As a result Bell, in his rewriting of *Brown*, has to dissent against the majority opinion. He writes that: 'While declaring racial segregation harmful to black children, the majority treats these policies as though they descended unwanted from the skies and can now be mopped up like a heavy rainfall and flushed away.'[93] Racism serves a purpose, that of distracting poor white people from their place in a system that transforms them into wage slaves. As Woodward puts it: 'It took a lot of ritual and Jim Crow to bolster the creed of white supremacy in the bosom of a white man working for a black man's wages.'[94] By 'rewiring' the rhetoric of equality *Brown* constructs racism and segregation as 'an eminently fixable aberration',[95] thus the Court dismisses *Plessy*. Instead, Bell argues in his dissenting opinion the Court should face up to the reality of a wide-ranging and systematic racism that characterises America, and serves as 'an ideological lens through which Americans perceive themselves, their nation, and their nation's Other'.[96] In this depiction of racism, the law is not immune from anti-racist critique, a possibility that *Brown* forecloses, but is implicit to it.

The courts and social change

Central to the 'story' of *Brown* is the portrayal of the Supreme Court as a producer of significant social change. The new orthodoxy however paints the ruling as an incidental legal outcome of a much wider political game. Can, and should, the icon of *Brown* be reduced to this extent? Rosenberg argues that: 'Courts can matter, but only some times, and only under limited conditions.'[97] These constraints are the limited nature of constitutional rights, where groups seeking change must articulate their arguments in the language of existing rights, by the judiciary's lack of independence, and by the judiciary's lack of implementation powers.

---

[92] W. E. B. Du Bois, 'Does the Negro Need Separate Schools?, p. 100.
[93] Bell, 'Dissenting Opinion', p. 196.   [94] Quoted in *ibid.* p. 188.   [95] *Ibid.* p. 198.
[96] *Ibid.* p. 198.   [97] Rosenberg, *The Hollow Hope*, p. 106.

These constraints can be overcome in certain circumstances. The first constraint can be overcome where there is ample legal precedent for change. The NAACP spent the 1930s and 1940s creating just such a groundwork. The judiciary's lack of independence can be overcome if the Congress and executive support change. Bell has demonstrated how the interests of Congress and the executive converged to make change possible, then diverged until the mid 1960s. Finally, the judiciary's inability to implement its decisions can be overcome in a number of ways but all the methods aim at producing support, or at reducing opposition, among the public.[98] There was not sufficient support among the public, nor sufficient willingness by the government to induce compliance, until the mid-1960s.

Unless these conditions are present the 'constrained court' view[99] is basically sound. The 'dynamic court' view,[100] which takes *Brown* as paradigmatic, overestimates, in Rosenberg's opinion, the power of the courts. He rejects the belief in their independence and rightly questions the extent to which they are open to all. He also challenges the assumption that courts have an indirect effect in mobilising activists who support change. He argues, along with Klarman, that all *Brown* really did was mobilise white resistance while lulling civil rights activists into a false sense of victory. In some respects this seems rather facile. No one was more aware of the power of pro-segregation Southern Americans than the African Americans they terrorised and oppressed. Nor did *Brown* cause activists to rest on their laurels. Such activists were intimately acquainted with the virulence of white racism. Rosenberg concludes that '[p]roblems that are unsolvable in the political and social context can rarely be solved by courts ... Turning to courts to produce

[98] The methods Rosenberg outlines are: 'Positive incentives ... offered to induce compliance ..., costs ... imposed to induce compliance ... Court decisions allow for market implementation ... or ... administrators and officials crucial for implementation are willing to act and see court orders as a tool for leveraging additional resources or for hiding behind' (Rosenberg, *The Hollow Hope*, p. 36).

[99] Rosenberg's constrained court view emphasises the courts' lack of budgetary and physical powers, arguing that 'the 'least dangerous' branch can do little more than point out how actions have fallen short of Constitutional or legislative requirements and hope that appropriate action is taken' (Rosenberg, *The Hollow Hope*, p. 3).

[100] The 'dynamic court' view believes that courts can produce significant social change. The failure of other branches of government to act does not impede their activism but rather increases their chances of success. Americans look to the courts to protect minorities and defend liberty from the democratically elected branches of government (Rosenberg, *The Hollow Hope*, p. 2).

significant social reforms substitutes the myth of America for its reality'.[101] Yet this position, while largely correct, is a little simplistic. Yes, courts cannot, and do not, stray far from the government line. Both courts and the law are inherently conservative but this does not mean that they can never produce unexpected or radical decisions. The argument that courts cannot solve problems that are unsolvable in the political context both demands too much from courts and underestimates what they can do. Rosenberg, and others, expect to see a level of power and efficacy to rival that of the government.[102] Courts and the law operate in a much more subtle manner, defining what truth and justice are. Moreover, the assumed neutrality and independence of law furthers their ability to be political. The courts should not be judged by the same criteria of power as the government. But Rosenberg too underestimates law: *Brown* happened because the executive wanted desegregation but the Congress was blocked by powerful Southern politicians. The wishes of the South were therefore subverted by the work of the Courts in *Brown*, something which the South was quick to realise and was the main focus of Southern anger. Finally, despite the thoroughgoing dismantling of *Brown* as a political icon in academic circles, the decision remains an important part of American folklore. That courts produce significant social change *is* one of the myths of America but to most the myth is much more powerful and appealing than the reality. This chapter has explored the myth of *Brown* and alternatives to it. *Brown* is undoubtedly a political and legal icon and as such the decision itself has grown to become a symbol of all types of equality. Indeed, the representation of *Brown* has come to mean more than the decision itself and any evaluation of its impact. But it is clear that whatever the symbolic importance of *Brown*, and this is where most of its impact lay, actual changes in the daily lives of African Americans were minimal, such was the force of American racism.

While this chapter supports a broadly critical interpretation of the role of social, political and economic pressures, there is an important aspect that the tension between the myth and its debunkers ignores: the importance of being in the legal domain at all. In both, the myth and critiques of it revolve around America's ideals: one seeing a triumph for equality and justice; the other seeing a triumph for stability and continuation of

---

[101] Rosenberg, *The Hollow Hope*, p. 338.

[102] Rosenberg accepts that he might be asking too much of the Courts. See his concluding chapter in *The Hollow Hope*.

an alternative set of ideals premised upon domination and discrimination. The fact that the NAACP and the civil rights movement could stake
a direct challenge to those ideals should not be dismissed. In a country
that legally sanctioned segregation at every stage of life and viewed
African Americans as inferior, arguing a case before the Supreme
Court, let alone winning it, was a considerable achievement. As Balkin
argues:

> *Brown* changed the playing field between supporters and opponents of
> Jim Crow ... because of *Brown* racial segregation was presumptively
> unconstitutional, and supporters now had to expend legal and political
> resources to defend it. Moreover, law has expressive and symbolic effects
> that should not be underestimated ... *Brown* provided a symbol that tied
> the Constitution and the Rule of Law itself to civil rights and racial
> equality. The power of that linkage in the country's political imagination
> was significant and long lasting. A deep connection between the
> Constitution, the Rule of Law, and equal citizenship has become an article
> of faith in the American civic religion. If *Brown* was not the sole cause of
> that powerful association, it certainly helped further and foster it.[103]

Brown and the law

How then should we understand *Brown*? And does it alter our understanding of law? Ultimately, given the present day reality of *de facto*
segregation in American schools and the overwhelming interest the
powerful within American society had in achieving segregation, it is
hard to be too romantic. For a brief and possibly unique period in
American history the interests of the white elite and African
Americans aligned. In 1896 the Supreme Court held that segregation
was constitutional, in 1954 they ruled the opposite. The similarity
between the two cases even extends to the fact that both were attempts
by civil rights activists to have segregation ruled unconstitutional. *Plessy*,
Brown and the question of segregation therefore provide an almost
unique opportunity to study the relationship between law and society,
and law and policy. The law and the Constitution had not significantly
changed so other variables must therefore be determinant. So what
differed between these two cases? There are two possible explanations.
First, society could have evolved and segregation was no longer considered acceptable. As Balkin argues there is little evidence that Supreme

---

[103] Balkin, *What* Brown v. Board of Education *Should Have Said*, p. 24.

Court decisions stray significantly from the national consensus. However, this explanation is undermined by the second: that it was the political elites who pushed hard for desegregation. Two factors point to the absence of widespread popular support for desegregation: 'massive resistance' in the South, and the deliberate slowness with which deseg-regation was undertaken.

Tushnet's characterisation of *Brown* as the enforcement of a national political view by a regional minority is instructive here. Had the South not had the power to block Congress, desegregation would probably have proceeded through the normal political channels. Truman had already used his executive power to integrate the armed forces. Had he been able to do the same with the entire principle of segregation, he would have done so. Instead Truman, his office and the Department of Justice placed political and legal pressure on the Supreme Court to rule that segregation was unconstitutional. Had this support been lacking it is hard to believe that the NAACP's litigation strategy would have produced a decision like *Brown* as early as it did. The difference between *Plessy* and *Brown* therefore is simply a shift in the willingness of certain parts of the white elite to fight for desegregation, which was in large part a hard-headed calculation about their own interests. In 1896 segregation was a necessary part of America's society and econ-omy. By 1954 it had started to cost America dear, both politically and economically.

Conclusion

From this exploration of *Brown* and the potential of law to deal with complex social problems and produce progressive social change, it is clear that law is an intrinsic part of its society. Not only is law infected by the ills of its society but it can also be a willing participant in their maintenance and propagation. The salutary lesson of *Brown* and the fight for desegregation is that law cannot and should not be immune from the charge of racism. Nor should we see the complex relationship between racism and the law as relegated to the past. If *Brown* should teach us anything it is that the law in popular understanding is capable of telling convenient truths about itself, painting itself as ending segrega-tion, fighting racism and defending equal rights. In conjunction with depicting itself in a favourable light, law masks its complicity in racism. When viewed in this way it is clear that not only does law lack the capacity to solve complex social problems; it frequently lacks the will.

Does *Brown* prove or disprove the common sense idea of law? This chapter started by exploring the popular understanding of *Brown* as the decision that ended segregation. In this view the law worked to produce justice: there was an injustice and, through a successful litigation strategy, it was rectified. The Supreme Court applied the Constitution and found segregation to be unconstitutional. The law operated as the common sense idea of law would expect it to, in both method and outcome. However, this chapter also considered a competing explanation of *Brown*, one which sees the law, not as that which ended segregation, but that which maintained it for so many years. The Supreme Court may have ruled that segregation was unconstitutional but the suit was not a class action: each individual school district would have to be taken to court in order to force desegregation. The decision may have served the interests of African Americans but it also served the interests of the white political elite and the government in its ideological fight against Communism. And the decision may have stopped segregation in the school districts party to the suit but desegregation itself did not happen in any meaningful way until a decade later.

Brown, and the competing understandings of it, therefore teaches us a number of things. It teaches us how the law actually operates and shows us the confusing reality of legal reasoning and method. It teaches us how courts and governments operate and how close appellate courts are to the sinews of power. It teaches us about how law and society interact. Even once a landmark decision like *Brown* has been reached, it does not necessarily mean that social change will happen. Law may not even be able to create social change when facing a complex and embedded social problem. And finally, *Brown* teaches us that the common sense idea of law, even when applied to a legal icon like *Brown*, has its limitations.

5

Constructing rape: defining the problem and finding the solution

Introduction

We saw in the previous chapter that our ideas about law may depart substantially from the reality. *Brown* is perhaps the most honoured and admired of all the Supreme Court rulings and it is underpinned by the common sense idea of law which forms a central part of a narrative about law. Law therefore is the path to justice; that which solves racism and desegregation in America rather than that which maintained and protected it. Counterpoising *Brown* against *Plessy* forces us to rethink the idea of law as unproblematically being able to solve serious social issues like racism. This chapter's focus on rape legislation and reform in the United Kingdom will push this issue further. In *Brown* and desegregation, injustice existed at the level of the wording of the law. The Supreme Court moved from stating that segregation did not violate the constitution to stating that it did. In changing the words, and the rules, of law, the Supreme Court changed society by removing segregation and removing the legal sanction from the doctrine of separate but equal. Justice was therefore produced by a change of rules.

Rape legislation will illustrate how this understanding of law needs to be complicated. In rape law we have a very clear statement of what the law is and at the level of the words of the law, there is no obvious unfairness or discrimination. Indeed, it is only relatively recently that the idea that there is a problem with the legal treatment of rape has become commonplace. So if the problem with rape law is not the legal rules itself, what is the problem? Where is it? And how do we fix it?

This chapter will compare different perceptions of the legal treatment of rape from the 1970s on and relate them to the reform undertaken. I will argue that assessments of what the rape problem is have naturally determined what reform will solve it. And yet, despite thirty-five years of attempted reform, the rape problem persists and I will conclude by asking what this should mean for our faith in law to solve complex social phenomena like sexism or racism.

However, before I start I offer the following caveat: it is extremely difficult to uncover the reality of rape. There are several reasons for this. As most people know, rape has historically been, and continues to be, significantly under-reported. According to Rape Crisis only 15 per cent of rapes are reported.[1] Even the British Crime Survey, which is a blunt tool for uncovering the extent of under-reporting found that only one in five rapes was reported to the police.[2] It also found that only 40 per cent of women[3] who had been raped considered their experience to actually be 'rape'. Where the attack was committed by the victim's date, only 44 per cent defined it as 'rape' and a further 18 per cent wrote the attack off as 'just something that happens'.

This is compounded by a lack of reliable statistics generally and a lack of directly comparable statistics. For example, Dave Gee, rape adviser to the Association of Chief Police Officers, found that 87 per cent of the rape cases he surveyed had corroborative evidence.[4] This contradicts the widely held belief that a significant part of the problem with rape is caused by the lack of corroboration. However, this statistic alone cannot form a reliable basis for making broader claims as it has not been replicated. Doing research which is statistically rigorous and sufficiently detailed is prohibitively expensive. It would require quantitative and qualitative analysis of hundreds of trials, potentially over a period of years and factoring in multiple variables. This has meant that research is, of necessity, partial.

It is also partial in the sense that those who conduct research into rape trials are generally those who believe there is something wrong or unfair in the legal treatment of rape. There is a strong tendency for researchers to 'self-select' as Brereton has argued, and this has the effect of skewing research. According to Brereton, because rape is the 'archetypal gendered

---

[1] See www.rapecrisis.org.uk/mythsampfacts2.php.

[2] Myhill and Allen, *Rape and Sexual Assault of Women* available at: http://rds.homeoffice. gov.uk/rds/pdfs2/r159.pdf (accessed June 2009). The British Crime Survey (BCS) aims to uncover the extent of victimisation in the United Kingdom each year. It surveys a randomly generated set of at least 1,000 respondents in each Police Force Area, with a 75 per cent response rate. Surveys are conducted in face-to-face interviews. See www. homeoffice.gov.uk/rds/bcs-methodological.html.

[3] The findings concerned only the sexual victimisation of women.

[4] Dave Gee quoted in Sean O'Neill and Fiona Hamilton, 'Rape Audit to Find Out Why So Few Win Justice' *The Times*, 14 May 2009.

crime'[5] it has been primarily studied by feminist researchers and this has produced an inaccurate perception of what the rape problem is. This is compounded by the lack of comparative research.

And finally, research is restricted by the legal prohibition on jurors discussing cases.[6] No research is therefore possible into how jurors have decided in real cases. Only mock juries are possible and these are costly and can in no way simulate the true atmosphere of a court case. Mock jurors do not spend weeks hearing evidence and deliberating. They are less likely to get bored or let their attention wonder. They are on their best behaviour and this can produce unreliable data. But despite all the limitations, research and statistics provide the only way to understand the reality of rape and rape trials. The government has funded research in order to understand what the rape problem is and how to solve it. Research and statistics therefore play a vital role in shaping government perceptions of the rape problem and it is this *perception*, underpinned by our faith in law to solve social conflict, that has created the repeated tendency to reform rape law. Whether this has proved successful remains to be seen.

The problem with rape

Rape has been viewed in different ways at different times throughout history. Events and social attitudes have shaped the perception of rape and this in turn has affected reform. How the 'rape problem' has been understood has also determined which reforms are instituted. Prior to 1975 the legal treatment of rape was not considered to be substantially limited or flawed. This changed in the *Morgan*[7] case of 1976, which I shall outline below. While rape activists had been arguing for a long time that rape complainants were treated poorly at all stages of the criminal justice system, it was only after *Morgan* the legal treatment of rape came to be seen as problematic by the public. And this perception produced reforms of a particular kind: those aimed at lessening the ordeal for rape complainants, from reporting to trial to verdict. Key among these reforms was the curtailment of the use of sexual history evidence (SHE). The assumption behind this was that defence counsel

---

[5] Brereton, 'How Different Are Rape Trials?', 243.
[6] Jurors are prohibited from talking about their jury service by s 8 of the Contempt of Court Act 1981.
[7] *DPP* v. *Morgan* [1976] AC 182, HL.

used irrelevant SHE to discredit and unnerve rape complainants. This created a perception that vulnerable rape complainants were being 'destroyed' by defence counsel[8] and this was affecting both the outcome of trials and the willingness of genuine rape victims to report their rape to the police. Throughout the 1970s and 1980s little attention was paid to the conviction rate because it was not particularly low at that time: in 1985 it was 24.4 per cent.[9]

In the late 1990s attention returned to the question of rape but in a different form. Concern now focused on the conviction rate. The attempt to curtail the use of irrelevant SHE, which was widely considered to have failed, was reviewed and further attempts to narrow the entry of such evidence began. However, this period was characterised by a recognition that, despite reforms dating back from the mid-1970s, the conviction rate had consistently fallen. The reform of the 1970s and 1980s seemed powerless to prevent this continued fall and more questions were asked about why rape was proving such a difficult crime to prosecute. Reform of the rules of evidence and extensive reform of the police and Crown Prosecution Service (CPS) were undertaken but to little avail.

In the past few years attention has moved once again, this time to the high attrition rate. The attrition rate is the number of complaints which fail to make it to trial. But this is a far from straightforward transition. Neither the conviction nor the attrition rate are incontestable indicators of the reality of rape. This new focus on the attrition rate has led to a reinterpretation of the conviction rate as no longer comparatively low. Instead, the conviction rate *as a percentage* of the number of cases that are tried is in line with other serious offences. The problem with rape therefore has now become the attrition rate and this has thrown the spotlight on the police and CPS. However, both the police and CPS have undergone substantial reform, so much so that continued reform is arguably of questionable merit. It is hard to know the extent to which the police and CPS discourage complainants or drop cases in expectation of how the court will find. Certainly it is widely believed nowadays that rape complainants find the trial traumatic and this might also be partially to blame for the high attrition rate. All these factors led the government to avoid

---

[8] Until the Youth Justice and Criminal Evidence Act 1999 a defendant who represented himself was allowed to cross-examine the complainant. After several high profile cases, including that of Ralston Edwards' cross-examination of Julia Mason during which he wore the same clothes that he attacked her in, the law was changed.
[9] Home Office statistics quoted in Lees, *Carnal Knowledge*, p. 278.

directly addressing the question of the attrition rate. This in turn left the government with two possible targets for reform: the judiciary and the jury. They chose the jury and the present government strategy targets 'rape myths' held by the jury. This locates the cause of the rape problem outside of the legal system but uses the legal arena to alter society-wide ideas of appropriate sexual behaviour.[10]

The 1970s and 1980s: treatment of complainants

As noted above the idea that there might be a problem with the legal treatment of rape only emerged in the 1970s and was largely a result of activism by rape crisis groups. The movement focused primarily on the way complainants were treated by the police and courts, with the belief that the fight for justice was like a 'second rape' becoming commonplace. Prior to this how rape was legislated and prosecuted was considered to be entirely satisfactory. Activism raised awareness of the plight of rape complainants and throughout this period the most general and consistent concern was treatment of complainants. For activists the idea that rape is a uniquely difficult crime to prosecute rests upon and is a direct consequence of a sexist belief system about rape. Historically this belief system about rape was articulated and made into law by men and reflects male interests. But such beliefs were neither widely known nor widely held and widespread public concern over the legal treatment of rape did not emerge until 1976 when the *Morgan* ruling provoked a furore.

Before 1976 there was little sense either throughout the criminal justice system or through the public that rape was problematic. Rape as a crime was not considered particularly different to other crimes and the conviction rate was broadly similar to other serious offences. In keeping with this there was no statutory definition of rape. Section 1(1) of the Sexual Offences Act 1956 simply stated: 'It is an offence for a man to rape a woman.' The only further elaboration was provided by section 1(2) which stated: 'A man who induces a married woman to have sexual intercourse with him by impersonating her husband commits rape.' In the absence of statute the common law definition was relied upon instead, where rape was 'unlawful sexual intercourse with a woman without her consent, by force, fear or fraud'.[11] However, this wording relied heavily on the presence of

---

[10] Constructivists would call these norms.
[11] Burke and Selfe, *Perspectives on Sex*, p. 58. The word 'unlawful' here means outside of marriage.

'force, fear or fraud', implying that without it, and relying solely on the woman's lack of consent, rape had not occurred.

And then there was the *Morgan* case. The circumstances of the case were that Mr Morgan invited three strangers to have sex with his wife. He told them that she was 'kinky' and was likely to struggle in order to get 'turned on'.[12] In court the three strangers claimed that they honestly believed Mrs Morgan was consenting. They were convicted of rape and Mr Morgan of aiding and abetting.[13] They appealed but their convictions were upheld. However, the House of Lords used the decision to reaffirm that there could be no conviction for rape if the man honestly believed that the woman was consenting *and* that his belief did not have to be reasonable. In *Morgan* such a belief was clearly unreasonable, yet as Lord Cross stated, they probably would have escaped conviction if they had made use of the mistaken belief defence rather than contesting Mrs Morgan's amply corroborated testimony.[14] He also argued that if the ordinary man (not woman) were asked if a man raped a woman but believed she was consenting, had he committed rape? 'No' he replied, 'If he was grossly careless then he may deserve to be punished but not for rape.'[15] This was because, as Lord Hailsham argued, the *mens rea* of rape consists of two parts: first, the man must intend to have sexual intercourse with the victim, and secondly, he must either know at the time that the person is not consenting, or be reckless, that is indifferent, to whether she is consenting. If the defendant made an honest mistake, he cannot be convicted of rape, however unreasonable his belief.

The so-called 'rapists' charter' provoked a public outcry. In response the government set up an Advisory Group on the Law of Rape, also known as the Heilbron Committee. The Committee's report argued that the law needed updating and that a statutory definition of rape was required. This led to the Sexual Offences (Amendment) Act 1976, section 1(1):

> A man commits rape if–
>
> (a) he has unlawful sexual intercourse with a woman who at the time of the intercourse does not consent to it; and

---

[12] Mrs Morgan's account differs considerably. She testified that her husband dragged her from her bedroom. She shouted to her children to go and fetch the police. Her assailants covered her face and pinched her nose to suffocate her. The men carried her by her wrists and feet into another bedroom where she was held down, raped and had a variety of sex acts performed upon her.

[13] Marital rape was not a crime until 1991.

[14] Quoted in Temkin, *Rape and the Legal Process*, p. 117.   [15] *Ibid.*

(b) at the time he knows that she does not consent to the intercourse or he is reckless as to whether she consents to it.

The Act introduced anonymity for complainants in the hope that this would encourage more women to report. The Act also introduced the 'rape shield law' whereby SHE could only be admitted in court if it was relevant, with the determination of relevancy to be made by the judge. This marks the beginning of a sustained battle to exclude irrelevant SHE from the courtroom and relied upon two assumptions. First, it was assumed that curtailing the use of irrelevant SHE would make the complainant's experience of trial less traumatic and more rape victims would therefore report the crime to the police. Secondly, it was assumed that by making it harder for defence counsel to discredit the complainant, conviction rates might increase.

But the issue of SHE, more than any other attempted reform, has been consistently asserted in law and consistently undermined in practice. Because the determination of relevance of SHE was and still is dependent upon judicial discretion, material that is irrelevant, and therefore inadmissible, may still find its way into the courtroom. In practice such evidence *was* considered relevant in most cases, usually in relation to the defendant's belief in consent. According to Lees the attempt to limit the cross-examination of the complainant about her sexual history and sexual character, was undermined by the decision to leave it to the judge's discretion. Lees' analysis of thirty cases found that judges frequently regarded such evidence as relevant 'even when it was *unconnected* to the offence'.[16] Even in 2000 Lees' research found that 'women were routinely made out to be promiscuous in court, with the implication that their testimony was therefore unreliable'.[17]

Because of the importance of *belief* in consent, SHE was deemed relevant on the grounds that how the defendant viewed the complainant, no matter how unreasonable or inaccurate, was of central importance. Thus despite the fact that the Act was *specifically designed* to prevent the gratuitous admission of the complainant's sexual past, court monitoring carried out twenty-four years after the amendment came into force showed that 'irrelevant sexual history and sexual character evidence ... [was] ... being admitted in a wide range of cases'.[18]

---

[16] Lees, *Carnal Knowledge*, p. xviii, emphasis added. Lees also surveyed 120 women who said they had been raped of which one quarter went to trial.
[17] *Ibid.* p. xxi.   [18] *Ibid.* p. xxiii.

Why did reform fail? According to Lees, it was quite simply because the admissibility of SHE was left to the discretion of judges. Lees places responsibility for both the poor treatment of complainants and the low conviction rate on judges. She argues that they are unrepresentative and bring outmoded and sexist attitudes towards women into the courtroom. Writing in 1996, Lees argued that: 'The judiciary, therefore, are largely comprised of a group of upper middle-class, predominantly white, elderly, highly paid men, many of whom have been educated in single-sex male public schools. It is exactly such institutions that tend to foster extreme forms of masculinity.'[19] Moreover, the institution of the criminal court and the criminal trial are very combative: trials are viewed by legal professionals as fights or contests between the two sides where witnesses are 'slammed'[20] or 'butchered'.[21] Reasonableness of belief only became a legal requirement in 2004. All these factors meant that the issue that provoked such public outrage in 1976 – that all a rapist need do was say he believed the victim was consenting in order to escape conviction – was not resolved until 2004.

New Labour reform: the preoccupation with conviction rates

By the late 1990s a new concern had reached the governmental level: the conviction rate. From the mid-1970s the conviction rate has continued to fall with a continuous annual drop to a low point in 2006 of 5.2 per cent. As a result, concern over the conviction rate overtook the traditional concern with the plight of rape complainants.

Reform

A second attempt to restrict the use of SHE was made in 1999 in the Youth Justice and Criminal Evidence Act (YJCEA). The Act represented the most radical reform yet of rape law, banning the introduction of evidence that the defendant had previously had sexual intercourse with the complainant. Section 41 of the Act repeals the Sexual Offences (Amendment) Act 1976 and further curtails the extent to which a complainant can be questioned about her sexual history and behaviour. Such evidence would only be admitted in court if sexual intercourse took place at, or about, the time of the alleged offence, or were so similar that it

[19] *Ibid.* p. 242.   [20] Rock, *The Social World of an English Crown Court*, p. 29.
[21] Ellison, 'Cross-examination in Rape Trials', 614.

might constitute a pattern of sexual behaviour. Evidence of the complainant's sexual history could also be introduced to refute evidence presented by the prosecution, for example, if the prosecution claimed that the complainant was a virgin at the time of the attack and the defence could prove otherwise. Evidence of this kind would only be admissible because the prosecution had raised the matter and had essentially 'thrown down the shield'. However, as the Bill passed through parliament an exemption was added: that SHE was relevant to *belief* in consent. In other words, section 41 lays down that sexual history is not relevant to consent. However, the exemption stated that such evidence was relevant to *belief* in consent. This meant that consent could continue to be inferred from previous behaviour and reputation (which may be unfounded) rather than actual consent.

The incorporation of the European Convention on Human Rights into British law in 2000 further complicated matters. The day after it became law it was used to challenge the rape shield laws introduced by the YJCEA on the grounds that curtailing the use of SHE contravened the defendant's right to a fair trial, as protected by Article 6. In *R* v. *A*[22] the House of Lords interpreted section 41 as admitting SHE where 'it was so relevant to the issue of consent that to exclude it would endanger the fairness of the trial'.[23] This meant that the defendant was not precluded from introducing evidence if he and the complainant had recently had consensual sex. As Judge Goldstein commented 'the sexual activity of a prostitute or someone as "chaste as a nun" will never be known because it cannot be explored in court by lawyers'.[24]

Despite the changes introduced by the YJCEA the law on sexual offences was still deemed to be in need of revision and updating, and in May 2004 the Sexual Offences Act came into force. The Act was designed to be a modern and clear framework and introduced a number of significant changes.[25] First, the Act further updated the law on bad character. The 2003 Criminal Justice Act had only allowed previous

---

[22] *R* v. *A* [2001] UKHL 25, [2001] 3 All ER 1.   [23] *Ibid.*

[24] Lees, *Carnal Knowledge*, pp. xxvii–xxviii. This also ignores the fact that in court a complainant is unable to defend her character against the standard defence tactic of destroying her credibility and thereby creating a reasonable doubt.

[25] The Act reworks existing offences into three new categories: rape, assault by penetration and sexual assault. Rape is defined as penetration of the vagina, anus or mouth with a penis. Assault by penetration covers penetration by any other body part or with an object, if the penetration is sexual. Sexual assault covers any kind of intentional sexual touching without consent, clothed or unclothed, with the offender's body or with an object.

1. *A genuine rape victim would report the attack immediately.* The Court of Appeal ruled on 24 October 2008 that where a defendant raises the issue of delayed reporting to undermine the credibility of the complainant, a judge is entitled to direct juries that delay can also be due to the trauma caused by the rape.

2. *False allegations are common.* There is no evidence that false allegations are made more often in rape cases than in any other crime.

3. *Most rapes are committed by strangers.* In fact, the vast majority of rapists are known to the victim and the stereotypical stranger rape is rare.

4. *Rape victims will attempt to fight off their attacker and will be injured. It will be clear from a medical examination that rape has occurred.* In reality, women do not resist or show significant injury for many reasons: many women freeze, many do not resist because of threats made to them or to their family, many simply recognise the fact of their physical inferiority and the inevitability of the rape. Moreover, it may not be clear from the physical examination that a rape has definitively occurred. Frequently, the injuries sustained can be explained away as 'rough sex'.

5. *Consent to sex can be assumed from dress, flirting or drinking.*[42] This is to counter the assumption that victims are often partly responsible for their rape. Juries would be given the following analogy: if a man 'flashed his bulging wallet around in a pub and then had it stolen, no one would say that the person who stole it was not really a thief',[43] or, more to the point, conclude that he was 'asking for it' and should bear partial responsibility.

6. *Stranger rape is more traumatic than rape by a known person.* This would be corrected by the assertion that all rape is traumatic and can be more traumatic if a breach of trust is involved.

It is clear then that Baird's proposed rape myths focus on the jury, society at large and not the judiciary. However, in New South Wales (NSW), Australia, judicial education has proved successful. A study of reforms instituted found evidence of good practice, mainly by judges rather than

---

[42] Unpublished research commissioned by the Metropolitan Police found that more than half of the men accused of raping women who had been drinking, where the cases were 'no crimed', had a history of sexual offences against women. (Woman Against Rape letter in *The Times*, 14 March 2009, available at www.guardian.co.uk/commentisfree/2009/mar/14/worboys-rape-women.)

[43] Gibb, 'Beware Rape Myths'.

barristers. The report notes that much of what has been achieved in NSW has been due to proactive and forward-thinking work by members of the judiciary and the Judicial Commission of NSW and extensive training. NSW also introduced model directions for judges to give to juries. The study found that Bench Books compiled by the Judicial Commission 'go a long way in standardising the comments and directions Judges make to the jury and ensure there is some consistency amongst the judiciary'.[44]

However, researchers in the United Kingdom are sceptical of the judiciary's commitment to transforming the way the criminal justice system deals with rape or even recognises that change within the judiciary might be needed. Temkin and Krahé interviewed seventeen judges and seven barristers about the existence of the justice gap for sexual assault and only one was prepared to concede that a gap existed. The other interviewees 'denied or showed resistance to this idea, and some were plainly annoyed at the suggestion'.[45] Many of Temkin and Krahé's interviewees considered the idea of a justice gap to be based on fundamental misunderstandings about the nature of rape cases 'in which so frequently it was one person's word against another so that the burden of proof would necessarily be very difficult for the prosecution to discharge'.[46]

For Lees it is the 'engrained complacency' of the Bar that is the primary obstacle to producing fair rape trials. Lacey reached a similar conclusion in her assessment of the Home Office's review of sexual offences.[47] She concluded that the changes proposed by the government to restrict SHE and the introduction of the reasonableness of belief would simply result in strategic adjustments to defence tactics which will relate SHE more closely to the question of *belief* in consent. Because SHE is still considered relevant to belief in consent, the door is still emphatically open and it seems inevitable that irrelevant and unfair SHE will make it into court. The resistance of the judiciary to change means that 'one has to ask how much can be achieved by even radical changes'.[48]

However, the latest government proposals sidestep the judiciary altogether. In 2006 the government published proposals to amend the law to allow prosecutors to adduce 'general' expert witness testimony in rape trials. Expert testimony would be 'general' in the sense that it would not relate specifically to the case at hand. Instead it would draw upon

[44] NSW Department of Women, *Heroines of Fortitude*.
[45] Temkin and Krahé, *Sexual Assault and the Justice Gap*, p. 139.
[46] *Ibid.* p. 141.   [47] Lacey, 'Beset by Boundaries, 1–14.   [48] *Ibid.* 12.

generalised social science data to provide jurors with a more accurate sense of the social and psychological context. Provided the expert is properly instructed, she should be able to give the jury a neutral summary of the relevant research, having corrected any incorrect assumptions the jury may have held. Keeping expert testimony general means that only one expert would be needed and she would be neutral. There would be no need for each side to bring their own expert and this would avoid a costly and time-consuming 'battle of the experts'.

According to the Home Office this will help to dispel 'myths and stereotypes concerning how a victim should behave'.[49] The Home Office argue that defence counsel frequently portrays the ordinary responses of rape complainants as unusual or abnormal as a means of discrediting her testimony. The report acknowledged therefore that there was a need to 'level the playing field between the prosecution and defence'.[50] According to Ellison and Munro such measures are warranted because 'mock jurors generally displayed limited appreciation of psychological responses to rape, often drawing negative, damaging inferences from the complainant's failure to appear more obviously distressed whilst testifying, to report the offence immediately or to fight back physically during the course of an assault'.[51]

The government has yet to decide how best to proceed with the issue of juror education and might yet opt to achieve juror education through extended judicial instruction to the jury. Research by Ellison and Munro set out to test the effectiveness of juror education in both possible methods. They created three separate trials which between twenty-four to twenty-six participants observed. Participants were then streamed into three juries and either given additional direction by a judge, expert testimony or no additional direction or information. The facts were identical for each trial and the judge, barristers, witnesses and experts were all played by actors: the same rape with the same actors.[52] The trial itself had three sets of variables: lack of resistance, delayed reporting and calm complainant behaviour. The actors adjusted their behaviour accordingly but the script did not alter. The jury were then allowed

---

[49] Home Office, *Convicting Rapists and Protecting Victims*, p. 16.   [50] *Ibid.*
[51] Ellison and Munro, 'Turning Mirrors into Windows?', 363.
[52] The scenario was that the complainant alleged that the defendant had raped her in the hallway to her apartment after their first date. The defendant claimed the sex was consensual. Ellison and Munro, 'Reacting to Rape', 202–19.

ninety minutes to deliberate and these deliberations were observed. Jurors also completed questionnaires afterwards.

The research found juror education was successful for some of the variables tested but not for others. It worked to counteract negative inferences drawn from the complainant's calm demeanour and delayed report but not for lack of resistance. According to Ellison and Munro: 'Whilst jurors appeared to accept that a woman could [freeze] ... they were generally only willing to countenance this reaction in a stranger rape situation.'[53] Both educated and uneducated groups believed that a victim of rape would inevitably suffer physical injury despite expert testimony to the contrary. Ellison and Munro also found that many jurors cited the absence of genital injury when justifying their not-guilty verdicts to peers, 'despite being advised in the trial that the medical examiner's failure to find internal damage was essentially neutral, neither supporting nor rebutting the rape allegation'.[54] Moreover where lack of resistance was concerned 'comments made by jurors in the education conditions (whether involving expert testimony or judicial instruction) echoed – in terms of both substantive strength and frequency – comments made by their uneducated counterparts'.[55]

However, the authors did not find any evidence that jurors disregarded elements of the defence evidence because of education or had misread the generic guidance offered, either by the judge or by an expert, as vouching indirectly for the complainant's credibility. Their study therefore concluded that general juror education did not unfairly skew the trial in favour of the complainant and as a result, Ellison and Munro conclude that the introduction of such guidance would be a 'pragmatic, defensible and efficient means of redressing at least some of the unfounded assumptions and attitudinal biases that prevent too many victims of sexual assault from accessing justice'.[56]

Competing narratives of the rape problem

It is clear from the latest government reform that the government believes, first, that there is a problem with the legal treatment of rape in the United Kingdom, either in low conviction rates or high attrition rates. Secondly, they have located the source of the problem in the jury and juror misconceptions about rape, rape victims and rapists. It should

---

[53] Ellison and Munro, 'Turning Mirrors into Windows?', 372.   [54] Ibid. 373.
[55] Ibid. 374.   [56] Ibid. 379.

be clear from the earlier part of the chapter exploring the changing perception of rape and in particular the role of activists, that this is a legacy of rape activism since the 1970s. The governmental response throughout the 1970s and 1980s was to focus on reforming the police first of all, and then the CPS. Indeed, police treatment of rape victims has been a core concern among rape activists from the 1970s onwards.

But activists have always argued that rape complainants are systematically disadvantaged in the trial process. This led to new attention being paid to the role of the CPS and the need for reform. The government seems to have accepted finally the long-standing activist argument that, not only is there a problem with rape, but the problem is specific to rape. In other words, rape complainants are treated uniquely badly and the low conviction and high attrition rates for rape are not seen in other serious offences. For many activists and writers on rape, this is because of institutionalised sexism within the legal system. They see bias operating at a number of levels. Historically it existed in the very language of the law; in the legal rules themselves. As this has been corrected over time, activists have fought to have bias in other areas of the law acknowledged, specifically in the personnel of law.

Judges in particular have come under attack, with writers like Lees and Kennedy arguing that they are unrepresentative, riddled with sexist attitudes towards women and disconnected from modern sexual mores.[57] This has led, they claim, to the perfectly normal behaviour of young women being portrayed as provocative and dangerous, and implicitly (and sometimes explicitly) blaming women for their own violation.

As the composition of the judiciary has changed over time attention has focused on the nature of the legal system itself. Feminists have long argued that the adversarial system is a 'male' way of doing things, in which women fare particularly badly. I will explore feminist explanations of rape legislation and reform below but the point I wish to make here is that the idea of what the problem with rape is, where its cause is located, and therefore the solution, has evolved over time. It is only very recently, in the last decade, that ideas touted by activists for many years have

---

[57] Kennedy argues that: 'Judges are also isolated and receive very little feedback. The people they mainly mix with socially are their own peers . . . they are in charge and wield great power over people's lives. They are not used to being challenged and it is hard for them to accept questioning of their function as creative' (Kennedy, *Eve was Framed*, p. 267). According to Kennedy, this is why they resist the pressure to be educated so strenuously and until at least 30 per cent of the judiciary are female, little will change (*ibid.* p. 269).

finally made it into the governmental debate and subsequent under-standing of the nature and cause of the rape problem.

Thus, at present, the government sees the rape problem as specific to rape itself. This is not a problem which afflicts, say, all violent crime, or crimes in which women are generally the victims. How the government understands, or constructs, the rape problem dictates to a very great extent how it will attempt to solve it. What the problem is not, is also significant. By arguing that it is juror misperception that is to blame, the government avoids the criticism made by many activists and writers on rape that the judiciary itself is to blame. The government have rejected two related notions here: first, that judges and barristers are biased; and secondly, that even if they are not, then they exploit and deploy jury bias in order to win their case or, in the case of judges, help the jury to reach the 'right' verdict. For many activists, who believe that judges are, in the main, sexist and hold outdated notions about female sexuality, this means reinforcing what Smart refers to as 'what is known about women – by women and men'.[58] Focusing on the jury neatly sidesteps the tricky proposition of blaming judges and barristers for the outcome of rape trials. This decision may be as pragmatic as it is politic: judge education was mooted and quite forcefully rejected. According to Temkin and Krahé judges are 'notoriously difficult to educate' and hold firm to two ideas about their profession: that only judges can and should educate judges, and that judges should ignore social science data.[59] When judges have been challenged about their lack of contact with modern society, many have responded by arguing that this is a virtue.[60] This enables them to be free from the passing fads of society and to judge solely by applying the relevant law to the case before them.

Given this construction of the rape problem, the solution that the government proposes – jury education – seems logical. And it is sup-ported by the majority of writing on rape law and reform. Ellison and Munro in other work have argued that rape myths, or socio-sexual scripts in their terminology, do exist and skew trials unfairly in favour

[58] Smart, *Law, Crime and Sexuality*, p. 84.
[59] Temkin and Krahé, *Sexual Assault and the Justice Gap*, p. 188.
[60] A 1997 survey by Labour Research found that 'today's judges are even less in touch with the life experience of those on whom they deliver judgements than a decade ago. Mr Justice Jeremiah Herman, the High Court judge who had never heard of Bruce Springsteen or Gazza, is not alone.' *Labour Research Bulletin*, vol. 86, no. 7 (1997) quoted in Lees, *Carnal Knowledge*, p. 244.

of the defendant. The general public's ideas about rape are inaccurate. They also acknowledge that juries are prone to misinterpreting the requirement of 'reasonable doubt'. Juries tend to over-interpret it to mean that there could be no feasible other explanation for events and that if there is any doubt at all, they cannot convict. This means that, as Ellison and Munro found in their mock jury experiment, that jurors would invent quite fantastical explanations for a rape complainant's bruising, despite an expert having testified that it was consistent with the use of force. These explanations included the complainant being bruised by jewellery that the juror imagined she might have been wearing, and being bruised from riding a rollercoaster, doing aerobics or going sailing, even though she had done none of these activities and there was no mention of them.[61] Indeed, the issue of lack of resistance was a significant stumbling block for the jurors in Ellison and Munro's trial. Jurors would frequently assert that freezing would not happen and they believed that a woman, when faced with a potential sexual assault, would not only resist, but be strong enough to fend off her attacker. Neither expert testimony nor judicial direction could sway them from this belief. Certain rape myths may therefore prove to be resistant to education.

Ultimately, however, Ellison and Munro believe that juror education is an important and necessary step. But for Temkin and Krahé, in their influential study of rape law and the psychology of rape, juror education may not go far enough. In common with both the government and Ellison and Munro, Temkin and Krahé believe that the problem with rape is specific to rape. They agree that the problem is rape myths but disagree that these myths only afflict jurors. As Temkin has consistently argued, judges and barristers have undermined attempted reform for many decades.[62] Until their attitudes are changed, juror education will be wasted in a courtroom environment that treats rape complainants with scepticism. They suggest a number of possible reforms. First of all, the use of expert evidence. This would counteract bias and ignorance among both juries and legal professionals. Secondly, they argue that education of judges is necessary. Without education, any change in the wording or procedure of the law will be undermined. And finally, and most radically, they consider the possibility of abolishing juries for rape trials and using rape-ticketed judges instead to decide the case.

---

[61] Ellison and Munro, 'Reacting to Rape', 208.
[62] Temkin, 'Prosecuting and Defending Rape', 219–48; Temkin, *Rape and the Legal Process*.

Such a move is not without precedent. Only recently, the Lord Chief Justice ordered that the trial of John Twomey, Peter Blake, Barry Hibberd and Glen Cameron be heard without a jury. Previous trials have collapsed because of jury tampering and Lord Judge ruled that the risk of jury tampering was so severe that the judge alone, Mr Justice Treacy, will hear the case. Moreover, juryless trials have happened before. The Diplock trials in North Ireland were decided solely by judges.[63] In the eighteenth century, midwife juries were used in cases concerning childbirth or pregnancy where such knowledge would be critical to a reliable judgment.[64] And after repeated failure by the Serious Fraud Office to secure convictions in a number of trials, including the high profile Jubilee Line fraud trial,[65] there have been calls for juryless trials for fraud trials. In 2005 Attorney General Lord Goldsmith put forward plans for such trials. The concern here is not jury tampering, but rather that jurors are either unable or uninterested in the complex evidence of a fraud trial. Fraud trials are now so complicated, so the argument goes, that it takes experts to be able to correctly identify guilt or innocence. This complexity also produces a lengthy trial for which a jury trial might not be feasible. For Temkin and Krahé however, the purpose of focusing attention on legal professionals, rather than the general public is deeply pragmatic: it is easier and more efficient to educate the legal sector than the society as a whole.

But while thinking about rape has long accepted the notion that rape is uniquely beset by problems, some thinkers doubt that this is the case. Brereton confronts the long-standing argument that rape complainants are treated uniquely badly by the legal system. Instead of taking this as a given, we should start by asking first whether they *are* treated worse than other witnesses. He compares the cross-examination of rape complainants with that of assault complainants in Victoria, Australia. Brereton surveyed forty-eight rape trials and forty-six assault trials and found that treatment of witnesses did not significantly differ. In both assault and rape trials defence counsel relied 'primarily on a limited number of generic, "tried and true" cross-examination strategies which were adapted to fit the particular factual circumstances of the case'.[66] It

[63] Diplock courts were used for terrorist suspects in order to prevent jury tampering. They were used from 1973 to 2007.
[64] Minow, 'Stripped Like a Runner or Enriched by Experience', 1201–18.
[65] 'Massive Jubilee Line Trial Collapses', *The Times*, 22 March 2005.
[66] Brereton, 'How Different are Rape Trials?', 243.

has been argued, Brereton argues, that cross-examination in rape trials is more frequent because 'the rape trial normally turns on the issue of consent, where there is little in the way of strong confirmatory evidence, such as reliable eye witness testimony or physical injuries to the complainant'.[67] While Brereton found that rape complainants were painted as sexually provocative risk takers, and/or persons of suspect morality who did not live a normal lifestyle, he found that a complainant in an assault trial was 'depicted as a troublemaker or bully who "gave as good as he got" and deserved what had happened to him'.[68] Assault complainants were just as likely as rape complainants to be subject to attacks on their character and credibility, and to be asked questions about such matters as their alcohol consumption and emotional and mental stability. If there were inconsistencies in a complainant's evidence, defence counsel attempted to exploit these, regardless of the crime. Moreover, if the complainant had not acted as expected or had not reported promptly to the police, he or she was just as likely as a rape complainant to be cross-examined about it. This leads Brereton to conclude that what so horrified the majority of rape researchers are simply the 'standard "tools of the trade" for lawyers, rather than unique to the setting of the rape trial'[69] and that their failure to do comparative research meant that this misperception was never corrected.

Much of what happens in rape trials therefore is simply a function of broader systemic factors which operate in a wide range of trials. McBarnet's research has focused on the victimology of the rape complainant and she argues that rape researchers have mistakenly located 'the source of the victim's experience in court ... in the specific social prejudices underlying rape cases'[70] and have ignored the structure and function of the criminal trial itself. Her study of 105 criminal trials in Scotland concluded that the 'degradation' of the victim was an inevitable consequence of the adversarial process.

Matoesian's discursive analysis of three rape trials found that too much emphasis is placed on the content of what is said during such trials and that the far more important question is the structure and logic of courtroom talk. He too notes that lawyers use a number of tactics to undermine witnesses in all trials, not just rape trials. Interestingly, however, he argues that such tactics 'have nothing to do with patriarchy, even though drawing on patriarchal ideology in the rape trial'.[71] Such an

---

[67] *Ibid.* 252–3.   [68] *Ibid.* 253.   [69] *Ibid.* 259.
[70] McBarnet, 'Victim in the Witness Box', 294.   [71] Matoesian, *Reproducing Rape*, p. 20.

argument would seem to confirm the competing viewpoint's belief that general social attitudes do enter into the courtroom and may function to skew the trial unfairly in favour of the defendant.

Rock's analysis of the social world of the court and the role of the witness also highlights how witnesses are treated in *all* cases and is worth quoting at length:

> The chief purpose of the defence was to extract information and impressions that were favourable to the defendant and unfavourable to the prosecution. They sought to discredit the prosecution witnesses and their testimony, making them seem ... 'fragile' ... [Questions] would be asked with some show of acting, artfully, incredulously, and often fiercely. At a set point in cross-examination, usually in the final stages, counsel might work themselves up to climax, simulating a sternness of manner and goading the witness (... 'slamming' ...). They would repeatedly accuse the witnesses of falsehood.[72]

The problem therefore is the way in which lawyers are trained to cross-examine and interpret evidence, as well as courtroom work practices. Ellison, in her analysis of cross-examination in rape trials, concludes that 'the bullying and browbeating of rape complainants in court are rooted in the adversarial trial process and therefore an inescapable feature of cross-examination'.[73] When the criminal trial is structured as a dispute, it is inevitable that the art of advocacy will view cross-examination as a matter of 'breaking' or 'destroying' the witness. The aim is to 'butcher the witness' and boxing metaphors abound in advocacy manuals.[74]

The cause of this ultimately lies for Ellison in the inadequate regulation of cross-examination. Judges are under a common law duty to restrain unnecessary and improper cross-examination[75] but they must also ensure fairness, and a conviction may be overturned if it is decided that a trial judge's interventions compromised the ability of counsel to present her case. Moreover, in the English legal tradition the trial judge is 'an impartial umpire who is expected to remain somewhat aloof from the party contest. The non-interventionist judge who plays no part in the preliminary investigative stages of criminal proceedings and is largely confined to the evidence presented by the parties in court is fundamental to adversarial theory.'[76]

---

[72] Rock, *The Social World of an English Crown Court*, p. 29.
[73] Ellison, 'Cross-examination in Rape Trials', 606.   [74] *Ibid.* 614.
[75] *Hobbs* v. *Tinling* [1929] 2 KB 1 at 51.
[76] Ellison, 'Cross-examination in Rape Trials', 611.

Thus while many writers have claimed that '[t]he defence at rape trials uses a number of strands of attack to undermine the woman's evidence and to shake her story, all of which would be considered totally unacceptable if she had reported, say, a serious non-sexual assault',[77] this may not be true. According to Brereton, this depiction of rape complainants as singled out for special treatment and of the crime itself as unique, 'has been based largely on inference and theoretical argument'.[78] Newby has argued that, in common with many other writers, the emphasis on consent means that the complainant's credibility is far more likely to be attacked than in trial for non-sexual offences.[79] Similarly, much attention has been focused on repeated questioning. But as comparative research conducted by Brereton and McBarnet suggests, the problem of poor witness treatment by defence counsel is not unique to rape: it is an endemic feature of the adversarial system. However, as Matoesian noted in his research, patriarchal or sexist ideas are being exploited by defence counsel and this would seem to support the government's attempt to address rape myths. Given the failure of legal thinkers to give a definitive explanation, I turn now to feminist accounts of law and what they can tell us about law, justice and bias.

Feminist interpretations

Feminism is a diverse school of thought encompassing many different theoretical standpoints, but all challenge the idea that law and the legal system are impartial arbiters when it comes to women. Naffine identifies three phases of feminism, each corresponding to the development of feminist theory and approaches to law in recent years.[80] The first phase corresponds to liberal feminism which accepts law as a fair and rational institution for arbitrating conflict. The structure and ethos of law are basically sound and offer a tool for women to attain a greater measure of equality. All that is needed is the development of effective rights for women and for the legal system to live up to its professed principles of fairness and impartiality. The solution to the rape problem therefore is simply to have more female barristers and judges. However, in the United Kingdom the upper echelons of the judicial system have few women. Of the twelve Lords of Appeal in Ordinary only one is a woman, the five Heads of Division are all men and three of the thirty-six Lords Justice of Appeal are women. Even at the most junior end of

---

[77] Adler, *Rape on Trial*, p. 53.   [78] Brereton, 'How Different are Rape Trials?', 244.
[79] Newby, L. 'Rape Victims in Court', 118.   [80] Naffine, *Law and the Sexes*.

scale – Deputy Masters, Deputy Registrars, Deputy Costs Judges and Deputy District Judges – women make up only 34 per cent.[81] Although there has been an influx of female law students it will take a generation at least to reach the upper echelons.

The second phase, which Naffine identifies primarily with MacKinnon's work, extends the first phase's focus on the personnel of law. For second phase feminists it is not just the barristers and judges that are biased, but the entire edifice of law. Law embodies a male culture, a male way of doing things and viewing the world. The optimistic belief that law can be improved is not shared by these feminists because, for second phase thinkers, law *is* masculine so can offer little to women. The solution then is to radically alter the entire model of law with women in mind. Thus the 'harsh, uncaring, combative, adversarial style of justice'[82] which reflects the male way of reasoning and thinking will be replaced. Women need their own rules because the existing system can only offer them freedom as men and the right to live up to the male standard. MacKinnon argues that we should not try to 'fit women to an existing system' but instead 'ask [...] what the system would look like if women, not men, were its starting point'.[83]

In a system designed by men, for men, the definition of rape reflects what men define as violation. But such a definition only captures a very narrow range of sexual violation. MacKinnon argues that what women experience as violation, even if they might not term it rape, encompasses a wider range of abuses than what men define as violation. Thus '[t]he distance between most intimate violations of women and the legally perfect rape measures the imposition of an alien definition. From women's point of view, rape is not prohibited; it is regulated'.[84] To MacKinnon it is men who distinguish between rape and consensual sex, the abnormal and the normal. Yet for women 'sexuality in exactly these normal forms often *does* violate us'.[85] The line between rape and sex coincides with the line between violence and non-violence. The criminal justice system can only recognise, in most cases, rape as rape if it is accompanied by violence. Rape without violence, for the men in MacKinnon's world, is just sex. Rapists think that they 'were put in jail

---

[81] Data correct as of 1 April 2008. Source: www.judiciary.gov.uk/keyfacts/statistics/women. htm (accessed June 2009).
[82] Naffine, *Law and the Sexes*, p. 7.
[83] MacKinnon quoted in Naffine, *Law and the Sexes*, p. 8.
[84] MacKinnon, *Toward a Feminist Theory*, p. 179.
[85] MacKinnon, *Feminism Unmodified*, p. 86.

for something very little different from what most men do most of the time and call it sex'.[86] Equating rape with violence reflects a male understanding of rape and assumes that men and women operate in conditions of equality where women are not victims of structural disempowerment.

Further still MacKinnon argues that violence is a part of 'normal' intercourse for many women. This may not be violence as a man or the criminal system would define it, but it can be a subtle form of coercion or a woman's recognition of her subordinate position. Consenting to coercive sex may be the least worst option. This approach sidesteps the 'sex or violence' question. MacKinnon argues that feminists 'put this neutral, objective, abstract word *violence* on it all'[87] in order to avoid appearing anti-male. It also serves to remove the confusion and ambiguity that the male culture feels about rape. In jurisdictions where the rape law was changed to minimise the sexual aspect of rape and focus instead on the assault aspect, reform is considered a resounding failure.[88] Sidestepping the problematic issue of sex, and as a consequence consent, has only served to over-complicate the law and confuse the jury. MacKinnon's critique differs from this approach by asking 'a series of questions about normal, heterosexual intercourse and attempt[ing] to move the line between heterosexuality ... – intercourse – and rape ... rather than allow it to stay where it is'.[89]

To MacKinnon, sexuality is the linchpin of women's oppression. Women are oppressed because of and through their sexuality. Gender is a hierarchy, a division of power, and is acted out and expressed primarily sexually. The male gaze produces women as men wish to define them – as objects, with their sexuality as a commodity. This traditional sexual role of women leaves them vulnerable to rape. Both women and men are taught that men initiate and women respond, and men are expected to test the boundaries. For Smart '[b]eing a sexual predator is regarded as normal, even desirable for men. Sexualising all women is regarded as natural. Pressing a woman until she submits is a natural, pleasurable phallocentric pastime'.[90] She further argues that in a powerful discourse of female sexuality, where their reputation and economic survival depends upon their chastity this is not one-dimensional

---

[86] *Ibid.* p. 88.   [87] *Ibid.* p. 86.
[88] Temkin: 'many feminist commentators now regret what they regard as the desexualization of rape and believe that legislation which has sought to achieve this has been an unfortunate mistake', *Rape and the Legal Process*, p. 154.
[89] MacKinnon, *Feminism Unmodified*, p. 89.
[90] Smart, *Feminism and the Power of Law*, p. 42.

prudery; women are not genuinely asexual, but rather their resistance is just 'the mouthing of a convention'.[91] This apparent duplicity is seen throughout society: 'From the judge to the convicted rapist there is a common understanding that female sexuality is problematic and that women's sexual responsiveness is whimsical or capricious.'[92] However, male sexuality is constructed too, with men being depicted as sexually atavistic and one-dimensional. Phallocentric society, that is a culture which is structured to meet the needs of the masculine, may privilege men over women, but this does not mean that men are free from restrictions of a constructed sexuality.

So what do constructions of male and female sexuality contribute to our understanding of rape and its legislation? In a society where men are taught to be sexual aggressors and, in Smart's phallocentric world, not understanding female sexuality, rape is not a freak occurrence or deviation from the dominant male sexuality. It is a central part of male sexuality. Rape is indigenous and culturally dictated. When we understand rape in this way the troubling questions raised by the legislation of rape, its reform, depictions of it, become comprehensible. Second phase feminists like MacKinnon would view this as evidence that law is simply a tool of the masculine state, a straightforward assertion that law privileges men and oppresses women. Law can be rehabilitated once we remake it with women in mind. Whereas first phase feminists would correct law by correcting its personnel and occasional rule, second phase feminists would remake its very ethos and nature. Once this has been achieved, the law will be able to live an unproblematic existence as a tool of justice.

Third phase feminism

Things are not so simple for third phase feminists like Smart. She adopts a more complicated conceptualisation of law and its relationship to sexism. Smart adopts a Foucauldian notion of discourse.[93] Thus: 'Law has its own method, its own testing ground, its own specialised language and system of results.'[94] The trial system is accepted as a secure basis for distinguishing truth from lies and it is unproblematically assumed that

---

[91] *Ibid.* p. 30.   [92] *Ibid.* p. 31.
[93] Foucault underestimated the importance of law and relegated it to the pre-modern episteme, arguing that it would be irrelevant in disciplinary society.
[94] Smart, *Feminism and the Power of Law*, p. 9.

the law is a neutral arbiter. Law's claim to truth also serves to disqualify other knowledges and experiences. 'Non-legal knowledge is therefore suspect and/or secondary ... [Everyday experience] must be translated into another form in order to become "legal" issues and before they can be processed through the legal system.'[95] The parties are legally represented and this serves to render many rape victims mute. Women's experiences are, in the truest sense, disqualified; the court simply does not want to hear her experiences in her own words. The rape trial itself is a process of disqualification of women and celebration of phallocentrism,[96] confirming 'what is known about women – by women and men'.[97] The rape trial is a celebration of phallocentrism in that it presents men's sexual urges and their fulfilment as simply the natural order of things. It is therefore common sense that a woman who places herself in a certain situation, such as being alone with a man, or having kissed him, that he would expect sex and that the woman was partially responsible for her own victimisation. This is certainly backed up by Temkin's research on barristers on rape trials. Temkin identified the 'foolish behaviour' theme as being presented both in relation to consent and independently of it:

> The jury would be invited to think that the way the complainant behaved suggested that either she might have consented or that the defendant might have believed that she consented. Alternatively, although less explicitly, it is put to the jury that whatever happened on the occasion in question, it was at least in part the complainant's fault and that therefore the defendant does not deserve to be convicted and imprisoned for it.[98]

'Foolish behaviour' would be contrasted with 'common sense' where 'common sense' meant 'behaviour that respected the primacy of men's sexual urges and which judiciously sought to avoid them'.[99]

It is clear then that 'law does not sit on a shelf, so to speak, waiting to be lifted off when the occasion demands'.[100] Law frames our lives and constructs our identities as legal subjects, wives, rape victims, rape defendants. Naffine uses the notion of the official version of law and this broadly translates to what I have termed the common sense idea of law. Naffine argues that the 'official version of law' sees itself as divorced from politics and morality, an impartial and neutral arbiter. She further

[95] *Ibid.* p. 11.   [96] *Ibid.* p. 35.   [97] Smart, *Law, Crime and Sexuality*, p. 84.
[98] Temkin, 'Prosecuting and Defending Rape', 232.   [99] *Ibid.*
[100] Smart, *Law, Crime and Sexuality*, p. 2.

highlights the important link between legal education and the perpetua-
tion of the official 'version' of law. Law schools teach students how legal
method views social problems as a series of disconnected disputes,
masking the systemic nature of discrimination in which law will often
be compliant.[101] 'Inevitably there is a vital connection between law and
social values which is obscured by the official version of law ... the
wheels of law are oiled by deeply held assumptions about the nature of
people and about the purpose of society.'[102] Law's much prized neutrality
lies in its refusal to look beyond the immediate facts of the case to wider
social and political problems, and reflects a liberal model of society and
law. This supposed objectivity enables law to present opinion as truth.
Naffine further argues that law lacks the degree of rationality, coherence
and consistency that it pretends to have. Both Smart and Naffine argue
that much feminist work, including second phase feminism, has bought
into the official version of law and that viewing law as unified and
powerful only serves to empower it further.

Smart too views law as lacking consistency and posits the notion of the
uneven development of law. By this she refers to the way in which law
incorporates conflicting principles and often produces contradictory
outcomes. Law operates on a number of dimensions at the same time.
The law cannot be relied upon to meet fully the goals of any one system of
politics. There can be unforeseen and unregulated outcomes for the state
as well as for individuals. 'Hence the law is not the mere instrument of an
omnipotent state. Its effects are uneven in all dimensions, and the aims of
legislators and even governments may be thwarted by the relative "independence" of law and the judiciary.'[103] So when we ask: is a woman
treated the same way by the law as a man? Smart responds that: 'The
answer must be yes and no, and even maybe.'[104] In some areas of law
women *are* advantaged, for example, in child custody, yet this recognition does not change the fact of the systematic and deep-rooted sexism of
society and the methods it uses to regulate our behaviour and morality.
Thus to Smart law is not a simple tool of patriarchy or capitalism and it
does not privilege all men over all women in all circumstances. Both
Smart and Naffine strongly argue that gender should not be the only
variable in seeing law's discrimination: class must be considered too, as

---

[101] Critical legal studies also shares this focus on how law is taught. See Kennedy, 'Legal
Education as Training for Hierarchy', pp. 40–61.
[102] Naffine, *Law and the Sexes*, p. 44.   [103] Smart, *Law, Crime and Sexuality*, p. 156.
[104] *Ibid.* p. 80.

well as race. Naffine argues that while the law purports to deal with abstract individuals it has in truth a preferred person: the 'man of law'. Such a man flourishes and dominates the type of society conceived by law, and law reflects his priorities and concerns.

> He is one of the possessing classes. His gender takes the form of a certain style of middle-class masculinity: he is assertive, articulate, independent, calculating, competitive and competent. And these are precisely the qualities valued in the sort of society which law has in mind.[105]

Law performs well for those who approximate this model, even if they may differ from it in a single variable. An articulate, self-assured, middle-class woman would arguably fare better in the legal system than a working class uneducated black man. 'Law may benevolently or malevolently confirm us in our discursive place as woman; the point is that it does so.'[106] Thus law is neither just repression or liberation but both. Feminist jurisprudence therefore faces two tasks:

> The first is to grasp the nettle that law is not a set of tools or rules which we can bend into a more favourable shape ... The second is to recognise the power of law as a technology of gender, but not to be silenced by this realisation. Thus we should see the power of law as more than the negative sanction that holds women down. Law is also productive of gender difference and identity, yet this law is not monolithic and unitary.[107]

Conclusion

The problem therefore is not the wording of law, or its personnel. It is not even the nature of the system itself. It is what Smart calls the 'imperialist reach of law':[108] the legalisation of everyday life. This has created the belief that 'every social problem has a legal solution ... and when law fails the solution is often posited as more law to cover the inadequacies of existing law'.[109] But this idea of law empowers it and further narrows down our awareness of and ability to deploy alternative forms of being in and conceptualising the world. If the experience of rape complainants is unified by one theme it is the feeling of being denied justice, the justice upon which our faith in law relies.

Shklar calls this same phenomenon legalism[110] and she offers a more complete extrapolation of it than Smart. In brief, legalism holds

---

[105] Naffine, *Law and the Sexes*, p. 22.   [106] Smart, *Law, Crime and Sexuality*, p. 156.
[107] *Ibid.* p. 198.   [108] Smart, 'The Woman of Legal Discourse', 41.   [109] *Ibid.* 41.
[110] Shklar, *Legalism*.

that moral conduct is a matter of rule-following and that all human relations can be put into the form of claims and counterclaims over rights and duties. This ethos has percolated throughout our society from the highest courts in the land to the village green, to the way we understand human relations. We understand the world through the idea of rights, so much so that envisaging justice as anything other than the 'equal application of rules'[111] is almost impossible. This is both what justice is and how we achieve it. It sees the legal rules as both necessary and neutral and as applied by impartial legal technicians. It is not only a way of resolving disputes but of being in and seeing the world.

Law is seen as simply 'there', meaning that it is self-regulating, immune from the unpredictable pressures of politicians and moralists, manned by an impartial judiciary that at least tries to maintain justice's celebrated blindness. It is 'a series of impersonal rules which fit together neatly'.[112] Law is also a superior mode of social action to politics: what Shklar calls the policy of justice. Legalism is so prevalent as to be beyond reproach: who would argue against justice? But, as Shklar writes:

> It is the rigidity of legalistic categories of thought, especially in appraising the relationships of law to the political environment within which it functions, that is so deleterious. This is the source of the artificiality of almost all legal theories and is what prevents its exponents from recognising both the strengths and weaknesses of law and legal procedures in a complex social world.[113]

Legalism is so problematic because of what we believe and our (misplaced) faith in law to solve complex social problems like racism and sexism.

---

[111] *Ibid.* p. 109.   [112] *Ibid.* p. 35.   [113] *Ibid.* p. 8.

6

Law and normative backsliding: torture since 9/11

Introduction

In Foot's account of the evolution of the torture norm,[1] she traces its origins back to the Enlightenment thinker Beccaria.[2] However, it was not until the end of the Second World War that such moral reasoning gained a foothold in international law. The 1948 Universal Declaration of Human Rights was the first to outlaw torture, followed swiftly by the Geneva Conventions in 1949. However, according to Foot, it was not until the emergence of Amnesty International that commitment to ending torture moved beyond words and into deeds.

It was in this climate, Foot argues, that torture came to be established as illegal and publicly condemned. Donnelly also claims that this period marked the establishment of a new standard of civilisation in which membership in international society depended on the extent to which governments observed human rights standards.[3] And no norm in the human rights pantheon is as admired or well-established as the norm against torture, enshrined in the 1984 Convention Against Torture. Sussman argues that: 'In philosophical and political discussion, torture is commonly offered as one of the few unproblematic examples of a type of act that is morally impermissible without exception or qualification.'[4]

Part of the reason for this is the depth of the torture norms' legal embeddedness. Torture is a peremptory norm: a legal rule that is binding on all states and from which no derogation is permitted. As Robertson says: 'There can be no doubt that the rule against torture has evolved into a *jus cogens* prohibition which every state has a duty owed

---

[1] By which I mean the norm against torture.   [2] Foot, 'Torture', 131–50.
[3] Donnelly, 'Human Rights', 1–23.   [4] Quoted in Bellamy, 'No Pain, No Gain?', 129.

to the international community to outlaw and punish.'[5] In addition there are numerous international and domestic laws prohibiting torture, the most important being the Convention Against Torture and Other Cruel, Inhuman, or Degrading Treatment or Punishment; the International Covenant on Civil and Political Rights; and the Geneva Conventions and Protocols. All this has meant that the torturer is, in a word, *hostis humani generis*, an enemy of mankind.

The evolution of torture is depicted by many as the ineluctable march towards moral progress. But with the value of hindsight, many thinkers are now arguing that the roots of the torture norm are relatively shallow. Rather than emphasising the long pedigree of ideas of human rights and physical autonomy, such accounts emphasise instead the use of torture by the West until comparatively recently. Torture was common throughout the colonies and secretly endorsed by the West during the cold war. It was even more widespread throughout the rest of the world. Torture therefore was honoured more in the breach.

Yet the significance of the torture norm has been in how it is viewed, rather than the mundane reality of its daily use. The torture norm is a rare beast. Studying the torture norm should therefore enable us to assess the validity and accuracy of constructivist accounts of norms and normative evolution. It sheds valuable light on the story constructivists tell of how norms evolve. But the real value of looking at the torture norm lies in what it can tell us about law: the torture norm was widely considered to be the pre-eminent manifestation of the global commitment to human rights and as a consequence it sits atop the legal hierarchy as a peremptory norm. In the model of norm evolution put forward by constructivists, law and legalisation are the end stages of evolution. They are both evidence and a guarantee of norm internalisation. The torture norm offers a way of assessing how accurate their assumptions about norm evolution are but also a way of exploring the role law plays in constructivist analysis.

The two preceding chapters use specific case studies to illuminate different aspects of law and to raise questions about what a better idea of law should look like. This chapter moves the argument on in two respects. First, we make the transition from the domestic legal arena to the international legal one. Secondly, we return to constructivism, this time focusing on the empirical and theoretical offshoots of constructivism's origins, as explored in chapter 1.

---

[5] Robertson, *Crimes Against Humanity*, p. 98.

The evolution of constructivism

Because constructivism has been the school of international relations (IR) theory that has spent the most time considering the role of law, I want to bring in more contemporary constructivist work. Onuf and Kratochwil's start point was very theoretical, relying on hypothetical examples and without empirical research. As Finnemore and Sikkink point out in their 'Taking Stock'[6] article, in 1988 the inchoate constructivist approach was challenged by Keohane to produce more empirical research. Keohane argued that the future survival and success of constructivism would depend on its ability to explain real life phenomena.[7] It was a call constructivists heeded and throughout the 1990s constructivist scholars produced a range of empirical case studies.[8] Because constructivism emerged in contradistinction to rationalism and sought to acknowledge and explore the role of ideational factors in international politics, analysis focused on cases that existing rationalist approaches could not explain. This meant that constructivism arguably cornered the market on a specific form of case study: unexpected normative evolution, that is, where norms that are contrary to state interests, as rationalists would define them, emerge and become dominant.

Klotz's work on the end of apartheid is a good example. She sought to explain how US foreign policy went from seeing sanctions against South Africa as inimical to key US interests like containment and access to minerals, to seeing sanctions as essential and instituting them.[9] Traditional rationalist accounts are unable to explain the move from one state of affairs to the other because the United States' material interests had not significantly changed: the cold war was still ongoing and the United States still needed South African minerals. The explanation, according to Klotz, lies in a sustained campaign to link racism in South Africa with racism in the United States and emphasise the centrality of a norm of racial equality to American identity.

Price makes a similar point in his work on the creation of the chemical weapons taboo and the construction of the anti-personnel land mine

---

[6] Finnemore and Sikkink, 'Taking Stock', 391–416.   [7] *Ibid.* 391.
[8] See Crawford, 'Decolonization as an International Norm', pp. 37–61; Lumsdaine, *Moral Vision*; Nadelman, 'Global Prohibition Regimes', 479–526; Price and Tannenwald, 'Norms and Deterrence', pp. 114–52.
[9] Klotz, 'Norms Reconstituting Interests', 451–78; Klotz, 'Transnational Activism and Global Transformations', 49–76; Klotz, *Norms in International Relations*.

ban.[10] Using rationalist accounts it is hard to explain why these two weapons technologies were de-legitimised and consequently prohibited. As Price points out, both are 'hard cases' because questions of national security are considered *the* core areas of state power and prerogative. The influence of civil society is very weak here and the assumption is that if a weapon has any military value at all, a government will not eschew it. Thus, under rationalist analysis, it becomes almost impossible to explain why governments would willingly do things that are contrary to their interests. The answer for Price, like Klotz, lies in adopting a broader notion of interests, one which can include questions of identity and concern for reputation, and how in turn these can be exploited by an orchestrated civil society campaign.

Constructivism made a number of key contributions to IR theory. First, and most significantly, it questioned rationalism's exclusive focus on material factors. Constructivists argued that while material factors were important, it was ideational factors that were *primary*.[11] By making ideational factors central to analysis, rather than just adding them as another variable, constructivists were able to explain the previously inexplicable. Rather than an ontology comprised of material factors and states with exogenously given interests, constructivists drew upon Onuf and Kratochwil's notion of intersubjective context. In a socially constructed world, it was how we understood and viewed material factors that was significant, not the material factors themselves. National security, threat, even anarchy, are all constructed. And this threw the emphasis onto how our shared ideas were created and changed. In relation to international politics this often meant focusing on the identities of states and the argument that identity could determine interests. The idea that good liberal states do not torture became a fairly frequently cited example.

This emphasis on ideas led to constructivism's second contribution: the move away from statism. Because of the new focus on the process of idea and identity construction, the explanandum became how ideas and identities were formed and who or what did the forming. This created a new focus on the hitherto ignored role of civil society and non-state actors.

It also brought a new politics, befitting a new, more optimistic period of history. Constructivism is very much a product of its time. This era

[10] Price, 'Reversing the Gun Sights', 613–44.
[11] Finnemore and Sikkink, 'Taking Stock', 393.

started with the end of the cold war and may potentially have ended with 9/11. The end of the cold war opened up unprecedented possibilities for peace and cooperation. The cold war had inhibited almost all progress towards human rights and it had forestalled the possibility of any meaningful humanitarian intervention. Now that it was over, and liberalism had won,[12] the opportunities for international politics to move beyond anarchy and conflict and towards higher moral values seemed finally to have arrived.

Arguably this optimism permeated constructivism, both in its view of the world, the case studies it explored and the values it saw as coming to prominence. We can see this most clearly in human rights, a key focus of constructivist research. It is hard to account for the establishment and 'rise and rise' of human rights using rationalist accounts of international politics.[13] Constructivists argued that a (better) explanation lay in the question of state identity. Good liberal, Western states supported human rights and encouraged their spread. And they did so because of their *identity* as members of the Western liberal 'club'. Because human rights help to define the identities of liberal states they have become the 'yardstick used to define who is in and who is outside of the liberal club of states'.[14] In this way human rights help to constitute liberal identity. As Fearon and Laitin argue, people sometimes follow norms because they want others to think well of them, and because they want to think well of themselves.[15] Actors' ability to think well of themselves is influenced by norms held by their relevant community of actors, in this case, states.

Such states therefore were not simply pushing human rights for instrumental reasons – for example, to foment revolution in communist countries – they were attempting to establish their own identities and to reaffirm their distinctness from other states. But there is also 'something in the intrinsic quality of the human rights norms that gives them their force and influence'.[16] States were in that sense, 'true believers'. In Keck and Sikkink's *Activists Beyond Borders: Advocacy Networks in International Politics* they argue that two categories of norms are particularly effective transnationally and cross-culturally: those violating bodily integrity and prevention of bodily harm for

---

[12] Fukuyama, *The End of History and the Last Man.*
[13] Sellars, *The Rise and Rise of Human Rights.*   [14] Sikkink, 'Transnational Politics', 520.
[15] Fearon and Laitin, 'Violence and the Social Construction of Ethnic Identity', 845–77.
[16] Sikkink, 'Transnational Politics', 520.

vulnerable or 'innocent' groups, especially when there is a short causal chain between cause and effect; and norms for legal equality of opportunity.[17]

Foot argues that in the 1990s 'no one questioned whether human rights should be a part of foreign policy ... the expectation that global actors would – indeed should – be concerned about human rights in any part of the world where they might be being abused was broadly understood.[18] And according to Foot it was in this climate that torture came to be established as illegal and publicly condemned as a moral outrage. This even extended to sovereignty. Sovereignty was no longer enough; it was now about responsible sovereignty and membership of international society depended on human rights observance. And the torture norm held a central place in the new human rights regime.

The torture norm also plays an important role in the norms literature. It is *the* archetypal internalised norm, and relatedly, is seen as evidence of moral progress. It is the end point at which other norms may one day arrive. Because of this, the evolution of the torture norm is rather taken for granted. Only Risse, Ropp and Sikkink's book is the exception. It explores torture as part of a core of human rights norms whose evolution they chart in a number of different countries. It may seem strange that it was considered unnecessary to study the torture norm itself when the prevalence of torture throughout the world, even pre-9/11, was extensive.[19] However, while the practice of torture was relatively commonplace, justification and defence of torture were not. States that tortured would not admit to it and this was seen as evidence of the torture norm's prevalence and internalisation. Conversely, denial indicated the power of the norm. This assumption, however, may well be called into question by the post-9/11 expansion of torture. But first we must outline the life-cycle theory itself, before applying it to the torture norm.

I start with Finnemore and Sikkink's seminal piece 'International Norm Dynamics and Political Change'.[20] Here they argue that norms evolve through three stages: first, there is norm emergence; secondly, broad norm acceptance and a 'norm cascade'.[21] This is when a 'critical mass of states ... become norm leaders and adopt new norms, we can say

---

[17] Keck and Sikkink, *Activists Beyond Borders*.   [18] Foot, 'Torture', 137.
[19] Blakeley, 'Why Torture?', 373–94.
[20] Finnemore and Sikkink, 'International Norm Dynamics', 887–917.
[21] Sunstein, *Free Markets and Social Justice*.

the norm reaches a threshold or tipping point'.[22] Once the tipping point is reached the norm will cascade, meaning that the adoption rate will increase and a kind of 'contagion' will occur.[23] And when this has happened we enter stage three: internalisation. Internalisation is when the norm becomes 'taken-for-granted'[24] and conformance is 'almost automatic'.[25] Such norms are, according to Finnemore and Sikkink, extremely powerful because behaving according to the norm is not questioned. It can however be difficult to discern when a norm is internalised 'because actors do not seriously consider or discuss whether to conform'.[26] It would be fair to assume therefore that lack of contestation would indicate, but not definitively prove, internalisation.

Each stage works slightly differently. In the first stage persuasion by norm entrepreneurs is the mechanism. Norm entrepreneurs are those who actively build notions about appropriate or desirable behaviour, like Red Cross founder Henry Dunant or suffragette Emmeline Pankhurst. They call attention to issues and may even 'create' them. They work by changing our minds and ideas about how we should behave. And as people's minds are changed, some of them join the fight to expand the norm. Often this means joining non-governmental organisations (NGOs) and becoming part of civil society. This civil society is frequently transnational. As the campaign spreads it may use other organisational platforms besides NGOs and use state or international organisations like the World Bank or the United Nations. Individuals are motivated by altruism, empathy and commitment to the idea.

At the second stage, all three elements – the mechanisms, the actors and the motives – change. Now states are involved, along with international organisations and transnational advocacy networks (TANs)[27] and they are motivated by reputation, legitimacy and esteem. The mechanisms behind this are socialisation, demonstration and institutionalisation. In other words, as states are socialised into adopting the norm, they start to institutionalise it and this serves as an example to other states. Once the norm has cascaded we are in distinctly different territory. States conform because the norm is now law. In part, this is

---

[22] Finnemore and Sikkink, 'International Norm Dynamics', 901. It is impossible to say precisely how many states it takes but Finnemore and Sikkink point to empirical studies that place the number at around one-third of the world's states: *ibid.* 901.
[23] *Ibid.* 902.   [24] *Ibid.* 904.   [25] *Ibid.* 904.   [26] *Ibid.* 904.
[27] Keck and Sikkink coin this term in their book: *Activists Beyond Borders.* I use it throughout this chapter as a synonym for terms used by other authors like transnational civil society and transnational activists.

instrumental – states recognise that the norm is now law, but also, as time goes on, they comply increasingly out of habit.

Finnemore and Sikkink's three stage model is fleshed out by Sikkink's work with Risse and Ropp, where they develop a five-stage spiral model.[28] It specifically charts the socialising process by which norms are internalised domestically. Because an exhaustive study of all human rights would not be feasible, Risse, Ropp and Sikkink choose a central core of rights to study: the right to life (which they define as the right to be free from extrajudicial execution and disappearance) and freedom from arbitrary arrest and detention, and from torture.[29] Because the spiral model builds upon work already done by Finnemore and Sikkink, it shares many of the same core assumptions about the centrality of activists and TANs. According to Risse and Sikkink's introductory chapter, the diffusion of international norms in the human rights area 'crucially depends on the establishment and sustainability of net-works'.[30] Identity and the process of socialisation are also key. Norm entrepreneurs work by targeting states identities and human rights norms are seen by Risse and Sikkink as having 'special status because they both prescribe rules for appropriate behaviour, and help define identities of liberal states'.[31] International norms are internalised and implemented domestically because states become socialised into com-plying with them.[32] Internalisation happens as the result of three causal mechanisms: first, processes of instrumental adoption and strategic bargaining; secondly, processes of moral consciousness-raising, argu-mentation, dialogue and persuasion; and thirdly, processes of institu-tionalisation and habitualisation. Although the model separates these three stages, Risse and Sikkink argue that in reality, these processes occur simultaneously. However, they note that '[o]ur task ... is to identify which mode of interaction dominates in which phase of the socialisation process'[33] and that separating them out into distinct stages is necessary.

The first stage is the start point: repression. Risse and Sikkink note that this stage 'might last for a long time, since many oppressive states never make it on to the agenda of the transnational advocacy network'.[34] It is only when a repressive state attracts the attention of a TAN, which are predominantly based in the West, that the spiral out of human rights

---

[28] Risse, Ropp and Sikkink (eds.) *The Power of Human Rights.*   [29] *Ibid.* p. 2.
[30] Risse and Sikkink, 'The Socialization of International Human Rights Norms', p. 5.
[31] *Ibid.* p. 8.   [32] *Ibid.* p. 5.   [33] *Ibid.* p. 11.   [34] *Ibid.* p. 22.

abuse starts. Once the TAN has started to act, using its various strategies of raising awareness, persuading and attempting to shame the repressors, we move into stage two: denial. That a state feels compelled to deny charges is, according to Risse and Sikkink, evidence of the start of the socialisation process. The process is most vulnerable in its transition into the next stage: tactical concessions. What makes the key difference here is that the domestic opposition has come to life, empowered by the TAN. The repressive regime is now faced with both international and domestic opposition. Here we see the emergence of a key constructivist argument: that governments become 'entrapped in their own rhetoric'.[35] And the more the government argues, the more they are drawn into debate and 'the more likely they are to make argumentative concessions and to specify their justifications and the less likely they are to leave the arguing mode'.[36] Although Risse and Sikkink are not explicit, I would infer from this that the reason this works is because it is assumed that human rights abuses cannot be logically justified.

The tide begins to turn as popular opinion swings behind the TAN and domestic opposition and 'norm-violating governments no longer have many choices'.[37] Yet this stage is fraught with danger and governments can react in one of two ways: they can make tactical concessions, moving the model onto stage four, or they can increase their repression and destroy the domestic opposition. This will have the effect of freezing the model until such time as a domestic opposition builds up again. But the model does not run backwards: the achievements of the international opposition are not lost and we do not return to either stage one or two. The only consequence is that the inevitable progress along the spiral model will take longer.

Once the state makes the precarious transition beyond mere tactical concessions we are into the fourth stage of prescriptive status. This means that 'the actors involved regularly refer to the human rights norm to describe and comment on their own behaviour and that of others . . . validity claims of the norm are no longer controversial'.[38] We know a norm has acquired prescriptive status when governments do certain things: they ratify the respective human rights conventions and protocols, the norms are institutionalised into the constitution or domestic law, and there is institutionalised mechanism for citizens to complain about human rights violations. In other words, the norm is institutionalised and legalised. But the norm has only just made it into

---

[35] *Ibid.* p. 28.   [36] *Ibid.* p. 28.   [37] *Ibid.* p. 28.   [38] *Ibid.* p. 29.

law and it is only in the final stage, stage five, that 'international human rights norms are fully institutionalised domestically and norm compliance becomes a habitual practice of actors and is enforced by the rule of law. At this point, we can safely assume that the human rights norms are internalised'.[39] Clearly then it is law, and enforcement of that law, that is the endpoint of the spiral model. It is the norm's guarantor.[40]

And reaching the final stage is akin to falling off a precipice. Indeed, at no stage of the model is reverse possible; the spiral does not run backwards. It can stop but, like a ratchet, it cannot go in the opposite direction. Theoretical models of norm evolution, like Finnemore and Sikkink's norm life cycle, and Risse, Ropp and Sikkink's spiral model, are relatively unusual in the norms literature. As I noted above, since Keohane's injunction to turn to more empirical work, this is predominantly where constructivist analysis of norms has been. I therefore want to supplement these two related models by looking at the work of Price and Klotz. Neither author looks at human rights specifically and both study what could be termed 'hard cases'. They should therefore provide a more balanced picture of constructivism as a whole.

Price's study of the anti-personnel land mine ban addressed the core state prerogative of national security and Klotz explores the decision to use sanctions against South Africa despite the geo-political importance of South Africa in the cold war context and American reliance on South African minerals. Both areas would seem fairly immune to activist pressure because activists would be working directly contrary to key state interests. However, both accounts share a number of core constructivist assumptions with the models outlined above. All the authors are

---

[39] *Ibid.* p. 33.

[40] There are also some other assumptions I want to draw attention to, notably the very particular focus of Risse, Ropp and Sikkink's study: repressive regimes throughout the developing world. The book's empirical case studies include Uganda, Kenya, Guatemala, and the Philippines. While there is nothing wrong with this per se, it tells a particular story about where human rights abuses happen and who human rights abusers are. Western states here are, at worst, hypocrites and at best actively involved in promoting human rights around world. They are the focus of TANs who 'alert Western public opinion and Western governments' (*ibid.* p. 5). It is simply inconceivable to Risse, Ropp and Sikkink that the West might be abusing human rights or, as it was to the majority of thinkers, that it might start. But it is not just Western states that are the harbingers of human rights: the entire process of norm evolution could not exist, according to Risse, Ropp and Sikkink, without TANs. In stages one and two they are the sole actors, in stage three they work with domestic opposition. It is only once the norm has acquired prescriptive status, i.e. people's minds have been changed, that TANs cease to be crucial actors.

self-consciously working in the constructivist vein and define their approach in distinction to both realism and liberal institutionalism. One of the key constructivist criticisms of these approaches is their exclusively statist focus and both Price and Klotz make the point that, in order to explain the processes in question, they must see the role played by non-state actors. Both see the role of TANs as key. In fact, for both Price and Klotz, in common with the authors of the models above, the vast majority of the work of norm evolution is done by TANs. They essentially 'create' the issue by raising awareness, and documenting and publicising the norm they want to promote. They also persuade and cajole, and seek to recruit more, and more powerful, supporters to their cause. Once they have 'captured' decision-makers, it is simply a matter of ensuring that decisions are finally taken, laws passed and norms internalised. But the vast bulk of the work is done by TANs and TANs alone. In Price's words, TANs do no less than 'teach [. . .] governments what is appropriate to pursue in politics'.[41] What ultimately causes governments to do things which are seemingly contrary to their interests is the amount of pressure that activists can produce.[42]

This is particularly clear in Klotz's work. According to her, transnational and domestic activists tipped the balance towards sanctions by generating pressure in congress. She argues that: 'Declining congressional support demonstrated that Regan, unlike previous Presidents, could no longer rely on orthodox assumptions that white-minority rule would protect U.S. strategic and economic interests in South Africa.'[43] Activists managed to 'capture' congress members by 'both framing the apartheid issue in the context of the prevailing civil rights discourse of equality and increasing their institutional access to decision-making power'.[44] By linking tolerance of apartheid to tolerance of racism at home, activists made it politically unwise *not* to support sanctions. By altering the interests of congress members, activists managed to move the issue up the food chain to alter US interests and therefore foreign policy. For Klotz then activists worked by altering the domestic political debate in America by linking apartheid and racism in South Africa with racism in the United States and thereby altering the costs to politicians who are keen to stay in power.

---

[41] Price, 'Reversing the Gun Sights', 639.
[42] Of course, norm entrepreneurs may fail to produce that pressure and Sikkink argues it is a necessary but not a sufficient condition. See Sikkink, 'Transnational Politics'.
[43] Klotz, 'Norms Reconstituting Interests', 471.   [44] *Ibid.* 462.

Klotz's account thus shows some fairly marked differences from the theoretical model of human rights evolution. First of all, identity does not feature at all. Klotz does not argue that activists managed to change US *identity*, only its understanding of its interests. Secondly, while the campaign did manage to persuade key decision-makers to support a policy they had previously rejected, they did so by targeting politicians' self-interest. It is therefore irrelevant for Klotz's analysis whether decision-makers were true believers in the wrongness of apartheid, or simply instrumental adopters responding to a change in the political climate. Nor does Klotz argue that there is anything intrinsic to the norm of racial equality that predisposes it to spread. What mattered was the resonance the global norm of racial equality could be made to have in American political culture. In this respect, Klotz's work echoes the argument made by both Kratochwil and Onuf that it is resonance, or fit, with the existing intersubjective context, that determines whether an emerging norm will survive.[45] However, the question of resonance does relate to the question of whether processes of norm evolution can run backwards, to which I will return later.

Price's account differs from Klotz's and is broadly speaking more similar to both the norm life cycle and spiral models of norm evolution. For Price the key element is 'moral persuasion and the social pressure arising from identity politics'.[46] As already noted, Price believes that norm entrepreneurs can teach states what is appropriate behaviour. Networks of norm entrepreneurs 'provide the classroom, the site that brings state and society together'.[47] Teaching works because of and through identity: we only know what is appropriate behaviour in relation to our identity. Price outlines four 'pedagogical techniques'.[48] First, norm entrepreneurs or activists generate issues by disseminating information. Secondly, they establish networks for proselytising to generate broad support for normative change within, across and outside government channels. Thirdly, norm entrepreneurs use a process that Price calls 'grafting' whereby the emergent norm is grafted onto existing norms. This involves a 'combination of active, manipulative persuasion and the contingency of genealogical heritage in norm germination'.[49] It is not simply that the emergent norm resonates, as in Kratochwil and Onuf's work, but that it is *made* to resonate. And finally, a transnational Socratic method whereby civil society's demands on states to publicly

---

[45] See chapter 1.   [46] Price, 'Reversing the Gun Sights', 616.
[47] *Ibid.* 627.   [48] *Ibid.* 617.   [49] *Ibid.* 617.

justify their positions reverse the burden of proof involved in contesting norms, thereby legitimising political space for change. According to Price the campaign to ban land mines used all these techniques to great effect. Like Klotz, Price sees these techniques as working to convert decision-makers to the cause but unlike Klotz he also sees this conversion operating in tandem with the 'social pressures of international reputation'.[50] Because identity and reputation are central to Price's analysis, shaming is an important technique for both helping a norm to evolve and for bringing non-compliant states into line. Whether or not shaming works is, according to Price, 'both predicated on and evidence for the existence of a norm'.[51]

Identity and reputational concerns are extremely potent. Price found that for reluctant states like Poland reputational pressures overcame their resistance. According to Price, '[t]he leaders of those nations evidently felt it intolerable to be left outside of the club of responsible international citizens once they judged that the balance had tipped such that resistance signalled outlier status'.[52] Even in key states like Britain and South Africa, whose militaries did not want to abandon land mines, 'political decisions' overrode resistance.[53]

But for Price, just because states agreed to and ratified the ban, does not mean that they are true believers. As indicated above, governments may have adopted the norm for purely instrumental reason.[54] For the model of norm evolution instrumental adoption is a necessary stage before the norm becomes internalised and compliance becomes unthinking. The difference between instrumental adoption and true belief is not considered any further by the model but Price does consider the question of internalisation. He argues that the 'existence of a norm does not mean it cannot be violated, only that the justification of unusual, even extraordinary, circumstances is required to engage in noncompliance'.[55] The bar is therefore raised. Unfortunately Price never clarifies what the difference, or maybe distance, is between a

---

[50] *Ibid.* 617. [51] *Ibid.* 635. [52] *Ibid.* 635.

[53] *Ibid.* 634. Price offers no evidence to support his claim in the case of Britain and only interview evidence with South African members of the land mine ban campaign for the South African case.

[54] Price writes that: 'Few if any politicians or governments that have agreed to a ban on AP [anti-personnel] land mines adopted the new norm directly for instrumental reasons ... – in other words, elections or leadership struggles would not be won or lost because of the land mine issue' (*ibid.* 631).

[55] *Ibid.* 641. See also Price, *The Chemical Weapons Taboo*.

norm existing and it being internalised. If we turn to Katzenstein's definition of a norm as a standard of appropriate behaviour for actors with a given identity[56] there is no necessary indication of whether a norm has to be internalised or not. For Price norms are 'an inherently contested phenomenon',[57] which implies that norms never slip into our consciousness.

  Ultimately there is a lack of clarity but there appear to be two ideas at play here. First, there is the idea of internalisation as when norms are never questioned. They are internalised so completely that we do not even see them. As such it is almost impossible to challenge such norms. This idea is found in Kratochwil, Onuf and Finnemore and Sikkink's work. However, Price's work indicates that internalised norms can still be challenged. Internalisation has the effect of making it harder to challenge them, and better, more extensive justifications will be needed, but no norm is ever immune to challenge. However, the first idea of internalisation found in Kratochwil and Onuf's work is itself unclear and, while they agree that an internalised norm is one which has sunk into our collective subconscious, they also believe that we can disobey a norm, if we so choose. And this question of internalisation speaks directly to the question of whether norms can be de-internalised and whether the models of norm evolution put forward by various authors can 'run backwards' to account for the regression of the torture norm.

Theories of norm evolution post-9/11

Post-9/11 there has not been a large amount of constructivist work which has specifically identified or addressed the challenge posed to constructivist assumptions of norm evolution by the return of torture. One exception has been McKeown, whose work addresses both these issues and argues that models of norm evolution can, with a little tinkering, explain normative back-sliding into torture. He argues that models of norm evolution have erred only in their focus, but not in their fundamental assumptions. McKeown builds upon Finnemore and Sikkink's norm life cycle. In their model norms progress through three stages. First, they emerge and are proselytised by norm entrepreneurs. If the norm resonates with a larger audience it may cascade and towards the end of this cascade norms may be internalised. McKeown

---

[56] Katzenstein, *The Culture of National Security*, p. 5.
[57] Price, 'Reversing the Gun Sights', 637.

then simply adds on his own three stage 'norm death series'. At the start point the norm is internalised but comes under challenge by 'norm revisionists'. This challenge can consist of 'quiet changes in policy away from compliance with the norm'[58] and can be a change in discourse, policy and/or practice. It can even be secretive. If the norm challenge has resonance there may be a reverse norm cascade. There are two parts to this. First, there is a discursive battle between defenders and revisionists. This can occur within public discourse or within government institutions or both. The 'prize' is the direction of policy but also public opinion. Secondly, 'the norm loses salience in the international arena through a process of emulation by leaders of other states who note that the normative stigma for breaking the norm is now significantly reduced'.[59] If the challenge is sufficiently echoed by other respected members of the system, the norms suffers an international crisis of legitimacy. For McKeown, reputation and respect for certain members of the community is still key. If this crisis is not resolved the norm will expire.

In applying this to torture, McKeown argues that the Bush adminis-tration and its supporters acted as 'norm revisionists' or agents of moral regress. They replace the key role played by TANs in Finnemore and Sikkink's model and they actively reframed torture as an acceptable and necessary tool in the War on Terror.[60] They did this by successfully depicting 9/11 as an exceptional event that required an exceptional response. They also exploited the fear, anger and xenophobia post-9/11 to portray enemies of the United States as unworthy of the legal or moral protections of the torture norm and depicted torture itself as both useful and necessary. This meant that the much-vaunted shaming mechanism[61] failed because of the hesitancy of the US media and 'a surprisingly acquiescent public'.[62] This called into question 'constructivist confidence regarding the exposure of hypocrisy as a useful tactic to change state behaviour'.[63] Even after the truth about torture was revealed there was a lack of popular condemnation. This meant that the norm regressed rapidly and with little impediment. McKeown argues that at present the norm is suffering a crisis of legitimacy. If this crisis continues and the international community

---

[58] McKeown, 'Norm Regress', 11.   [59] *Ibid.* 11.   [60] *Ibid.* 6.
[61] See Finnemore and Sikkink, 'International Norm Dynamics'; Linklater, 'Torture and Civilisation', 111–18; Risse, Ropp and Sikkink, *The Power of Human Rights*.
[62] McKeown, 'Norm Regress', 6.   [63] *Ibid.* 6.

does not start to condemn torture and America's actions, then the norm will die. For many, the future of the torture norm will be determined, in large part, by what President Obama does. While he has condemned the use of torture and ring-fenced the actions of two Bush administrations as a 'dark chapter', Guantánamo Bay and numerous black sites remain open.[64] Until the difficult problem of what to do with the detainees is resolved, the crisis of legitimacy seems unlikely to end.

Norm evolution as a ratchet

Although McKeown's account appears to solve the problem of reconciling the models of norm evolution with the reality of torture, there remain some serious problems. While McKeown attempts to save the norm evolution model, I argue that in so doing, he must alter constructivism's fundamental assumptions to such an extent that there is little left that is recognisably constructivist. Most significant among these problems is the fact that the original models never intended or foresaw norm regress. Although it is never explicitly stated, the model of norm evolution, indeed the very term itself, implies that the creation and spread of norms is an irreversible process. As McKeown points out, the very fact that it has an *end point* suggests as much. The predominant account of norm evolution depicts it as instigated and driven by activists. They start the process – they might even create it – and they do the vast majority of the hard graft of spreading the norm. Governments, on the other hand, are depicted as largely passive and reactive. There are some exceptional, middle-ranking states that may be 'early adopters', like Canada in the land mine ban, but on the whole governments and states are merely the target of activist strategy.

And the 'hard graft' that activists do consists of a gradual accumulation of support from different constituencies: at first, raising awareness in the general population and then trying to parlay that into pressure on politicians and officials. Through both genuine moral conversion and

---

[64] Barack Obama started his presidency by announcing that Guantánamo would be closed but a year on the camp remains open. On 22 January 2009 Obama signed three executive orders, one requiring Guantánamo to be closed within a year, one formally banning torture and reasserting the Army Field Manual as the authoritative source on prisoner treatment, and one establishing an intra-agency task force to lead a systematic review of detention policies and procedures and a review of all individual cases. However, there was no mention of 'black sites' across the world which may hold hundreds, potentially a thousand, detainees, according to Clive Stafford Smith: see www.reprieve.org.uk.

adoption for instrumental reasons, decision-makers are recruited to the cause. This is a long process of gradually building up pressure and working up the food chain until the campaign is able to start a debate and raise the issue in the corridors of power. Because the process is one of gradual accumulation of support and coalition-building, each new growth in support and each key decision brings the end point closer. Moreover, that process never runs backwards. The building of support does not suddenly disappear or dwindle. It may do so slowly, as enthusiasm may wane as progress stalls, but the process is gradual and unsuccessful campaigns stall, rather than crash. They may stop, but they do not reverse.

It is therefore reasonable to assume that, once a norm has been internalised, its de-internalisation would have to go through the same process by which it evolved. This means a process of gradual change in perception through increasing numbers of the population, and in increasingly important sections of the population, i.e. decision-makers. Normative evolution must happen gradually because it has to change people's perceptions and that, inevitably, takes time.

Also, because of the almost exclusive focus on TANs as the engine that drives norm evolution towards legalisation and internalisation, it is hard to see the process as capable of seeing or explaining norm regress. The difficulty may lie in attempting to run the model *backwards* per se. Maybe a more accurate explanation of normative change would characterise the process, not as norm regression or 'de-evolution', but as the emergence of a counter norm. In this way, the counter norm will simply run through the same process. However, this does not fit with the case of the torture norm. It is clearly not the case that a counter norm has emerged and achieved ascendancy over the existing norm which prohibits torture. The normative change that we have witnessed looks more like a successful challenge to the norm. Indeed, the majority of scholarly opinion of torture post-9/11 views it as a 'crisis of legitimacy' of the norm, not the end of the norm itself.[65] Most argue that the torture norm is in serious danger but that until we see what post-Bush foreign policy looks like, we cannot know for sure whether the norm will survive or die.

---

[65] See Dunne, "'The Rules of the Game are Changing'", 269–86 and see the Special Edition, 'Resolving International Crises of Legitimacy' of *International Politics* generally, vol. 44 (2007); Foot, 'Torture'; Linklater, 'Torture and Civilisation'.

I find myself in agreement with McKeown on this point: that the norm is in regression. The alternative view would be that the norm itself has not regressed but simply that we misunderstood it and overestimated the extent to which it was internalised. This would mean that key decision-makers were never convinced by the torture norm and all it took was a severe enough threat to national security for them to break their instrumental adoption of the norm. However, if the norm itself has not changed, only our assessment of its power, then people's view of torture would itself not change. But public opinion within the United States has changed significantly.[66] It would be illogical to separate off public opinion from political decision-makers as McKeown does. He argues that 'it is questionable that certain members in the Bush admin-istration *ever* fully internalized the norm against torture'[67] but he concedes that a large majority of Americans did. McKeown argues that we should distinguish between personal internalisation and public inter-nalisation, arguing that the torture norm was internalised by the American people but not by the Bush administration.

But the change in popular opinion is important. In constructivist terms, these people de-internalised the norm. Moreover, constructivism has never made the distinction between those in power and the rest of society. It has never recognised that certain individuals have more influence over the intersubjective context than others. I believe it should, as does Mckeown, but in doing so he fundamentally alters constructivism as a result.

The problem is, however, as McKeown acknowledges, that the mod-els of norm evolution cited above have an undeniably 'teleological flavour'[68] and that they have failed to 'adequately recognise the imper-manence of internalisation'.[69] However, despite McKeown's neat divi-sion of public and private internalisation, it sidesteps the very quintessence of constructivist orthodoxy, that normative change hap-pens through the argumentative process. My point here is that there is first, an assumption that argumentative processes happen in the open

[66] Traugott, Brader and Coral *et al.*, 'How Americans Responded', 511–16. The public debate about torture seemed to view torture as increasingly acceptable: on 5 November 2001 *Newsweek* ran an article called 'Time to Think About Torture?' and in January 2003 the *Economist*'s cover story asked 'Is Torture Ever Justified?'. These articles were reinforced by TV shows like *24* which depicted the extensive use of torture by hero, Jack Bauer but also upon him and other characters, once with the President watching on a monitor. Such depictions have arguably contributed to a normalisation of torture.
[67] McKeown, 'Norm Regress', 9, emphasis in original.   [68] *Ibid.* 7.   [69] *Ibid.* 9.

and in the public domain and secondly, there is a lack of clarity and specificity about how the argumentative process and the intersubjective context interact that goes right back to Kratochwil and Onuf.

But this does not fit with what happened to the torture norm. Let's accept (and I do) McKeown's argument that the Bush administration were never true believers and had not internalised the torture norm. They then started the systematic use of torture but hid it because they knew that it would be unpopular and might potentially have serious ramifications for both America's reputation and the prevalence of torture worldwide. They then started to attempt to alter the discursive field by using inflammatory rhetoric to make torture more acceptable. This combined with popular ambivalence about torture to create an atmosphere in which, even after the abuse at Abu Ghraib was revealed, the public outcry that many activists and scholars hoped for or expected did not materialise. The decision to use torture, and transgress or redefine the norm, was made away from the public domain by a small number of key decision-makers. There was no argumentative process *before* the norm regress. The return to torture, whether we characterise it as a normative change or not, preceded the argumentative process. And because constructivists argue that interests and actions are shaped by ideas – this is their central claim – then some ideational change in the intersubjective context must have happened. But there is no evidence of this.

Moreover, the relationship between the individual and the intersubjective context is problematic. There were many individuals who were perfectly able to disregard it and the much-vaunted 'shaming' strategy and regard for reputational concerns amounted to very little. These flaws in the foundations of constructivist meta-theory have not been noted or challenged by subsequent constructivist analysis and I argue this is because of the types of case studies selected. Analysis has focused on non-Western states and how predominantly Western-based advocacy networks, with the occasional help of Western states, help to spread human rights beyond the Western liberal club. There has also been a marked tendency to focus on 'good' norms: norms against torture, arbitrary detention, norms of racial equality.[70] Constructivists have therefore studied the end of apartheid, but not its beginning. What would the constructivist analysis of the emergence of a 'bad' norm look like? Would it be any different? Would the actors change? And if they did, what would that mean for their

---

[70] Finnemore and Sikkink acknowledge this in 'Taking Stock', 403.

foundational assumptions about how the argumentative process changes our normative universe? If the analysis were, for example, of anti-Semitism, would Hitler be a norm entrepreneur? Can those in power *be* norm entrepreneurs? It seems strange to exclude them from the calculation of how norms evolve, but this is precisely what the norm evolution models do because of their almost exclusive focus on non-state actors.[71]

The narrowness of the selection of case studies is compounded by the fact that models of norm evolution do not offer concrete prediction. This is because they do not see cause, at least in relation to norms or activist campaigns, as direct: cause is 'permissive and probabilistic'.[72] Norms and campaigns around them make it more likely the norm will evolve but they cannot cause it. They are necessary, but not sufficient conditions. These two factors the choice of particular cases and the concept of cause, mean that empirical analysis is prone to seeing everything as a nail, because all it has is a hammer. And this all leads to the very real possibility that normative accounts suffer from the error of *post hoc ergo propter hoc* logic.[73] That is, because the norm evolved *after* certain actions by groups designated by constructivists as norm entrepreneurs, it must therefore have been *caused by* it. It is only with the regress of the key norm of torture that these deficiencies have come to light.

The role of law in normative backsliding

However, my primary concern here is the law and the role law plays in models of norm evolution. All the flaws discussed above contributed to the failure by norms scholars to see that normative backsliding or de-internalisation were possible. In part this is a consequence of the foundations of constructivist theory, in part it is a consequence of the narrow range of empirical studies conducted by constructivists. But could their assumptions about law also be responsible? Did their inaccurate and flawed idea of law lead them to overstate the torture norm?

All accounts of norm evolution share the idea that norms evolve through a series of stages in which law appears only at the very end.

---

[71] Constructivist work which does not focus on the norm life cycle does see states as affecting norms. See Laffey and Weldes, 'Beyond Belief', 193–237; and Weldes, Laffey, Gusterson and Duvall (eds.), *Cultures of Insecurity*.

[72] Finnemore and Sikkink, 'Taking Stock', 394.

[73] This translates as 'after therefore because of'.

In Finnemore and Sikkink's model law is the final stage; in the spiral model it appears in both the penultimate and final stages. In the penultimate stage there is legalisation, where the emergent norm is enshrined in law, which is followed by the final stage of internalisation. Law is crucial to both. It is through the operation of law, both its symbolic value and its very real capacity to prosecute and punish transgressors, that internalisation is, in part, achieved. Law is both the path to internalisation and evidence of it. Legalisation therefore serves as a synonym for internalisation. Once a norm is legalised the pressure is off and internalisation will inevitably follow. Law then functions as a kind of guarantee: once a norm is legalised it cannot, or at least is very unlikely to, be de-legalised. Legalisation is the gold standard; the ultimate safety net. To a very great extent legalisation and the law are treated as a black box. Constructivism, despite its legally influenced origins, has not thought about law in any sustained or critical way and this has led them to rely upon the common sense idea of law outlined in chapter 2.

The teleology and the assumption of moral progress that pervades the norms literature also have an effect. If norms are implicitly moral and law represents the pinnacle of norm evolution, then law is insulated from possible critique and the constructivist reliance on the common sense idea of law is reinforced. But the reality is that the law not only failed to protect the torture norm: lawyers and the law played a significant role in undermining it. The Bush administration sought to redefine the use of torture by three tactics. First, the 9 January 2002 Yoo Memo categorised Taliban and al-Qaida detainees as 'unlawful enemy combatants', stripping detainees of the protections of the Geneva Protocols. President Bush accepted its conclusions in his memo of 7 February 2002. In the same memo President Bush affirmed that the Geneva Conventions did not apply as a matter of law and only as a matter of policy.[74] But the term 'unlawful enemy combatant' was a fiction, invented by the Office of Legal Counsel (OLC) within the Justice Department.[75] It was specifically created in order to cast detainees into a 'legal black hole'.[76] As John Yoo stated, 'what the Administration is trying to do [in Guantánamo] is create a new legal regime'.[77]

---

[74] Memorandum from President George W. Bush, 'Humane Treatment of al Qaeda and Taliban Detainees', 7 February 2002, in Greenberg and Dratel (eds.), *The Torture Papers*, pp. 134–5.

[75] The OLC provides legal advice to the President and all Executive Branch agencies.

[76] Steyn, 'Guantánamo Bay: The Legal Black Hole', 1.

[77] John Yoo quoted in Sands, *Lawless World*, pp. 153–4.

Secondly, the OLC attempted to justify more aggressive techniques by narrowing the scope of what counts as torture. The August 2002 memo, also known as the Bybee Memo, stated that physical torture: 'must be equivalent in intensity to the pain accompanying serious physical injury, such as organ failure, impairment of bodily function, or even death'.[78] Mental torture 'must result in significant psychological harm of significant duration, e.g., lasting for months or even years'.[79] Because the federal statute does not impose criminal liability for cruel and inhuman punishment, only torture, downgrading a number of interrogation techniques from torture to this designation served to minimise the risk of criminal liability for US officials. Thirdly, the OLC argued that the President, in his capacity as Commander-in-Chief, has an unlimited right to decide upon matters of national security and this includes the treatment of detainees.

These three strategies are underpinned by a broader desire to see 9/ 11 as an exceptional and unprecedented attack which warrants exceptional and unprecedented actions. Ring-fencing the post-9/11 period in this way, and the use of torture which characterises it, serves to legitimise it. However, the desire to recalibrate the relationship between international law and US domestic law did not start with 9/11: it predates it. Right-wing legal scholars like Goldsmith, Rabkin, Yoo and Posner[80] have argued since before 9/11 that international law has crept too far into American domestic law[81] and that it must be rolled back. They argue that the Constitution is superior to international law in every instance[82] and they also assert the need for a strong, unencumbered Presidency to be able to tackle potential threats. But

---

[78] Memorandum from Assistant Attorney General Jay S. Bybee for Alberto R. Gonzales, 1 August 2002, in Greenberg and Dratel (eds.) *The Torture Papers*, p. 176, hereafter the Bybee Memo.

[79] Bybee Memo, p. 172.

[80] Goldsmith, 'Should International Human Rights Law Trump US Domestic Law?', 327–40. Goldsmith argues that domestication of international conventions such as the ICCPR 'would generate enormous litigation and uncertainty, potentially changing domestic civil rights law in manifold ways. Human rights protections in the United States are not remotely so deficient as to warrant these costs ... It would constitute a massive, largely standardless delegation of power to federal courts to rethink the content and scope of nearly every aspect of domestic human rights law' (*ibid*. 332–3). See also, Goldsmith and Posner, *The Limits of International Law* and Rabkin, *The Case for Sovereignty*.

[81] Sinclair and Byers, 'The US, Sovereignty and International Law Since 9/11', 318–40.

[82] Yoo and Posner, 'International Court of Hubris'. See generally the American Enterprise Institute, a right-wing think tank, for other work: www.aei.org.

even prior to the emergence of right-wing legal thinkers who were handed the reins of power by Bush, there has always been a strong American resistance to international law. Raustiala shows how America has always sought to assert its jurisdiction extra-territorially while protecting its own citizens from the jurisdiction of other states.[83]

Nor was the attempt to legally justify systematic torture limited to the OLC. For a start, there is a clear line of responsibility to Secretary of Defense Donald Rumsfeld, if not President Bush.[84] Moreover, the OLC is not a small or insignificant office: it is responsible for giving legal advice to the President and the Executive Branch agencies. Finally, justification of torture spread beyond the OLC. Luban argues that there were over a dozen memoranda pertaining to the status and treatment of detainees circulated between the White House, the Department of Defense, the State Department and the Justice Department.

Despite the systematic nature of torture, or its justification at many levels of the chain of command, many still see torture as limited and exceptional. By ring-fencing the use of torture post-9/11 such thinkers hope to protect the torture norm from challenge. They see the two Bush administrations as anomalous and, now that Bush is no longer president, the torture norm will emerge from its crisis of legitimacy and be reaffirmed. And law can either play a central role in this, or, if change is not forthcoming, can provide a 'site of resistance'.[85] For thinkers like Dunne, the law and the independence of the judiciary can provide the solution.

Ring-fencers also try to paint torture as originating from the bottom up, rather than the top down. Clark argues that the move to torture began with a request by Central Intelligence Agency (CIA) officials to use harsher techniques in their interrogation of Abu Zubaydah. They wanted a clarification of the techniques they could use without violating the Convention Against Torture and implementing federal legislation which makes it a crime to torture under colour of law anywhere

---

[83] Raustiala, 'The Evolution of Territoriality: International Relations and American Law', pp. 219–50. Raustiala states that: 'My primary claim is that the existing pattern of legal spatiality reflects power and interest … But US courts, litigants, Congress, and the Executive have all engaged in instrumental assessments of the benefits and detriments of a reliance on territorial location as a legal principle in particular instances' (p. 220).

[84] Alex Bellamy, David Luban and Philippe Sands all trace responsibility to Rumsfeld at a minimum. See Bellamy, 'No Pain, No Gain?'; Luban, 'Liberalism', *VLR*, 1425–61; Sands, *Torture Team*.

[85] Dunne, '"The Rules of the Game are Changing"', 283.

in the world. Had this request not been made, Clark implies, then the torture memos would not have been written.

But Sands contests this. He sets out specifically to find out whether the desire to torture came from the bottom up or the top down. He argues that the need to clarify what was allowed and what was prohibited was created by the President's decision that Geneva did not apply to detainees. Diane Beaver, the Judge Advocate General who had to sign off on techniques used at Guantánamo, was a junior lawyer, with little experience who was deliberately isolated at Guantánamo, and without proper legal sources. She was also pressured by David Addington, Alberto Gonzales and Jim Haynes, who all went to Guantánamo, to 'do whatever needed to be done' to get results.[86] Beaver's legal advice was 'a fig-leaf: the real but undeclared legal advice came from Bybee and Yoo'.[87] Sands argues that Rumsfeld was not merely responding to a request from Guantánamo but that: 'he and his office were actively involved from an early stage, pressuring and bullying so that a request came'.[88] It was a 'preordained policy of aggression that came from the very top, which the most senior lawyers approved: they gave their names as jurists to cloak the policy with a veneer of legality'.[89]

Similar to the ring-fencing argument is the claim that the torture memos and other legal arguments put forward by the OLC were bad or incorrect law.[90] Luban claims that there is a 'near consensus that the legal analysis in the Bybee Memo was bizarre' and points to the memo's reliance on a health care statute for its definition of torture.[91] He also cites Brooks' argument that the memo 'offers a remarkable example of textual interpretation run amok – less "lawyering as usual" than the work of some bizarre literary deconstructionist'.[92] According to Clark the legal arguments offered in the Bybee Memo are 'so inaccurate that they seem to be arguments about what the authors (or the intended recipients) wanted the law to be rather than assessments of what the law actually is'.[93] She terms it 'indefensible'[94] and argues that Bybee and Yoo breached the ethics rules which apply to all lawyers. According to Clark, they failed to do their ethical duty to give objective legal advice

---

[86] See Sands' interview with Beaver in *Torture Team*, p. 76.   [87] *Ibid.* p. 274.
[88] *Ibid.* p. 274.   [89] *Ibid.* p. 275.
[90] Compare this with the branding of *Plessy* as 'incorrect' law in chapter 4.
[91] Luban, 'Liberalism', *VLR*, 1455.   [92] Brooks quoted in *ibid.* 1455–6.
[93] Clark, 'Ethical Issues', 458.   [94] *Ibid.* 462.

and slipped into legal advocacy, spinning out creative arguments that fit with the finding their client, White House Counsel Alberto Gonzales, wanted to hear.[95] They failed to warn Gonzales that their opinions were not shared by the majority of lawyers and therefore failed to give candid legal advice. However, these ethical rules assume that the client is not a lawyer. It is faintly ridiculous that White House Counsel Gonzales would not have known, at least in outline, what the law on torture was. This leads Luban to speculate that the Bybee Memo was not intended as legal advice at all but was an immunising document, designed to ensure that CIA officials who engaged in torture would be safe from prosecution.[96]

Luban calls this 'loophole lawyering'. The OLC exploited the fact that the United States had only implemented the Torture Convention's prohibition of cruel, inhuman or degrading treatment and not its prohibition on torture. The point of the Bybee Memo was to downgrade torture to cruel, inhuman or degrading treatment because this avoided criminal liability. The OLC also sought to exploit a further loophole to argue that even the prohibition on cruel, inhuman or degrading treatment does not apply extra-territorially.[97] Indeed, as Clark argues, the legal arguments put forward by Bybee were so indefensible that they did not withstand scrutiny and the memo was withdrawn in June 2004 and formally replaced on 30 December 2004 by an opinion by Daniel Levin, the Acting Assistant Attorney General of the OLC. However, the Levin Memo does not significantly alter the legal arguments put forward by Bybee. It retains a very narrow definition of torture, it avoids discussion of the necessity defence and it evades the Commander-in-Chief question and the President's ability to authorise torture.

According to Luban the fact that the Levin Memo replaces and repudiates the Bybee Memo does not matter; indeed, it illustrates even more graphically that the illegality (or not) of torture is shrouded in legal obscurity. 'In other words' he argues, 'from this date forward the mere existence of the Bybee Memo covers the ass of any interrogator who

---

[95] According to Clark this means that Bybee and Yoo violated District of Columbia Rules of Professional Conduct 2.1 (failure to give candid legal advice) and 1.4 (failure to inform their client about the state of the law of torture). *Ibid.* 468.

[96] Luban, 'Liberalism' in Greenberg, p. 55.

[97] This is because when the US ratified the Convention it attached a reservation that interpreted cruel, inhuman or degrading treatment to mean treatment which violates the 5th, 8th or 14th Amendments, none of which applies extra-territorially.

tortures under color of superior orders.'[98] The purpose was to create legal confusion and in that respect the work of the OLC has succeeded in making sure that torture, at least for America, has lost its manifest illegality. A seed of doubt has been sown and this means that legal arguments for and against it are now possible.

Nor does it matter particularly what the Supreme Court has ruled. In *Hamdan* v. *Bush*, the Supreme Court ruled that Geneva was applicable and subsequently the Pentagon reinstated the applicability of Common Article 32 to all detainees to the conflict. Foot argues that while the US court system has 'played a role in reigning in some of the circumstances that have contributed to the abuse',[99] the United States continues to abuse detainee rights, no high-level figure has ever been brought to account for these abuses and hundreds, possibly thousands, remain in black sites. Fiss goes further. He argues that the Supreme Court has done less than it should have and has been cowardly in its decisions. For Fiss, while the Supreme Court judges are committed to the rule of law and the protection of the Constitution, they also see themselves as responsible for protecting the interests of the nation they serve. Their aim therefore was to honour the Constitution without compromising vital national interests.

> As a result, they told Jose Padilla to start over in another court, provided Yaser Hamdi with an opportunity to contest the legality of his classification but made it possible for that hearing to be conducted by a military tribunal, and allowed the prisoners in Guantanamo to begin habeas proceedings without telling them in any clear way what rights they might assert in those proceedings.[100]

The torture memos and the role played by lawyers illustrates the ease with which legal arguments in support of torture can made. It is very tempting to see torture as a transgression of law. Doing so protects the torture norm by arguing that the legal status of torture has not changed and it remains illegal for every state. It also places the blame on the Bush administration and views the law as having been corrupted by a small group of lawyers. The work of the OLC post-9/11 has been characterised by many as simply bad or incorrect law. In a sense this allows normal service to be resumed. But this ring-fencing is inaccurate and responsibility for torture must spread much wider. Responsibility extends to Rumsfeld and possibly to Bush. And as Fiss points out, the

---

[98] Luban, 'Liberalism' in Greenberg, p. 55.   [99] Foot, 'Torture', 141.
[100] Fiss, 'The War Against Terrorism', 256.

expense of forests'.[2] Such an approach also minimises our capacity to see and ask broader questions about the nature of *all* law, be it domestic or international. It is precisely these theoretical, or maybe I should say jurisprudential, questions that need to be addressed. Only by doing so will IR theorists truly understand the nature of law.

Kratochwil and Onuf's work differs from these accounts because both their approaches are explicitly theoretical. Yet there are flaws in their analyses, principally their technical focus. This, I believe, is a consequence of the Habermasian speech act theory that both use to unpack the inter-relationship of norms, language and behaviour. This leads them to create a notion of an intersubjective context that each individual can and does shape, in more or less equal ways. Because each of us is capable of shaping our shared normative universe, we all have roughly equal power and there is no sense of hierarchy within society or individuals who may have disproportionate influence. This focus on the empowered individual also creates an approach in which it is hard to see society-wide prejudices or disempowerment. Arguably this produces an idea of society as consensual. Or such theorisation is a *consequence* of a pre-existing assumption that society is consensual. Indeed, in a consensual, mostly fair society there is no danger in viewing legal rules in a technical manner. Because there is no pressing social injustice to remedy, the law and its practitioners can focus on the fine-tuning of the legal rules that regulate our society.

Clearly, then, this idea of law as essentially benign, and society as consensual and most importantly *just*, substantially overlaps with the common sense idea of law outlined in chapter 2. We have all internalised certain ideas about law and many of these ideas reflect a formalistic understanding of law. While formalism has been largely debunked in jurisprudence, it retains a powerful hold on our collective notions of what law is and how it works – notions that provide the foundations for the constructivist project. By exploring what these ideas are, in both the general ideas that we hold about law providing justice most of the time, to unpicking how we think the everyday business of law operates, chapter 2 started to question their accuracy. This chapter offered alternative, critical explanations and explored a range of theories of legal reasoning. At one extreme there is formalism, at the other radical indeterminacy. Where formalism sees law as the impartial application of neutral rules to disputes, the radical indeterminacy

[2] Kennedy, 'Legal Education as Training for Hierarchy', p. 40.

thesis rejects this idea in its entirety. The certainty and determinacy of formalism is replaced by the idea that there is no necessary connection between what the law says and the legal decision that will be reached. If decisions are random or contingent then the decision is determined by the decision-maker herself and we are left with the reality of one human being deciding the fate of another.

But there is a middle way which argues that the idea of radical indeterminacy actually bears little resemblance to what courts actually do. The idea that judges decide on a whim belies the extent to which they are socialised into a certain legal mindset and this mindset imposes restrictions on judicial caprice. Moreover, radical indeterminacy ignores the extent to which legal professionals are 'true believers': they are committed to justice and the process of deciding between competing interpretations of the facts of a case. Further restrictions are imposed by the nature of legal argumentation and reasoning. A lawyer cannot argue anything she pleases. There are only so many legal arguments possible and even if an argument can be made, this does not mean that it will be convincing. Finally, the innate restrictions of law upon itself lies in its function in society. Thompson argues that social relations, in his case study, class relations, were expressed 'not in any way one likes, but *through the forms of law*'.[3] And the empirical second half of the book gave me the opportunity to assess whether this may be true.

We started with the legal battle for desegregation in America and the landmark decision *Brown* v. *Board of Education*. *Brown* is a beloved political and legal icon and the 'story' of *Brown* tells a powerful message about what law is. In the popular consciousness *Brown* is most straightforwardly the decision that ended segregation and law therefore is cast as the tool that provided justice. But upon closer examination we find *Plessy*: the Supreme Court's 1896 ruling that segregation did not violate the Constitution. Fifty-eight years later, the Supreme Court ruled that it did. There is also a second complicating factor: a competing narrative of *Brown*. In it, the law is not the tool that provided justice to African Americans but the tool that maintained segregation for so long. Law, in Bell's metaphor, allowed the majority to see segregation as though it had 'descended unwanted from the skies and can now be mopped up like a heavy rainfall and flushed away'.[4] But what would be a more accurate depiction of law? That it solved racism in America in a single decision or that it was

---

[3] Thompson, *Whigs and Hunters*, p. 262. [4] Bell, 'Dissenting Opinion', p. 196.

complicit in racism for centuries before that? Which law do we look at? The law before or after 17 May 1954? Even after *Brown*, desegregation was slow; a deliberate slowness mandated by *Brown II*. Significant desegregation did not start until at least a decade later. And while *Brown* instituted *de jure* desegregation and imposed it through the deeply unpopular bussing, *de facto* economic segregation has since returned to America's schools. Perhaps what the beloved icon of *Brown* should teach us is that law may not be able to solve complex social phenomena as deeply entrenched as racism.

This possibility is taken up by the case of rape legislation and reform in the United Kingdom. Again, there are two competing narratives at play here, and I argue that it is the *perception* of the legal treatment of rape that has dictated reform, rather than the reality. After thirty-five years of consistent reform, the rape problem has yet to be solved and, if anything, has worsened during that time. In *Brown* discrimination existed at, and was removed from, the level of words. This was how justice was achieved. Where the legal treatment of rape is concerned, such bias has been gradually removed: it is now illegal for a husband to rape his wife, belief in consent must be reasonable and so on but the injustice remains. But re-jigging the wording of the law has not succeeded in solving the rape problem and attention has turned to the nature of the legal system itself.

In the first narrative the problem with rape is specific to it: we do not see the same problems in other crimes. The solution therefore is to alter the law and the legal system. The latest incarnation of this approach is educating the jury in order to dispel 'rape myths' – inaccurate perceptions, held by the public, about rape and how a genuine rape victim would react and the evidence she would present. The second narrative, however, disputes the idea that the problem with rape is specific to it. Instead, the cause of the rape problem lies in the nature of the legal system itself and all crimes are similarly affected. This is not to say that rape does or should have the same conviction or attrition rate as other crimes: rape is clearly different in that respect. Rather, the cause of the difference between rape and other crimes does not lie in the legal system. Law treats all complainants roughly: rape complainants are treated no worse than anyone else and cross-examination which accuses the complainant of lying is common to both rape and assault trials. And if this is true can legal reform ever solve the rape problem?

However, while all lawyers employ standard 'tools of the trade' to discredit witnesses, in rape trials defence counsel do tend to exploit patriarchal ideas in order to win. Or to put it differently, lawyers use the (assumed) prejudice of the jury in order to win. Indeed, the focus of the government's latest initiative on juror education certainly seems to be a recognition that the problem might not be the law but society itself.[5] Thus, we find ourselves again faced with the limited capacity of law to deal with embedded, society-wide prejudices. And if law lacks this capacity, the question is: does this fundamentally undermine either the common sense idea of law or the more sophisticated 'middle-way' of limited indeterminacy? Is expecting the law to solve such complex problems asking too much? And if it is, what does this mean for 'justice'? Can justice be limited or partial? Can entire swathes of society be denied justice and it still be meaningful to believe that law can and does produce justice?

And so we return again to constructivism and the book's *raison d'être*. The interceding chapters have worked towards identifying and re-evaluating IR's ideas about law. Why? Because IR theorists are not, on the whole, legally trained. And this makes us prone to falling back on the common sense idea of law, in my opinion, colouring our analysis. The case of the torture norm allows me to unpick what this tendency means for our ability to explain international politics.

I argue, first, that part of constructivism's inaccurate idea of law is caused by its theoretical foundations. The focus on language and articulation has created a tendency to view law technically, in the same way that non-legal rules are treated technically. Similarly the individualism of Kratochwil and Onuf's work has produced a strong notion of agency and a weak notion of structure. These have combined in the norms literature to place a heavy reliance on norm entrepreneurs: activists who build norms and see them through to internalisation. And the process of norm evolution functions like a ratchet: each stage builds upon the preceding one but evolution does not run backwards. It would be meaningless to speak of 'de-evolution' and so the model of norm evolution does not consider the possibility that a norm

---

[5] I refer here to the Labour government. The Coalition came to power at the very end of this book but early indications are that it intends to pursue a very different approach to rape, focusing instead on the plight of the falsely accused. To do so misunderstands the nature of the rape problem. The plight of the falsely accused is not a cause but a symptom: a symptom of a legal system where an acquittal for rape is little indication of innocence.

could run backwards. The process may stop, but it does not reverse. Law is crucial to both legalisation and internalisation. It is through the operation of law, both its symbolic value and its very real capacity to prosecute and punish transgressors, that internalisation is, in part, achieved. Law is both the path to internalisation and evidence of it, and therefore serves as a synonym for internalisation. Once a norm is legalised internalisation will inevitably follow. To a very great extent legalisation and the law are treated as a black box. Constructivism, despite its legally influenced origins, has not thought about law in any sustained or critical way and this has led it to rely upon the common sense idea of law.

And it is in its perception of law that constructivism bears the imprint of the common sense idea of law. Law is seen as (a) good. It is 'a force of linear progress, a beacon to lead us out of darkness':[6] the darkness of politics. In this respect more sophisticated constructivist ideas of law stray towards the middle way: that you cannot argue anything you like (and win). But the case of torture powerfully challenges this assumption. The Office of Legal Counsel *did* argue precisely what it wanted. The prohibition on torture was absolute and the legal norm against torture has achieved the highest level of legal normativity: torture was a peremptory legal norm from which no derogation is permitted. It is almost impossible to find an international legal norm of comparable strength. And yet it was overturned with shocking ease. And what is most striking is that its overturning happened *because of and through the forms of law*. The law and its method were sufficiently flexible to justify that which it prohibited. The restrictions upon which we have come to rely may not be as powerful as we would hope, nor give law the capacity to solve society-wide injustice. Relying upon the assumption that law contains within it the seeds of its own limitation, and thereby justice, produces questionable theory.

[6] Smart, *Feminism and the Power of Law*, p. 12.

BIBLIOGRAPHY

Abbott, K. W., Keohane, R. O., Moravcsik, A., Slaughter, A.-M. and Snidal, D., 'The Concept of Legalization', *International Organization*, 54(3) (2000), 401–19.

Abbott, K. W. and Snidal, D., 'Hard and Soft Law in International Governance', *International Organization*, 54(3) (2000), 421–56.

Adams, J. N. and Brownsword, R., *Understanding Law*, 4th edn (London: Sweet and Maxwell, 2006).

Adler, Z., *Rape on Trial* (London: Routledge & Kegan Paul, 1987).

Alexandrowicz, C. H. (ed.), *Studies in the History of the Law of Nations* (The Hague: Martinus Nijhoff, 1970).

Allison, J. A., and Wrightsman, L. S., *Rape: The Misunderstood Crime* (London: SAGE Publications, 1993).

Alston, P., 'Conjuring Up New Human Rights: A Proposal for Quality Control', *American Journal of International Law*, 78 (1984), 607–21.

Alston, P., 'Review Essay: Transplanting Foreign Norms: Human Rights and Other International Legal Norms in Japan', *European Journal of International Law*, 10 (1999), 625–32.

Armstrong, D., Farrell, T. and Lambert, H., *International Law and International Relations* (Cambridge University Press, 2007).

Balkin, J. M. (ed.), *What* Brown v. Board of Education *Should Have Said: The Nations' Top Legal Experts Rewrite America's Landmark Civil Rights Decisions* (New York University Press, 2001).

Barnett, H., *Introduction to Feminist Jurisprudence* (London: Cavendish Publishing Limited, 1998).

Beirne, P. and Quinney, R., *Marxism and Law* (Chichester: John Wiley & Sons, 1982).

Bell, D. A. Jr., '*Brown v. Board of Education* and the Interest-Convergence Dilemma', *Harvard Law Review* 93 (1980), 518–33.

Bell, D. A., 'Dissenting Opinion' in J. M. Balkin (ed.), *What* Brown v. Board of Education *Should Have Said: The Nations' Top Legal Experts Rewrite America's Landmark Civil Rights Decisions* (New York University Press, 2001), pp. 185–200.

Bell, D. A., *Silent Covenants:* Brown v. Board of Education *and the Unfulfilled Hopes for Racial Reform* (Oxford University Press, 2004).

Bellamy, A. J., 'No Pain, No Gain? Torture and Ethics in the War on Terror', *International Affairs*, 82(1) (2006), 121–48.

Berman, H. J., *Law and Revolution: The Formation of the Western Legal Tradition* (London: Harvard University Press, 1983).

Bix, B., *Jurisprudence: Theory and Context*, 3rd edn (London: Sweet & Maxwell, 2003).

Blair, I., *Investigating Rape: A New Approach for Police* (London: Croom Helm, 1985).

Blakeley, R., 'Why Torture?', *Review of International Studies*, 33 (2007), 373–94.

Breitman, G. (ed.), *Malcolm X Speaks* (London: Seeker & Warburg, 1965).

Brereton, D., 'How Different are Rape Trials? A Comparison of the Cross-examination of Complainants in Rape and Assault Trials', *British Journal of Criminology*, 37(2) (1997), 242–61.

Burke, V. and Selfe, D., *Perspectives on Sex, Crime and Society* (London: Cavendish Publishing Limited, 1998).

Burns, H. W., 'Law and Race in America' in D. Kairys, *The Politics of Law: A Progressive Critique* (New York: Pantheon Books, 1982), pp. 89–95.

Byers, M., *Custom, Power and the Power of Rules: International Relations and Customary International Law* (Cambridge University Press, 1999).

Byers, M. (ed.), *The Role of Law in International Politics* (Oxford University Press, 2000).

Cain, M. and Harrington, C. B., (eds.) *Lawyers in a Postmodern World: Translation and Transgression* (Milton Keynes: Open University Press, 1994).

Cain, M. and Hunt, A., *Marx and Engels on Law* (London: Academic Press, 1979).

Calhoun, L., Selby, J., Cann, A. and Keller, T., 'The Effects of Victim Physical Attractiveness and Sex of Respondent on Social Relations to Victims of Rape', *British Journal of Social and Clinical Psychology*, 17 (1978), 191–2.

Carr, E. H., *The Twenty Years' Crisis: 1919–1939*, 2nd edn (London: Macmillan, 1946).

Carter, A., *Direct Action and Liberal Democracy* (London: Routledge, 1973).

Carty, A., *The Decay of International Law: A Reappraisal of the Limits of Legal Imagination in International Affairs* (Manchester University Press, 1986).

Cassese, A., *International Law* (Oxford University Press, 2001).

Charlesworth, H. and Chinkin, C., *The Boundaries of International Law: A Feminist Analysis* (Manchester University Press, 2000).

Chayes, A., *The Cuban Missile Crisis* (Oxford University Press, 1974).

Clark, K., 'Ethical Issues Raised by the OLC Torture Memorandum', *Journal of National Security, Law and Policy*, 1 (2005), 455–72.

Coleman, J. L. and Shapiro, S. (eds.), *The Oxford Handbook of Jurisprudence and Philosophy of Law* (Oxford University Press, 2004).

Collins, H., *Marxism and Law* (Oxford: Clarendon Press, 1982).

Collins, H., 'The Decline of Privacy in Private Law' in P. Fitzpatrick and A. Hunt (eds.), *Critical Legal Studies* (Oxford: Blackwell, 1987), pp. 91–103.

Cook, R. J. (ed.), *Human Rights of Women: National and International Perspectives* (Philadelphia: University of Pennsylvania Press, 1994).

Cook, R., *Sweet Land of Liberty? The African-American Struggle for Civil Rights in the Twentieth Century* (London: Longman, 1998).

Copelon, R., 'Intimate Terror: Understanding Domestic Violence as Torture' in R. J. Cook (ed.), *Human Rights of Women: National and International Perspectives* (Philadelphia: University of Pennsylvania Press, 1994), pp. 116–52.

Cotterrell, R., 'Power, Property and the Law of Trusts: A Partial Agenda for Critical Legal Scholarship' in P. Fitzpatrick and A. Hunt (eds.), *Critical Legal Studies* (Oxford: Blackwell, 1987), pp. 77–90.

Cotterrell, R., *The Politics of Jurisprudence: A Critical Introduction to Legal Philosophy* (London: Butterworths, 1989).

Cotterrell, R., *The Sociology of Law: An Introduction* (London: Butterworth & Co., 1984).

Council of HM Circuit Judges, 'Convicting Rapist and Protecting Victim: A Consultation' (Response of the Council of HM Circuit Judges, 2006).

Crawford, N. C., 'Decolonization as an International Norm: The Evolution of Practices, Arguments, and Beliefs' in L. W. Reed and C. Kaysen, *Emerging Norms of Justified Intervention* (Cambridge, MA: American Academy of Arts and Sciences, 1993), pp. 37–61.

Criminal Bar Association, Response to Consultation Paper, 'Convicting Rapists and Protecting Victims' (London: Criminal Bar Association, 2006).

Cuklanz, L. M., *Rape on Trial: How the Mass Media Construct Legal Reform and Social Change* (Philadelphia: University of Pennsylvania Press, 1996).

Davies, M., *Asking the Law Question* (London: Sweet & Maxwell, 1994).

DeLaMothe, C. M., 'Liberta Revisited: A Call to Repeal the Marital Exemption for All Sex Offenses in New York's Penal Law', *Fordham Urban Law Journal*, 23 (1996), 857–97.

Dershowitz, A., 'Tortured Reasoning' in S. Levinson (ed.), *Torture: A Collection* (Oxford University Press, 2004), pp. 257–80.

Doherty, M., *Jurisprudence: The Philosophy of Law*, 2nd edn (London: Old Bailey Press, 2001).

Donnelly, J., 'Human Rights: A New Standard of Civilisation?', *International Affairs*, 74(1) (1998), 1–23.

Du Bois, W. E. B., 'Does the Negro Need Separate Schools?' extracted in W. E. Martin, *Brown v. Board of Education: A Brief History with Documents* (Boston, MA: Bedford/St. Martins, 1998).

Dudziak, M. L., 'Desegregation as a Cold War Imperative', *Stanford Law Review*, 41 (1988), 61–120.

Dunne, T., '"The Rules of the Game are Changing": Fundamental Human Rights in Crisis After 9/11', *International Politics*, 44 (2007), 269–86.

Dworkin, R., *Law's Empire* (London: Fontana Press, 1986).

Dworkin, R., *Taking Rights Seriously* (London: Duckworth, 1977).

Dyzenhaus, D., *Legality and Legitimacy: Carl Schmitt, Hans Kelsen and Hermann Heller in Weimar* (Oxford: Clarendon Press, 1997).

Ellison, L., 'Closing the Credibility Gap: the Prosecutorial Use of Expert Witness Testimony in Sexual Assault Cases', *International Journal of Evidence and Proof*, 9 (2005), 239–68.

Ellison, L., 'Cross-examination in Rape Trials', *Criminal Law Review* (September 1998), 605–15.

Ellison, L., 'Witness Preparation and the Prosecution of Rape', *Legal Studies*, 27(2) (2007), 171–87.

Ellison, L. and Munro, V., 'Reacting to Rape: Exploring Mock Jurors' Assessments of Complainant Credibility', *British Journal of Criminology*, 49 (2009), 202–19.

Ellison, L. and Munro, V., 'Turning Mirrors into Windows? Assessing the Impact of (Mock) Juror Education in Rape Trials', *British Journal of Criminology*, 49 (2009), 363–83.

Falk, R., *Legal Order in a Violent World* (Princeton University Press, 1968).

Farrar, J. H. and Dugdale, A. M., *Introduction to Legal Method*, 3rd edn (London: Sweet & Maxwell, 1990).

Fearon, J. D. and Laitin, D. D., 'Violence and the Social Construction of Ethnic Identity', *International Organization*, 54(4) (2000), 845–77.

Fine, B., 'Law and Class' in B. Fine, R. Kinsey, J. Lea, S. Picciotto and J. Young (eds.), *Capitalism and the Rule of Law: From Deviancy Theory to Marxism* (London: Hutchinson, 1979), pp. 29–45.

Fine, B., Kinsey, R., Lea, J., Picciotto, S. and Young, J. (eds.), *Capitalism and the Rule of Law: From Deviancy Theory to Marxism* (London: Hutchinson, 1979).

Fine, B. and Millar, R. (eds.), *Policing the Miners' Strike* (London: Lawrence & Wishart, 1985).

Finley, L. M., 'Breaking Women's Silence in Law: The Dilemma of the Gendered Nature of Legal Reasoning', *Notre Dame Law Review*, 64 (1989), 838–85.

Finnemore, M. and Sikkink, K., 'International Norm Dynamics and Political Change', *International Organization*, 52(4) (1998), 887–917.

Finnemore, M. and Sikkink, K., 'Taking Stock: The Constructivist Research Program in International Relations and Comparative Politics', *Annual Review of Political Science*, 4 (2001), 391–416.

Finnemore, M. and Toope, S. J., 'Alternatives to "Legalization": Richer Views of Law and Politics', *International Organization*, 55(3) (2001), 743–58.

Fiss, O., 'Objectivity and Interpretation', *Stanford Law Review*, 34 (1982), 739–63.

Fiss, O., 'The War Against Terrorism and the Rule of Law', *Oxford Journal of Legal Studies*, 26(2) (2006), 235–56.

Fitzpatrick, P. and Hunt, A. (eds.), *Critical Legal Studies* (Oxford: Blackwell, 1987).

Foot, R., 'Torture: The Struggle over a Peremptory Norm in a Counter-terrorist Era', *International Relations*, 20 (2006), 131–50.

Franck, T. M., *The Power of Legitimacy Among Nations* (Oxford University Press, 1990).

Frank, J., 'Are Judges Human? Part One: The Effect on Legal Thinking of the Assumption That Judges Behave Like Human Beings', *University of Pennsylvania Law Review*, 80(1) (1931), 17–53.

Frank, J., 'Are Judges Human? Part Two: As Through a Class Darkly', *University of Pennsylvania Law Review*, 80(2) (1931), 233–67.

Frank, J., *Courts on Trial* (Princeton University Press, 1973).

Freeman, M. D. A., *Lloyd's Introduction to Jurisprudence*, 6th edn (London: Sweet & Maxwell, 1994).

Freestone, D. and Davidson, S., 'Nuclear Weapon-Free Zones' in I. Pogany (ed.), *Nuclear Weapons and International Law* (Aldershot: Avebury, 1987), pp. 176–216.

Fukuyama, F., *The End of History and the Last Man* (Harmondsworth: Penguin, 1992).

Fuller, L. L., *The Morality of Law* (New Haven: Yale University Press, 1969).

Fuller, L. L., 'The Speluncean Explorers', in M. D. A. Freeman, *Lloyd's Introduction to Jurisprudence*, 6th edn (London: Sweet & Maxwell, 1994), pp. 61–71.

Gabel, P. and Feinman, J. M., 'Contract Law as Ideology' in D. Kairys, *The Politics of Law: A Progressive Critique* (New York: Pantheon Books, 1982), pp. 172–84.

Garcia, I. and Salter, K. W., *The Trial of Inez Garcia* (Berkeley, CA: Editorial Justa Publications, 1976).

Gibb, F., 'Beware Rape Myths, Judges to Tell Jurors' *The Times*, 15 June 2009.

Glennon, R. J., 'The Role of Law in the Civil Rights Movement: The Montgomery Bus Boycott, 1955–57', *Law and History Review*, 9(1) (Spring 1991), 59–112.

Goldsmith, J., 'Should International Human Rights Law Trump US Domestic Law?', *Chicago Journal of International Law*, 1 (2000), 327–40.

Goldsmith, J. L. and Posner, E. A., *The Limits of International Law* (Oxford University Press, 2005).

Goodrich, P., *Reading the Law: A Critical Introduction to Legal Methods and Techniques* (Oxford: Basil Blackwell, 1986).

Goodwin, B., *Using Political Ideas*, 4th edn (Chichester: John Wiley & Sons, 1997).

Gordon, R. W., 'Critical Legal Histories', *Stanford Law Review*, 36 (1984), 57–125.

Gordon, R. W., 'Law and Ideology', *Tikkun*, 3(1) (1988), 14–18 and 83–6.

Gordon, R. W., 'New Developments in Legal Theory' in D. Kairys, *The Politics of Law: A Progressive Critique* (New York: Pantheon Books, 1982), pp. 281–93.

Gowlland-Debbas, V., 'The Functions of the United Nations Security Council in the International Legal System' in M. Byers (ed.), *The Role of Law in International Politics* (Oxford University Press, 2000), pp. 277–313.

Gray, F., *Bus Ride to Justice: Changing the System by the System. The Life and Works of Fred D. Gray* (Montgomery: New South Books, 1995).

Gray, J., *Liberalism* (Milton Keynes: Open University Press, 1986).

Graycar, R. (ed.), *Dissenting Opinions: Feminist Explorations in Law and Society* (Sydney: Allen & Unwin, 1990).

Greenberg, J., *Crusaders in the Courts: How a Dedicated Band of Lawyers Fought for the Civil Rights Revolution* (New York: Basic Books, 1994).

Greenberg, K. (ed.), *The Torture Debate in America* (Cambridge University Press, 2006).

Greenberg, K. and Dratel, J. L. (eds.), *The Torture Papers: The Road to Abu Ghraib* (Cambridge University Press, 2005).

Greer, E., 'Antonio Gramsci and "Legal Hegemony"' in D. Kairys, *The Politics of Law: A Progressive Critique* (New York: Pantheon Books, 1982), pp. 304–9.

Greer, G., 'A Phallocentric View of Sexual Violence' *Guardian*, 3 April 1995, p. 20.

Greer, G., 'Call Rape by Another Name' *Guardian*, 6 March 1995, p. 20.

Greer, G., 'The Refusal to be Bowed by Brutality' *Guardian*, 20 March 1995, p. 18.

Gregory, J. and Lees, S., 'Attrition in Rape and Sexual Assault Cases', *British Journal of Criminology*, 36 (1996), 1–17.

Gregory, J. and Lees, S., *Policing Sexual Assault* (London: Routledge, 1999).

Grigg-Spall, I. and Ireland, P., *The Critical Lawyers' Handbook* (London: Pluto Press, 1992).

Habermas, J., *The Theory of Communicative Action, Volume 1: Reason and the Rationalization of Society*, translated by T. McCarthy (Boston: Beacon Press, 1984).

Hägerström, A., *Inquiries into the Nature of Law and Morals*, edited by K. Olivecrona and translated by C. D. Broad (Stockholm: Almqvist & Wiksell, 1953).

Hamilton, C. V., 'Federal Law and the Courts in the Civil Rights Movement' in C. W. Eagles, *The Civil Rights Movement in America* (Jackson and London: University Press of Mississippi, 1986), pp. 97–117.

Hampsher-Monk, I., *A History of Modern Political Thought: Major Political Thinkers from Hobbes to Marx* (Oxford: Blackwell, 1992).

Harris, J. and Grace, S., *A Question of Evidence? Investigating and Prosecuting Rape in the 1990s*, Home Office Research Study 196 (London: HMSO, 1999).

Harris, J. W., *Legal Philosophies* (London: Butterworths, 1980).

Harris, P., *An Introduction to Law*, 7th edn (Cambridge University Press, 2007).

Hart, H. L. A., *Law, Liberty and Morality* (Oxford University Press, 1963).

Hart, H. L. A., 'Positivism and the Separation of Law and Morals' in *Essays in Jurisprudence and Philosophy* (Oxford: Clarendon Press, 1983).

Hart, H. L. A., *The Concept of Law*, 2nd edn (Oxford: Clarendon Press, 1994).

Hayek, F. A., *Constitution of Liberty* (London: Routledge, 1960).

Henkin, L., 'Comment' in A. Chayes, *The Cuban Missile Crisis* (Oxford University Press, 1974), pp. 149–54.

Higgins, R., *Problems and Process: International Law and How We Use It* (Oxford: Clarendon Press, 1994).

HMCPSI and HMIC, *A Report on the Joint Inspection into the Investigation and Prosecution of Cases Involving Allegations of Rape* (London: Home Office, 2002) available at http://inspectorates.homeoffice.gov.uk/hmic/inspections/thematic/aor/them02-aor.pdf?view=Binary (accessed July 2009).

HMIC and HMCPSI, *Without Consent: HMCPSI and HMIC Thematic Report* (London: Home Office, 2007).

Holland, J. A. and Webb, J. S., *Learning Legal Rules*, 3rd edn (London: Blackstone Press, 1996).

Holmes, O. W., 'The Path of the Law', *Harvard Law Review*, 10(8) (1897), 457–78.

Holmas, O. W., *The Comman Law* (American Bar Association, 2009).

Home Office, *Convicting Rapists and Protecting Victims: Justice for Victims of Rape* (London: Home Office, 2006).

Honderich, T., 'Hierarchic Democracy and the Necessity of Mass Civil Disobedience', *Conway Memorial Lecture* at the South Place Ethical Society (London: Aldgate Press, 1995).

Hunt, A., 'The Critique of Law: What is Critical about Critical Legal Theory?' in P. Fitzpatrick and A. Hunt (eds.), *Critical Legal Studies* (Oxford: Blackwell, 1987), pp. 5–19.

Hunt, A., *The Sociological Movement in Law* (London: Macmillan, 1978).

Hunt, A. and Wickham, G., *Foucault and Law: Towards a Sociology of Law as Governance* (London: Pluto Press, 1994).

Hurrell, A., 'International Law and the Changing Constitution of International Society' in M. Byers (ed.), *The Role of Law in International Politics* (Oxford University Press, 2000), pp. 327–47.

Hutchings, K., 'Political Theory and Cosmopolitan Citizenship' in K. Hutchings and R. Dannreuther (eds.), *Cosmopolitan Citizenship* (London: Macmillan, 1999), pp. 3–32.

Hutchinson, A. C. and Monahan, P. J., 'Law, Politics, and the Critical Legal Scholars: The Unfolding Drama of American Legal Thought', *Stanford Law Review*, 36 (1984), 199–245.

Hutchinson, A. C. and Monahan, P. J., *The Rule of Law: Ideal or Ideology* (Toronto: Carswell, 1987).

Hutchings, K. and Dannreuther, R. (eds.), *Cosmopolitan Citizenship* (London: Macmillan, 1999).

Huysmans, J., 'International Politics of Insecurity: Normativity, Inwardness and the Exception', *Security Dialogue*, 37 (2006), 11–29.

Isin, E. F. and Turner, B. S. (eds.), *Handbook of Citizenship Studies* (London: Sage, 2002).

Kairys, D., 'Legal Reasoning' in D. Kairys, *The Politics of Law: A Progressive Critique* (New York: Pantheon Books, 1982), pp. 11–17.

Kairys, D., *The Politics of Law: A Progressive Critique* (New York: Pantheon Books, 1982).

Kalven, H. Jr. and Zeisel, H., *The American Jury* (Boston: Little Brown, 1966).

Katzenstein, P. J. (ed.), *The Culture of National Security: Norms and Identity in World Politics* (New York: Columbia University Press, 1996).

Keck, M. and Sikkink, K., *Activists Beyond Borders: Advocacy Networks in International Politics* (Ithaca: Cornell University Press, 1998).

Kelley, R. D. G., '"We Are Not What We Seem": Rethinking Black Working-Class Opposition in the Jim Crow South', *The Journal of American History*, 80(1) (June 1993), 75–112.

Kelly, L., Lovett, J. and Regan, L., *A Gap or a Chasm? Attrition in Reported Rape Cases*, Home Office Research Study 293 (London: HMSO, 2005).

Kelman, M. G., 'Trashing', *Stanford Law Review*, 36 (1984), 293–348.

Kelman, M. G., *A Guide to Critical Legal Studies* (Cambridge, MA: Harvard University Press, 1987).

Kennedy, D., 'Legal Education as Training for Hierarchy' in D. Kairys, *The Politics of Law: A Progressive Critique* (New York: Pantheon Books, 1982), pp. 40–61.

Kennedy, H., *Eve was Framed: Women and British Justice* (London: Chatto & Windus, 1992).

King, M. L., *Stride Towards Freedom: The Montgomery Story* (New York: Harper & Row, 1958).

King, M. L., *Why We Can't Wait* (New York: Signet Books, 1964).

Klare, K. E., 'Critical Theory and Labour Relations Law' in D. Kairys, *The Politics of Law: A Progressive Critique* (New York: Pantheon Books, 1982), pp. 65–88.

Klarman, M. J., *From Jim Crow to Civil Rights: The Supreme Court and the Struggle for Racial Equality* (Oxford University Press, 2004).

Klarman, M. J., 'How *Brown* Changed Race Relations: The Backlash Thesis', *Journal of American History*, 81(1) (June 1994), 81–118.

Klotz, A., *Norms in International Relations: The Struggle Against Apartheid* (London: Cornell University Press, 1995).

Klotz, A., 'Norms Reconstituting Interests: Global Racial Equality and US Sanctions Against South Africa', *International Organization*, 49(3) (1995), 451–78.

Klotz, A., 'Transnational Activism and Global Transformations: The Anti-Apartheid and Abolitionist Experiences', *European Journal of International Relations*, 8(1) (2002), 49–76.

Kluger, J., *Simple Justice: The History of* Brown v. Board of Education *and Black America's Struggle for Equality* (London: Deutsch, 1977).

Koskenniemi, M., *From Apology to Utopia: The Structure of International Legal Argument* (Helsinki: Finnish Lawyers' Publishing Company, 1989).

Koskenniemi, M., *The Gentle Civiliser of Nations* (Cambridge University Press, 2001).

Koslowski, R. and Kratochwil, F. V., 'Understanding Change in International Politics: the Soviet Empire's Demise and the International System', *International Organization*, 48 (1994), 215–47.

Kratochwil, F. V., 'How Do Norms Matter?' in M. Byers (ed.), *The Role of Law in International Politics* (Oxford University Press, 2000), pp. 35–68.

Kratochwil, F. V., *Rules, Norms, and Decisions: On the Conditions of Practical and Legal Reasoning in International Relations and Domestic Affairs* (Cambridge University Press, 1989).

Kratochwil, F. V. 'Rules, Norms, Values and the Limits of "Rationality"', *Archiv für Rechts- und Sozialphilosophie*, 73 (1987), 301–29.

Kratochwil, F. V., 'Sovereignty as *Dominium*: Is There a Right of Humanitarian Intervention?' in G. M. Lyons and M. Mastanduno, *Beyond Westphalia? State Sovereignty and International Intervention* (Baltimore: Johns Hopkins University Press, 1995), pp. 21–42.

Kratochwil, F. V., 'Thrasymachos Revisited: on the Relevance of Norms of International Relations', *Journal of International Affairs*, 37 (1984), 343–56.

Kurki, M., *Causation in International Relations: Reclaiming Causal Analysis* (Cambridge University Press, 2008).

Lacey, N., 'Beset by Boundaries: the Home Office Review of Sexual Offences', *Criminal Law Review* (January 2001), 1–14.

Laffey, M. and Weldes, J., 'Beyond Belief: Ideas and Symbolic Technologies on the Study of International Relations', *European Journal of International Relations*, 3(2) (1997), 193–237.

Laville, S., 'Rape Conviction Rates Remain Near Record Low' *Guardian*, 20 July 2007.

Lees, S., *Carnal Knowledge: Rape on Trial* (London: The Women's Press, 2002).

Lees, S., 'Rape on Trial' *Guardian*, 9 March 1995.

Lees, S., 'Small Steps Toward a Fairer Law' *Guardian*, 7 April 2000.

Lees, S., 'What Should You Do if a Man is About to Rape You?' *Guardian*, 17 August 2000.

Levinson, S. (ed.), *Torture: A Collection* (Oxford University Press, 2004).

Liberty, *Liberty's Response to the Consultation Convicting Rapists and Protecting Victims* (London: Liberty, 2006).

Linklater, A., 'Cosmopolitan Citizenship' in K. Hutchings and R. Dannreuther (eds.), *Cosmopolitan Citizenship* (London: Macmillan, 1999), pp. 35–59.

Linklater, A., 'Cosmopolitan Political Communities in International Relations', *International Relations*, 16(1) (2002), 135–50.

Linklater, A., 'Torture and Civilisation', *International Relations*, 21 (2007), 111–18.

Llewellyn, K. N., *Jurisprudence: Realism in Theory and Practice* (Chicago: University Press, 1962).

Llewellyn, K. N., *The Bramble Bush: On Our Law and its Study* (New York: Oceana Publications Inc., 1951).

Lloyd, D., *The Idea of Law* (Middlesex: Penguin Books, 1983).

Locke, J., *Two Treatises of Government* edited by P. Laslett, student edition (Cambridge University Press, 1988).

Lomax, L. E., *To Kill a Black Man: The Shocking Parallel Lives of Malcolm X and Martin Luther King Jr.* (Los Angeles, CA: Holloway House, 1968).

Loriaux, M. and Lynch, C. (eds.) *Law and Moral Action in World Politics* (University of Minnesota Press, 2000).

Luban, D., 'Liberalism, Torture, and the Ticking Bomb', *Virginia Law Review*, 91(6) (2005), 1425–61.

Luban, D., 'Liberalism, Torture, and the Ticking Bomb' in K. J. Greenberg, *The Torture Debate in America* (Cambridge University Press, 2006), pp. 35–83.

Lumsdaine, D. H., *Moral Vision: The Foreign Aid Regime 1949–1989* (Princeton University Press, 1993).

MacCormick, N., *Legal Reasoning and Legal Theory* (Oxford: Clarendon Press, 1978).

MacCormick, N., 'Rhetoric and the Rule of Law' in A. C. Hutchinson and P. Monahan (eds.), *The Rule of Law: Ideal or Ideology* (Toronto: Carswell, 1987), pp. 163–77.

MacKinnon, C. A., *Feminism Unmodified: Discourses on Life and Law* (London: Harvard University Press, 1987).

MacKinnon, C. A., *Toward a Feminist Theory of the State* (London: Harvard University Press, 1989).

MacMaster, N., 'Torture: From Algiers to Abu Ghraib', *Race and Class*, 46(2) (2004), 1–21.

Mansell, W., Meteyard, B. and Thomson, A., *A Critical Introduction to Law* (London: Cavendish Publishing, 1995).

Martin, W. E.Jr., *Brown v. Board of Education: A Brief History with Documents* (Boston, MA: Bedford/St. Martins, 1998).

Matoesian, G. M., *Law and the Language of Identity: Discourse in the William Kennedy Smith Rape Trial* (Oxford University Press, 2001).

Matoesian, G. M., *Reproducing Rape: Domination Through Talk in the Courtroom* (Chicago: University of Chicago Press, 1993).

Matoesian, G. M., *Reproducing Rape: Domination Through Talk in the Courtroom* (London: Polity Press, 1993).

McBarnet, D., 'Victim in the Witness Box: Confronting Victimology's Stereotype', *Contemporary Crises*, 7 (1983), 293–303.

McColgan, A., *Women Under the Law: The False Promise of Human Rights* (Harlow: Longman, 2000).

McKeown, R., 'Norm Regress: US Revisionism and the Slow Death of the Torture Norm', *International Relations*, 23(1) (2009), 5–25.

McLeod, I., *Legal Method*, 2nd edn (London: Macmillan, 1996).

McLeod, I., *Legal Theory* (London: Macmillan, 1999).

Mensch, E., 'The History of Mainstream Legal Thought' in D. Kairys, *The Politics of Law: A Progressive Critique* (New York: Pantheon Books, 1982), pp. 18–39.

Miller, D., 'Bounded Citizenship' in K. Hutchings and R. Dannreuther (eds.), *Cosmopolitan Citizenship* (London: Macmillan, 1999), pp. 60–80.

Minow, M., 'Stripped Like a Runner or Enriched by Experience: Bias and Impartiality of Judges and Jurors', *William and Mary Law Review*, 33 (1991–1992), 1201–18.

Morgenthau, H. J., *Politics Among Nations: The Struggle for Power and Peace*, brief edition, revised by K. W. Thompson (London: McGraw-Hill, Inc., 1993).

Morreall, J., 'The Justifiability of Violent Civil Disobedience' in H. A. Bedau (ed.), *Civil Disobedience in Focus* (London: Routledge, 1991), pp. 130–43.

Morrision, W., *Jurisprudence: From the Greeks to Post-modernism* (London: Cavendish Publishing Ltd, 1997).

Myhill, A. and Allen, J., *Rape and Sexual Assault of Women: Findings from the British Crime Survey*, Home Office Research Findings 159 (London: Home Office, 2002).

Nadelman, E., 'Global Prohibition Regimes: The Evolution of Norms in International Society', *International Organization*, 40 (1990), 479–526.

Naffine, N., *Law and the Sexes: Explorations in Feminist Jurisprudence* (Sydney: Allen & Unwin, 1990).

Naffine, N. and Owens, R. J., (eds.), *Sexing the Subject of Law* (London: Sweet & Maxwell, 1997).

Newby, L., 'Rape Victims in Court – the Western Australian Experience' in J. A. Scutt, *Rape Law Reform* (Canberra, Australian Institute of Criminology, 1980).

New South Wales Department of Women, *Heroines of Fortitude: The Experience of Women in Court as Victims of Sexual Assault* (Canberra: Department for Women, 1996) available at: www.women.nsw.gov.au/__data/assets/pdf_file/0009/81684/Heroines1.pdf (accessed July 2009).

Olivecrona, K., *Law as Fact*, 2nd edn (London: Stevens, 1971).

Onuf, N. G., 'A Constructivist Manifesto', in K. Burch and R. A. Denemark, *Constituting International Political Economy* (London: Lynne Rienner, 1997) pp. 7–17.

Onuf, N. G., 'Constructivism: A User's Manual' in V. Kubálková, N. G. Onuf and P. Kowert (eds.), *International Relations in a Constructed World* (London: M. E. Sharpe, 1998), pp. 58–78.

Onuf, N. G., 'Do Rules Say What They Do? From Ordinary Language to International Law', *Harvard International Law Journal*, 26(2) (1985), 385–410.

Onuf, N. G., *World of Our Making: Rules and Rule in Social Theory and International Relations* (Columbia: University of South Carolina Press, 1989).

Pateman, C., *The Sexual Contract* (Cambridge: Polity Press, 1988).

Patterson, J. T., Brown v. Board of Education: *A Civil Rights Milestone and its Troubled Legacy* (Oxford University Press, 1994).

Polan, D., 'Toward a Theory of Law and Patriarchy' in D. Kairys, *The Politics of Law: A Progressive Critique* (New York: Pantheon Books, 1982), pp. 294–303.

Posner, R. A., *The Problems of Jurisprudence* (Cambridge, MA: Harvard University Press, 1993).

Posner, R. A., 'Torture, Terrorism, and Interrogation' in S. Levinson (ed.), *Torture: A Collection* (Oxford University Press, 2004), pp. 291–8.

Pound, R., *An Introduction to the Philosophy of Law* (London: Yale University Press, 1922).

President's Committee on Civil Rights, 'Excerpts from the To Secure These Rights: The Report of the President's Committee on Civil Rights (1947)' in S. F. Lawson and C. Payne, *Debating the Civil Rights Movement, 1945– 1968* (Lanham: Rowman & Littlefield Publishers Inc, 1998).

Price, R., 'A Genealogy of the Chemical Weapons Taboo', *International Organization*, 49(1) (1995), pp. 73–103.

Price, R. (ed.), *Moral Limit and Possibility in World Politics* (Cambridge University Press, 2008).

Price, R., 'Reversing the Gun Sights: Transnational Civil Society Targets Land Mines', *International Organization*, 52(3) (1998), 613–44.

Price, R., *The Chemical Weapons Taboo* (Ithaca: Cornell University Press, 1997).

Price, R. and Tannenwald, N., 'Norms and Deterrence: The Nuclear and Chemical Weapons Taboos' in P. J. Katzenstein (ed.), *The Culture of National Security: Norms and Identity in World Politics* (New York: Columbia University Press, 1996), pp. 114–52.

Rabinowitz, V., 'The Radical Tradition in the Law' in D. Kairys, *The Politics of Law: A Progressive Critique* (New York: Pantheon Books, 1982), pp. 310–18.

Rabkin, J. A., *The Case for Sovereignty: Why the World Should Welcome American Independence* (Washington: The AEI Press, 2004).

Rape Crisis Federation: England and Wales, available at www.rapecrisis.co.uk.

Raustiala, K., 'The Evolution of Territoriality: International Relations and American Law' in M. Kahler and B. Walter (eds.), *Territoriality and Conflict in an Era of Globalisation* (Cambridge University Press, 2006), pp. 219–50.

Rawls, J., *A Theory of Justice* (Oxford: Clarendon Press, 1972).

Raz, J., 'Civil Disobedience' in H. A. Bedau (ed.), *Civil Disobedience in Focus* (London: Routledge, 1991), pp. 159–69.

Raz, J., *The Authority of Law* (Oxford: Clarendon Press, 1979).

Raz, J., *The Morality of Freedom* (Oxford: Clarendon Press, 1986).

Raz, J., 'The Rule of Law and Its Virtue', *Law Quarterly Review*, 93 (1977), 195–211.

Risse, T., Ropp, S. C. and Sikkink, K. (eds.), *The Power of Human Rights: International Norms and Domestic Change* (Cambridge University Press, 1999).

Risse, T. and Sikkink, K., 'The Socialization of International Human Rights Norms into Domestic Practices: Introduction' in T. Risse, S. C. Ropp and K. Sikkink (eds.), *The Power of Human Rights: International Norms and Domestic Change* (Cambridge University Press, 1999), pp. 1–38.

Robertson, G., *Crimes Against Humanity: The Struggle for Global Justice* (London: Penguin, 2000).

Rock, P., *The Social World of an English Crown Court* (Oxford: Clarendon Press, 1993).

Rock, P., 'The Sociology of Deviancy and Conceptions of Moral Order', *The British Journal of Criminology*, 14 (1974), 139–49.

Rosenberg, G. N., *The Hollow Hope: Can Courts Bring About Social Change?* (University of Chicago Press, 1991).

Ross, A., *On Law and Justice*, translated by M. Dutton (London: Stevens, 1958).

Rowland, J., *Rape: The Ultimate Violation* (London: Pluto Press, 1985).

Rumney, P., 'False Allegations of Rape', *Cambridge Law Journal*, 65 (2006), 128–58.

Sands, P., *Lawless World: America and the Making and Breaking of Global Rules* (London: Penguin, 2005).

Sands, P., *Torture Team: Deception, Cruelty and the Compromise of Law* (London: Allen Lane, 2008).

Scheuerman, W. E., *Carl Schmitt: The End of Law* (Lanham, Md: Rowman and Littlefield Publishers, 1999).

Schneider, E. M., and Jordan, S. B., 'Representing Women Who Defend Themselves in Response to Physical or Sexual Assault', *Women's Rights Law Reporter*, 4 (Spring 1978), 149.

Sellars, K., *The Rise and Rise of Human Rights* (Stroud: Sutton, 2002).

Shapiro, S. J., 'The "Hart-Dworkin" Debate: A Short Guide for the Perplexed', University of Michigan Law School Public Law and Legal Theory Working Paper Series, Working Paper No. 77 (March 2007).

Shklar, J. N., *Legalism: Law, Morals and Political Trials* (London: Harvard University Press, 1986).

Shklar, J. N., 'Political Theory and the Rule of Law' in A. C. Hutchinson and P. Monahan (eds.), *The Rule of Law: Ideal or Ideology* (Toronto: Carswell, 1987), p. 1.

Sikkink, K., 'Transnational Politics, International Relations Theory, and Human Rights', *PS: Political Science and Politics*, 31(3) (1998), 516–23.

Simmonds, N. E., *Central Issues in Jurisprudence: Justice, Law and Rights* (London: Sweet & Maxwell, 1986).

Simmonds, N. E., *Law as a Moral Idea* (Oxford University Press, 2008).

Sinclair, A., 'The Role of Law in Political Action: The Case of Trident Ploughshares', unpublished PhD manuscript, University of Wales, Aberystwyth (2005).

Sinclair, A. and Byers, M., 'The US, Sovereignty and International Law Since 9/11', *Political Studies*, 55(2) (June 2007), pp. 318–40.

Sitkoff, H., *The Struggle for Black Equality, 1954–1992, revised edition* (New York: Hill and Wang, 1981).

Slagstead, R., 'Liberal Constitutionalism and its Critics: Carl Schmitt and Max Weber' in J. Elster and R. Slagstead (eds.), *Constitutionalism and Democracy: Studies in Rationality and Social Change* (Cambridge University Press, 1988), pp. 103–29.

Smart, C., *Feminism and the Power of Law* (London: Routledge, 1989).

Smart, C., *Law, Crime and Sexuality: Essays in Feminism* (London: SAGE Publications, 1995).

Smart, C., 'The Woman of Legal Discourse', *Social and Legal Studies*, 1 (1992), 29–44.

Soothill, K. and Soothill, D., 'Prosecuting the Victim? A Study of the Reporting of Barristers' Comments in Rape Cases', *The Howard Journal*, 32(1) (1993), 12–24.

Soothill, K. and Walby, S., *Sex Crime in the News* (London: Routledge, 1991).

Soothill, K., Walby, S. and Bagguley, P., 'Judges, the Media and Rape', *Journal of Law and Society*, 17(2) (1990), 211–33.

Steyn, Lord Johan, 'Guantánamo Bay: The Legal Black Hole', *International and Comparative Law Quarterly*, 53(1) (2004), 1–15.

'Still Getting Away With Rape' *Dispatches* programme transcript (2000), available at www.broadcaster.org.uk/section1/rapecampaign/date_rape_trans.htm (accessed 19 June 2004).

Stone, M., 'Formalism' in J. L. Coleman and S. Shapiro (eds.), *The Oxford Handbook of Jurisprudence and Philosophy of Law* (Oxford University Press, 2004), pp. 166–205.

Suber, P., *The Case of the Speluncean Explorers: Nine New Opinions* (London: Routledge, 1998).

Sunstein, C. R., 'Concurring opinion' in J. M. Balkin (ed.), *What* Brown v. Board of Education *Should Have Said: The Nations' Top Legal Experts Rewrite America's Landmark Civil Rights Decisions* (New York University Press, 2001).

Sunstein, C. R., *Free Markets and Social Justice* (Oxford University Press, 1997).

Sussman, D., 'What's Wrong with Torture?', *Philosophy and Public Affairs*, 33(1) (2005), 1–33.

Tannenwald, N., 'The Nuclear Taboo: The United States and the Normative Basis of Nuclear Non-Use', *International Organization*, 53(3) (1993), 433–68.

Taub, N. and Schneider, E. M., 'Perspectives on Women's Subordination and the Role of Law' in D. Kairys, *The Politics of Law: A Progressive Critique* (New York: Pantheon Books, 1982), pp. 117–39.

Temkin, J., 'Prosecuting and Defending Rape: Perspectives from the Bar', *Journal of Law and Society*, 27(2) (2000), 219–48.

Temkin, J., *Rape and the Legal Process*, 2nd edn (Oxford University Press, 2002).

Temkin, J., 'We Must Point the Finger' *Guardian*, 15 April 1995.

Temkin, J. and Krahé, B., *Sexual Assault and the Justice Gap: A Question of Attitude* (Oxford: Hart, 2008).

Thomas, T., *Sex Crime: Sex Offending and Society* (Cullompton: Willan Publishing, 2000).

Thompson, E. P., *Whigs and Hunters: The Origin of the Black Act* (London: Allen Lane, 1975).

Thomson, A., 'Foreword: Critical Approaches to Law: Who Needs Theory?' in I. Grigg-Spall and P. Ireland, *The Critical Lawyers' Handbook* (London: Pluto Press, 1992), pp. 2–10.

Tigar, M. E. and Levy, M. R., *Law and the Rise of Capitalism*, 2nd edn (New York: Monthly Review Press, 2000).

Timasheff, N. S., *An Introduction to the Sociology of Law*, reprint (Harvard University Press, 1939).

Traugott, M., Brader, T., Coral, D., Curtin, R., Featherman, D., Groves, R., Hill, M., Jackson, J., Juster, T., Kahn, R., Kennedy, C., Kinder, D., Pennell, B.-E., Shapiro, M., Tessler, M., Weit, D. and Willis, R., 'How Americans Responded: A Study of Public Reactions to 9/11/01', *PS: Political Science and Politics*, 35(3) (September 2002), 511–16.

Tushnet, M. V., 'Commentary' in C. W. Eagles, *The Civil Rights Movement in America* (Jackson and London: University Press of Mississippi, 1986), pp. 117–25.

Tushnet, M. V., 'Corporations and Free Speech' in D. Kairys, *The Politics of Law: A Progressive Critique* (New York: Pantheon Books, 1982), pp. 253–61.

Tushnet, M. V., *Making Civil Rights Law: Thurgood Marshall and the Supreme Court, 1936–1961* (Oxford University Press, 1994).

Tushnet, M. V., *Taking the Constitution Away from the Courts* (Princeton University Press, 1999).

Tushnet, M. V., *The NAACP's Legal Strategy Against Segregated Education, 1925–1950* (Chapel Hill & London: University of North Carolina Press, 1987).

Unger, R. M., *Law in Modern Society* (London: Collier Macmillan, 1977).

Unger, R. M., 'The Critical Legal Studies Movement', *Harvard Law Review*, 96(3) (1983), 561–675.

Ungerer, C. and Hanson, M. (eds.), *The Politics of Nuclear Non-Proliferation* (St Leonards, Australia: Allen & Unwin, 2001).

Ward, C. A., *Attitudes Towards Rape: Feminist and Social Psychological Perspectives* (London: SAGE, 1995).

Weldes, J., Laffey, M., Gusterson, H. and Duvall, R. (eds.), *Cultures of Insecurity: States, Communities, and the Production of Danger* (London: University of Minnesota Press, 1999).

Westmarland, N., 'Rape Law Reform in England and Wales' School for Policy Studies Working Paper Series, Paper No. 7 (April 2004), available at www. bristol.ac.uk/sps.

Wolchover, D. and Heaton-Armstrong, A., 'Debunking Rape Myths', *New Law Journal*, 158 (2008), 117–19.

X, Malcolm with the assistance of Haley, A., *The Autobiography of Malcolm X* (London: Penguin Books, 1965).

Yoo, J. and Posner, E., 'International Court of Hubris', *Wall Street Journal* (7 April 2004), available at www.aei.org/article/20245.

Zehfuss, M., *Constructivism in International Relations: The Politics of Reality* (Cambridge University Press, 2002).